GARDENS BY DESIGN

STEP-BY-STEP PLANS FOR 12 IMAGINATIVE GARDENS

Other Gardening Books by
Peter Loewer

The Indoor Water Gardener's How-To Handbook
Bringing the Outdoors In
Seeds and Cuttings
Growing and Decorating with Grasses
Growing Plants in Water
Evergreens: A Guide for Landscape, Lawn, and Garden
The Garden Almanac: For Indoor and Outdoor Gardening
with Bebe Miles: *Wildflower Perennials for Your Garden*

GARDENS BY DESIGN

STEP-BY-STEP PLANS FOR 12 IMAGINATIVE GARDENS

Written and illustrated by

Peter Loewer

Rodale Press, Emmaus, Pennsylvania

Library of Congress Cataloging-in-Publication Data

Loewer, H. Peter
    Gardens by design.

      Bibliography: p. 256
      Includes index.
      1. Gardening.   2. Gardens.   I. Title.
SB453.L73   1986   635.9   85–28343
ISBN 0–87857–601–0   hardback
ISBN 0–87857–602–9   paperback

2 4 6 8 10 9 7 5 3 1   hardcover

The Devil's Tongue and *A Winter Garden of Grasses* reprinted with the permission of *Green Scene,* The Pennsylvania Horticultural Society.
Building a Scree Bed, The Annual Garden, and *The Cutting Garden* reprinted courtesy of *Horticulture,* Copyright © 1984, 1985.
Life's Darkest Moment by Webster reprinted with the permission of Al Smith Features.

CONTENTS

LIST OF PLANTS ILLUSTRATED

PREFACE

In 1930 Milt Gross, a comic writer of some reputation wrote a book entirely of cartoons without words, called *He Done Her Wrong*. With a wry smile he said of his endeavor, "They laughed when I sat down to draw a novel," itself a play on the old 20s advertisement showing the wallflower at the party who turns away from the snickering crowd to say: "They laughed when I sat down to play the piano."

When I announced to family and friends the plans for this project, including the physical act of either nurturing or acquiring most of the plants mentioned in its pages—if they were not in the garden already—I could almost hear a Greek chorus: "They laughed when I sat down to grow a book!"

That was more than a year and a half ago; seeds have been propagated, ponds dug, pools lined, flowers picked, seed pods dried, and some 20 odd gardens planned, worked in, and completed. Although I am amazed that the project ever even got off the ground—much less was finished—now as winter winds blow again and I dot the final "i," another spring waits in the wings and the spirit of the gardener is ready to try again.

And I got a little help from my friends: my wife Jean who gracefully puts up with my moody behavior; my agent, Dominick Abel, for his continuing support; my editor at Rodale, Anne Halpin, whose advice was always needed and heeded; Nancy Land, a Texas flower, for changing my computer disks to type; Rosemary Porter for garden thoughts and all the wonderful books; plus the many garden friends or cronies whose names are carefully hidden throughout the text or concealed among the labels, leaves, and flowers in the art—this last done as a salute to two years spent in the army as a cryptographer.

Peter Loewer,
Cochecton, 1986.

INTRODUCTION

This is a book about my garden, its successes and its failures, and the plants it contains. It's also about garden design and ideas. No one of the many gardens described is complete in itself; there are not enough days in my week for such a feat. But individual parts of each garden do exist, spread about our backyard, back field, frontyard, the vegetable patch, and the perimeter of our pond.

And the plants themselves are real. Many have been gifts from garden friends and many purchased from nurseries in the United States and England. More have been grown from seed, either collected by friends or supplied by the various seed exchanges that are a most important part of plant societies today. Finally quite a few have been gathered in the wild and saved from the impending threat of bulldozers or overactive highway departments. These bureaucracies usually view a growing plant as something resembling the Black Death of the Fifteenth Century and wipe it out as fast as possible.

Our garden is in the Catskill Mountains of New York State at an elevation of 1300 feet. The USDA lists our area as Zone 5a or with a minimum winter temperature of − 20°F. But every few winters we hit a low of − 30°F., often accompanied by 30 mph winds—and sometimes with no snow cover at all—yet the gardens survive. There are times when the landscape can only be described as ravaged, but even then there is a barren beauty to it all. I am occasionally despondent when the deer invade the garden and nibble everything in sight (never with the sharp eye of a practiced pruner but only in the guise of Shiva, the Destroyer) and am often moved to tears at the sight of the plants that succumb to winter's chill, but each spring when the redwing blackbirds return and the sun again shines on the pond at 6:00 in the morning, we're ready to begin again.

Some years we have a surfeit of rain: Inch after inch will fall as though Mother Nature is without any knowledge of actuary tables; other years will be dry with weeks passing and nary a drop. But over a ten year period the inches will balance out and appear normal to an eye that only looks at decades and centuries. And still most plants survive.

Finally, this book deals with an American approach to gardening. I love English gardens and all they contain but after 15 years of working in the climate just described I'm enough of a realist to know that it's impossible for a Chartwell to exist in my own backyard and a Kew or

Sissinghurst right down the road: An English garden is right for England where vistas are comfortable, never broad—and that's as it should be.

In the appendixes are lists of suppliers, publications, and growers but they are far from complete. If you know of a source not listed, kindly advise by writing to me in care of Rodale Press, Inc., 33 East Minor Street, Emmaus, PA 18049.

On Naming Plants

Although it's true that many plants can be recognized by their common names, many more cannot. There are, for example, seven different plants known as snakeroot: common snakeroot, black snakeroot, button snakeroot, Sampson's snakeroot, Seneca snakeroot, Virginia snakeroot, and white snakeroot. All these names are now in general use. Now imagine the local variations on these seven across fifty states and Canada. Then imagine the confusion that would arise when one snakeroot is thought to be another in the order department of a nursery operated by someone who didn't like using scientific names to begin with. But if each were ordered by its Latin equivalent confusion

Life's Darkest Moment : : : BY WEBSTER

SALLY TELLS ME YOU LIKE FLOWERS, SO YOU WILL BE INTERESTED IN WHAT WE ARE GOING TO DO NEXT SPRING. RIGHT HERE WE WILL HAVE THE ACONITUM NAPELLUS, AND BEYOND THERE WILL BE THE GIANT HYBRID GAILLARDIA AND THE DINORPHOTHEDA — OR WOULD YOU PLANT THE INCARVILLEA DELAYAYI IN THIS SPOT? BY THE WAY, DID YOUR PRIMULA MALACOIDES DO WELL THIS YEAR?

ABLE TO DISTINGUISH A VIOLET FROM A ROSE --

would vanish. Those names in the same order are: *Asarum canadense, Cimicifuga racemosa, Eryngium yuccifolium, Gentiana catesbaei, Polygala senega, Aristolochia serpentaria,* and *Eupatorium rugosum.* And if you are worried about pronunciation, don't be. Very few people today can speak these names aloud with impunity and you will generally be using them in the written sense alone.

All plants known to man have been given these Latin or scientific names—each unique—and they are easily understood throughout the world. Whether in Japan, Turkey, Russia, or Buffalo, New York, and regardless of the language spoken by the native gardener, *Taraxacum officinale* is the common dandelion and quack grass is *Agropyron repens.*

Four terms are in general use: *genus, species, variety,* and *cultivar.* All reference books, most good gardening books, and nearly all catalogs and nurseries—even most seed packets—list the scientific name under the common.

In print, the *genus* and *species* are set off from the accompanying text by the use of *italics. Genus* refers to a group of plants that are closely related, while the *species* suggests an individual plant's unique quality, or color, or perhaps honors the individual who discovered it. Usually the *Genus* has an initial capital and the *species* is all in lower case, but when the species is derived from a former generic name, a person's name, or a common name, it too can begin with a capital letter.

The *variety* is also italicized and usually preceded by the abbreviation "var.", set in roman type. A *variety* is a plant that develops a noticeable change in characteristics that breeds true from generation to generation. A *cultivar* is a variation that appears on a plant while in cultivation (thus a change either by chance or design) and is derived from **culti**vated **var**iety and distinguished in type by being set in roman boldface inside single quotation marks.

The common garden flower called honesty, money plant, or moonwort is grown for its cheerful flowers and seedpods that are round and silvery. The botanical or scientific name is *Lunaria annua* (*Luna*, the moon and *annua*, annual). One form has leaves striped with white and is called *Lunaria annua* var. *variegata,* while another cultivar with especially large purple flowers is called *Lunaria annua* **'Munstead Purple'.** And though it would seem to violate a well-known rule of copyediting, any punctuation marks used after the single quote end of a cultivar name follow that quote and do not fall within.

A Little More Nomenclature

A few other terms in use are annual, biennial, and perennial. An annual completes its cycle of growth from seed to maturity and demise in less than one year.

A biennial follows the same pattern but requires two growing seasons to accomplish it all.

A perennial lives for many years, flowering and producing seeds every season. Within this classification are shortlived perennials that flourish for only a few years, then die, and longer-lived types that could last well over 50 years in one garden.

ON GARDEN DESIGN

When you drive through the average subdivision or suburban tract development you quickly see the contemporary approach to landscape and gardening in general. Everything in view is usually clipped and manicured with the expanse of lawn cutely marked here and there—usually in straight lines—with a few shrubs or small evergreens. Any trees, if trees there are, sit exactly in the center of the front yard. Flowers have a tendency to be marigolds, petunias, and other bright annuals, planted in concentric circles within a perfect circle of soil. For some reason any imagination that is exercised is often found within the vegetable garden where caution is thrown to the winds: Tepees of weathered branches hold green tangles of beans and peas; stalks of celery, posts of broccoli, and balls of cabbage are set off by the deep purples of eggplants and the yellow flowers, and the red fruit of tomatoes.

Now grass that is a bit too long doesn't disturb my sensibilities. Weeds, though not given out-and-out invitations, do not strike terror in my heart—at least not until they become so large as to detract from other plants in the neighborhood. So in the gardens featured in the following pages, I'd like to bring the gardeners' imagination to the fore—out of the vegetable patch and into the front yard—and replace some of that endless grass with blooming flowers and plants.

One major piece of garden advice that I think is a bit overdone is the overattention paid to the mismatching of colors. Photographic studies have been made of garden borders in the noonday sun to show how bright colors will bleach out or how the impact of one flower is diminished by the contrasting color of its nearest neighbor.

Of course a sprig of tiny white flowers scarcely a foot high would be overpowered if surrounded by three sunflowers each 3 feet tall. But going out of your way to match flower colors as though you were painting an abstract watercolor is not my idea of being a happy gardener.

That's not to say that one-color gardening as originally conceived by Gertrude Jekyll, the great English gardener, or as reported by Alice Morse Earle here in America is not to be practiced: The all-white garden planted by Vita Sackville-West at Sissinghurst in southern England or the moonlight garden of Major Poore of Massachusetts are singularly beautiful—but never become a slave to one approach.

So here are a few rules:

1. Pay attention to the eventual size of a plant, shrub, or tree. Try to visualize what it will become five years from the day you plant it. It's amazing how fast some things will grow.
2. Match the plant to the available conditions. Avoid planting a bush that requires perfect drainage next to another that revels in pure clay. You can probably rectify any mismatch but it often is more trouble than the effort is worth.
3. Avoid long straight lines: They are never found in nature and (to me) are boring to look at—and impossible to maintain. A gentle and sweeping curve looks much better and is easier to install and keep up.

4. Trust your own aesthetic judgment. After all, it is your garden and should reflect your likes and dislikes, not some expert's—and that could include me!
5. Never use garden ornaments not in scale with your garden. A small Japanese stone lantern—which can accommodate a candle for evening viewing—would probably look better in the average-size garden than a 6-foot marble statue of the Venus de Milo. If you wish to acquire some garden sculpture, keep in mind the specific requirements of your own site. You will find that scaled down ornaments add depth to a garden view rather than overpower it.

I realize it's never easy to accept advice—I ought to know as I've been fighting most offers for years. But if ever there was a time to listen up it's now: Before you start any garden—whether your own design or from suggestions in this book (or others like it)—FIRST, TAKE PAPER AND PENCIL AND SKETCH A SIMPLE MAP OF THE AREA TO BE DEVELOPED AND PLANTED! The map need not be complicated or artistic, and need not stifle your creativity; it just helps the gardener to arrive at the starting gate with some idea of what's coming on down the line. Large scale or small potatoes, planning it out beforehand saves time, energy, money, and much grief.

Only you can decide how much land is to be cared for and how much time you will have for weeding and cultivating. Is your garden going to be a weekend pastime—a sideline in the journey from spring to fall—or a year-round pursuit? And while you mull it over consider: Gardening always takes more time than you expect it will, and very few things can look more dismal to you—or your neighbors—than an abandoned site with a few malnourished plants overwhelmed by weeds.

Now on your map or plan indicate the presence of natural windbreaks, existing trees, the direction of the worst winter winds, possible obstructions to spring and fall sunlight, and all structures—whether already there or planned for the future. And if you are going into gardening with great abandon, leave a spot for a nursery bed (a temporary home for young and experimental plants) and a cold frame to winter over selected specimens and protect seedlings in the spring.

Checking the areas of natural and artificial windbreaks is very important, especially in the colder areas of the country. You might find that your projected garden is in Zone 5 with winter lows of − 20°F. but in a protected spot a plant from Zone 7 might survive.

We have one plant, a Himalayan honeysuckle (*Leycesteria formosa*) that is only hardy to Zone 7 (0°F.), about the climate found in New York City. It's a small bush and I tried for many years to keep a specimen alive, to no avail. Finally we tried planting a new seedling with the protection of a 6-foot bank and the back of the garage only 4 feet away. The combination worked—now the honeysuckle blooms.

A collection of various fritillarias including the crown-imperial (*Fritillaria imperialis*) bloom every year regardless of the winter's severity, as they are planted at the corner of the house just over the soil pipe that leads to the septic tank. The soil never quite freezes there due to the constant warmth radiating from the tank and its plumbing.

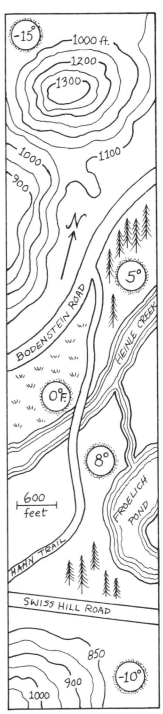

Temperature fluctuations over one square mile in January.

CLIMATE ZONES—TEMPERATURE AND WIND-CHILL FACTOR

MAKING A PLAN

The plans below show two sample garden layouts. The one on the left is especially suited to a shade or wildflower garden.

You will find no map of the United States in this book depicting zones for annual high and low temperatures. To illustrate these zones with any degree of clarity would require a chart 2 by 4 feet and even then such local variations created by natural and artificial barriers as hills, buildings, and even ponds would not be visible or the effects these objects have on the course of a wind that is whipping winter's chill.

This combination of wind and cold, by the by, is the hit of the T.V. weather forecasters and they all act as though it's a new invention of nature. "It's cold enough today at 0°F. but with that 25 mph wind it will seem like − 44°F. so be sure and dress warmly to prevent frostbite!" they say.

Well, that cold wind will have the same effect on your tender plants as it will on your nose. So when checking the zones listed in this

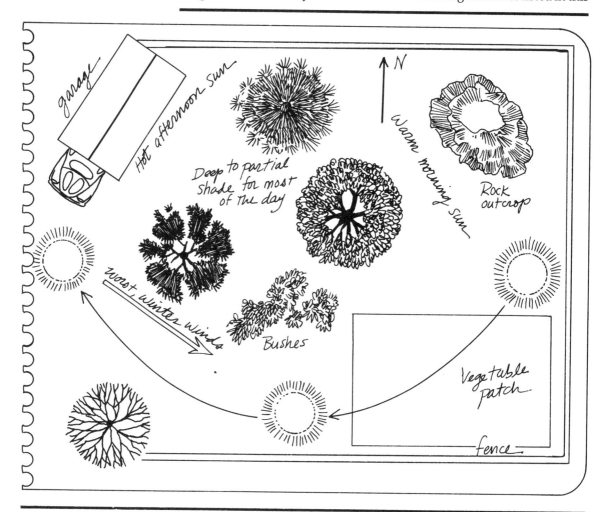

garage

Hot afternoon sun

Deep to partial shade for most of the day

N

Warm morning sun

Rock outcrop

most winter winds

Bushes

Vegetable patch

fence

book against your home zone (if in doubt call your local county extension agent) be sure and check on the average winter winds in your area. Then by looking at the wind-chill chart you'll see just how cold it can get in your back garden.

A word of warning: There are two hardiness zone maps at large in the United States and Canada. One is published by the Agricultural Research Service of the U.S. Department of Agriculture; the other is backed by the Arnold Arboretum of Harvard University. The two maps generate a great deal of confusion as they do *not* match.

When ordering plants from any catalog, check to see which system they are using. The temperatures for each are given on the next page. This book uses the USDA map. And as I write this book a move is afoot to create a new temperature chart for the country based on a computerized reading of zip codes (see bibliography).

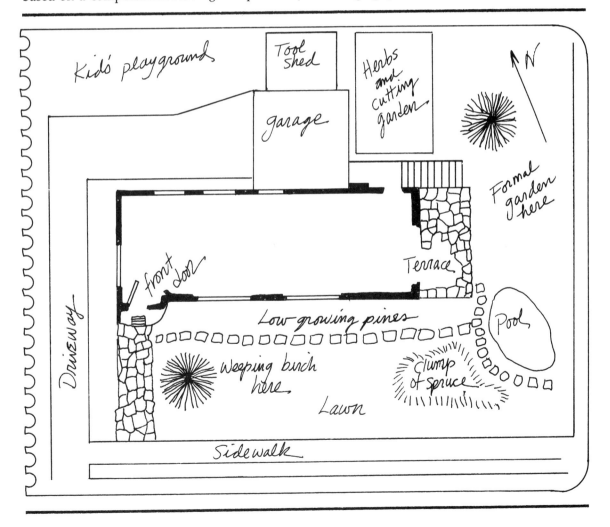

MORE GARDEN PLANS

The following sketches depict four more garden plans:

1. This is my own garden where the numbers refer to different planting areas.
2. The layout of Budd Myer's alpine garden.
3. A small backyard garden with dwarf conifers in pots upon the flagstone terrace.
4. A plan for a small suburban plot.

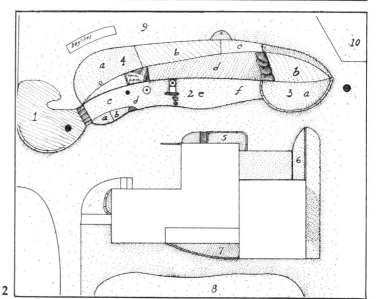

1

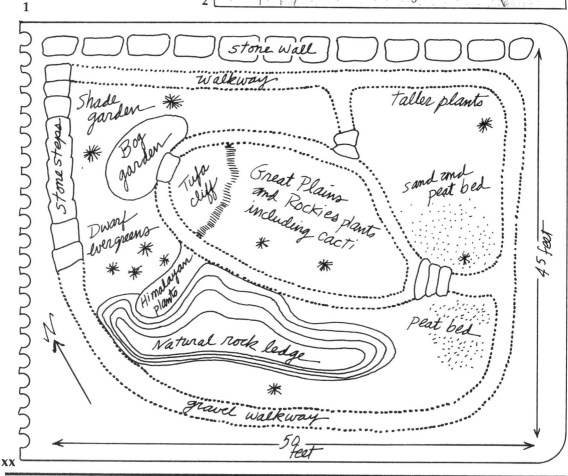

2

xx

Rug junipers

Bird bath

Flag-stones

Weeping birch

White impatiens

Ferns

Ivy

Terrace

Sliding doors

TABLE

Railroad ties

gravel

Rhododendrons

Japanese maple

French lilacs

Hostas

Small pool

Sedum 'Dragon Blood'

Lawn

Fence

Approximate Range of Average Annual
Minimum Temperature for Each Zone

	USDA		Arnold Arboretum	
Zone 1	Below -50°F	Zone 1		Below -50°F
Zone 2	− 50° to − 40°	Zone 2		− 35° to − 50°
Zone 3	− 40° to − 30°	Zone 3		− 20° to − 35°
Zone 4	− 30° to − 20°	Zone 4		− 10° to − 20°
Zone 5	− 20° to − 10°	Zone 5		− 5° to − 10°
Zone 6	− 10° to 0°	Zone 6		− 5° to 5°
Zone 7	0° to 10°	Zone 7		5° to 10°
Zone 8	10° to 20°	Zone 8		10° to 20°
Zone 9	20° to 30°	Zone 9		20° to 30°
Zone 10	30° to 40°	Zone 10		30° to 40°

Wind-Chill Factor

Temperature	Wind Speed								
	Calm	5	10	15	20	25	30	35	40
+ 50	50	48	40	36	32	30	28	27	26
+ 40	40	37	28	22	18	16	13	11	10
+ 30	30	27	16	9	4	0	− 2	− 4	− 6
+ 20	20	16	4	− 5	− 10	− 15	− 18	− 20	− 21
+ 10	10	6	− 9	− 18	− 25	− 29	− 33	− 35	− 37
0	0	− 5	− 21	− 36	− 39	− 44	− 48	− 50	− 53
− 10	− 10	− 15	− 33	− 45	− 53	− 59	− 63	− 67	− 69
− 20	− 20	− 26	− 46	− 58	− 67	− 74	− 79	− 82	− 85
− 30	− 30	− 36	− 58	− 72	− 82	− 88	− 94	− 98	− 100
− 40	− 40	− 47	− 70	− 88	− 96	− 104	− 109	− 113	− 116

Calm: Chimney smoke rises vertically.

1–12 mph: Leaves stir; you feel a breeze on your face.

13–24 mph: Branches stir; loose paper is blown about.

25–30 mph: Large branches move; wires whistle.

30–40 mph: Whole trees in motion; hard to walk against the wind.

WORKING THE LAND

On Soils and Soil Types

The plants described in this book range from those happy in water and wet to those that prefer the driest of sands; some that are happy in the most average of soils and some that demand a deep and luxurious loam; and a few that will persist in solid clay and a few that will grow in a red shale bank.

So when you start to plan a garden, your soil should be checked for its character: Is it solid clay, rich loam, or a combination of both? Is it well-drained or does water stand in puddles even after a light rain?

Clay soils are sticky. If you roll a lump of wet soil between your fingers as though rolling a cigarette and it forms a compact cylinder that does not break up, that's clay. Clay can become rock hard when completely dry. Instead of sinking into such soil, water simply rolls to the lowest level and sits. Sandy soil drains immediately; a soil that is rich and loamy, full of organic matter, strikes a balance between the two others.

Unless a plant demands special conditions, try to prepare a garden soil that strikes a balance between clay, sand, and loam. In addition the organic matter helps to provide food for healthy plant development.

There are many ways to improve soil. You can add sand, peat moss, or composted manure (fresh manure is usually too strong to plant in directly so mix it in the soil thoroughly in late fall, winter, or early spring, and wait a few months before direct planting). Or you can make your own compost by maintaining a compost pile for grass clippings, weeds, kitchen and garden refuse.

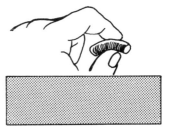

Clay

Sand

Loam

Checking the pH of Soil

pH is a method of measuring the relative acidity, or sourness, and alkalinity, or sweetness, of the soil. Most plants grow in pH ranges between 5.0 and 7.0. Swamps or bogs that have high percentages of peat are extremely acidic; in humid regions, and most woods and forests, the soil is moderately acidic to slightly alkaline; arid regions go up from a moderate to a strong alkaline content; and desert areas in the Southwest have vast alkali flats.

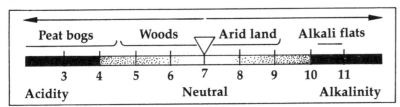

Most garden centers now stock an inexpensive paper pH tape that can be held against a moist soil sample and will turn colors to indicate the degree of acidity. Acid soils are usually corrected by the addition of lime. But to be really sure, call your county extension agent about the quality and character of your local soil.

Double-digging

If you've decided where to garden and the area picked has never been worked before, read on.

First clear the ground of all existing weeds or grass with a mower or—if you have the strength—a scythe. Rake the result into piles for later use at the bottom of the trenches that you will be digging. The following figure gives the general idea.

Don't use a Rototiller at this point: The idea of double-digging is to replace the subsoil with a better quality of fill, not to just work the surface soil about.

THE POLAROID—A GREAT TOOL FOR GARDEN DESIGN

I've got an old—and fairly cheap—Polaroid camera that I load with black and white film and carry off to any spot that I plan to develop or design (color works just as well). There I take a number of shots covering as many angles as possible and know before I return to the drawing board that I've plenty of pictures.

Back in the studio, while consulting plans and outlines, I take a felt-tip pen with a fine point and draw directly on the polaroid prints. This gives me a perfect picture of just how everything is going to look: plants and all are in scale with the existing features of the property. Here are a number of examples:

1. Hiding a blot on the landscape. 2. Adding a line of shrubs to a home in the woods. 3. Where to put a large shrub. 4. Sprucing up a back door. 5. Planning a new perennial border. 6. Hiding a fence. 7. Landscaping a country home. 8. Adding a garden of containers. 9. Finishing off a sunporch.

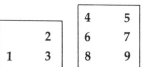

			4	5
	2		6	7
1	3		8	9

The foregoing advice is only for those who are starting out from scratch and are putting in an entire garden, not just adding new plants to an existing spread. And be advised that this is the time for being an ant not a grasshopper.

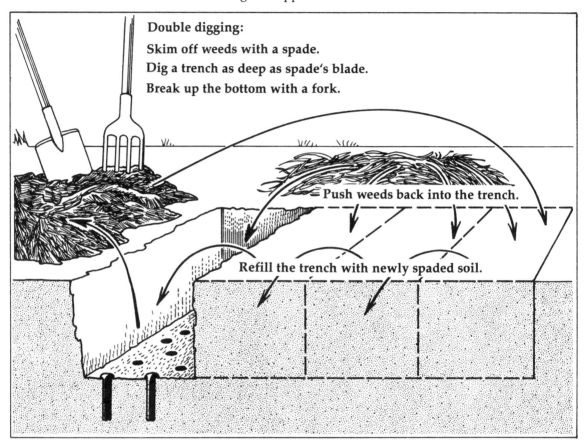

Double digging:

Skim off weeds with a spade.

Dig a trench as deep as spade's blade.

Break up the bottom with a fork.

Push weeds back into the trench.

Refill the trench with newly spaded soil.

Raised Beds

If your soil is really bad and not worth the effort to improve, try the concept of raised bed gardening. It will fit in with any of the gardens mentioned in this book. Instead of digging down, mark out your area and build it up about 2 feet above the ground level with railroad ties from the lumber yard—be careful they're not treated with creosote—or build a wall of concrete blocks, fieldstone, or even bricks. Then fill it with purchased top soil.

If you live on the side of a hill, this idea can be used to build terraces and prevent the rain from washing down the slopes.

Much of our garden is on a hill composed of granite with an overlay of red shale and a sprinkling of larger rocks. By building retaining walls of concrete blocks, topped with a layer of fieldstones from old stone walls (just for good looks), we've been able to have good soil and perfect drainage, and we don't have to stoop over all the time for cultivation jobs.

A Nursery Bed

If your garden keeps on expanding and you wish to try new plants, especially those grown from seed, try to include a nursery bed in your plan. It need not be large, but it should be in a protected spot, have good soil, and be out of the way so you are under no pressure to consider aesthetics.

Here you can raise seedling plants to maturity before planting them out in the garden proper.

Record Keeping

In the rush of planting and maintaining a garden, the job of record keeping often takes second place. You always think it's easy to remember a name and a date, but it really isn't.

There is an inherent desire in all human beings, especially plant people, to know the correct name of everything and if you ever plan on selling or trading plants, records and labels are a must.

Keep information on 3 by 5 file cards or in a notebook, the method is not important. Note the scientific and common name, the date you got the plant, its age, the nursery or plant supplier, its location in the garden and any propagation attempts.

At the same time a durable label should be prepared. This is not as easy as you might expect. The perfect label has yet to be devised; it's like the search for perpetual motion.

Plastic labels soon crack and shatter from exposure to sun and freezing in the North. They also heave out of the soil after winter thaws and once free the wind will blow them far and wide. Try metal labels that are provided with long wire supports and mark the names by scratching with a nail or knife, or print names on stainless steel or aluminum tape with a tapewriter.

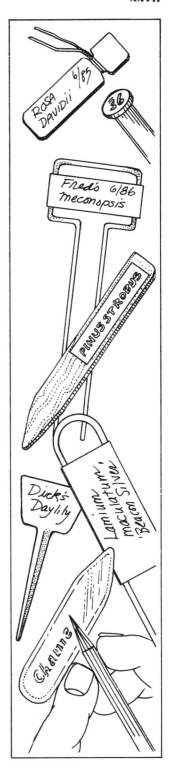

BOTANICAL NAME		
CRUCIANELLA STYLOSA [PHUOPSIS?]		
COMMON NAME		FAMILY
CROSSWORT		_CRUCIANELLA_
REC'D AS · DAY / MON / YEAR	SOURCE	LOCATION
SEED · 19 5 84	_T+M_	_BED 10_
PROPAGATION		
GERM. 15 DAYS @ 65°		

Hortus says annual
T+M, RHS. perennial
Verey says plants smell 'foxy' when wet.

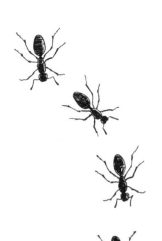

Pests and Disease

There is a dark side to the garden: All those creatures who feed and wreak havoc on flowers and leaves. But there are ways to defeat them without resorting to those brown plastic bottles with the colorful labels and the small type that warns you to wear rubber gloves when handling. You won't need an 800 telephone number to call if the spray gets in your eyes.

Pest control on the insect front should begin with good soil condition and fertility, adequate watering, and just plain good housekeeping about the garden. Never allow diseased or decaying plant material to lie about. And remember that a healthy plant can fight off many attacks that will kill a weaker cousin.

Our worst problem is the slug, simply one of nature's most disgusting creatures. These are snails without shells that glide about at night on a trail of slime and chew holes in just about everything. I've tried slug traps baited with beer—I refuse to use the poisoned bait because of possible danger to our garden cats (who effectively take care of any rabbit problem)—but have never found them to work so I resort to the easiest method: taking a flashlight out into the garden in the dead of night, spotlighting the slug, and sprinkling a few grains of salt on its tender body. The salt kills them without any damage to the garden. But if you are tender-hearted, use alcohol as the salt is a slow way to kill.

Japanese beetles are also a trial. I pick them off individually and drop them in a can of soapwater, the resulting mixture to be buried deeply when the can is full.

Insects like flea beetles and aphids are controlled by spraying with an insecticide derived from the dried flower heads of the pyrethrum daisy (*Chrysanthemum cinerariifolium*), a plant that resembles the common field daisy. The active ingredients are removed with solvents and the result is powdered concentrate that is used to formulate the spray. Pyrethrum has one problem: It is readily broken down chemically by the action of light, often in a matter of hours. So pyrethrum should be applied in the late afternoon.

Rotenone is another plant-based insecticide, manufactured from the roots of the tuba root (*Derris elliptica*) and the lancepods (*Lonchocarpus* spp.), but it can cause severe irritation to humans if inhaled. It is sold as a dust and is an extremely potent control for many insect species but the killing action is slow and like pyrethrum, it breaks down in the environment, although not as quickly.

Spider mites bite the dust when confronted with insecticidal soap.

For those gardeners who have the inclination to carry the war directly to the enemy there are firms who now supply the eggs of ladybugs (*Hippodamia* spp.), praying mantis (*Mantis* spp.), and green lacewings (*Chrysopa* spp.), for troops that will wage the war for you.

Finally, the gardener should remember that gardens are alive and not perfect.

Mulch: Keeping the Garden Moist

When the dog days of summer arrive and the hot sun beats down on your garden, soils bake and what water is there quickly evaporates. Laying on a garden mulch will help to conserve this water and also cut down on the growth of weeds. And a neatly applied layer of mulch often looks better between the plants than parched dirt. Remember to keep mulches away from the crowns of the plants to prevent rotting.

A number of types of mulch are available around the country, including: buckwheat hulls, cocoa husks, corn cobs, garden compost, hay, leaf mold, marble chips, oak leaves (soft leaves like maple will mat), pea gravel, peat moss, pecan hulls, pine bark chips, pine needles, and wood chips.

In addition there is black plastic film that can be made somewhat acceptable by covering it with another, more pleasing material. But I will always view this particular item as something created by the oil companies to get even with the organic movement.

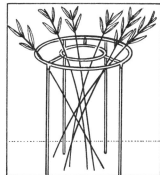

You have to be careful with peat moss because once it packs down it really repels water with a vengeance, so keep it fluffed up.

I don't use cocoa husks. Although I love the smell of chocolate, it can become overbearing and does not belong in a garden full of the delicate fragrance of flowers.

Holding Up the Garden

When some plants grow well, the flowers and leaves often become too heavy and topple over, especially during summer storms. So it becomes necessary to prop them up. Here are four methods:

Pea-staking is an English invention and involves placing branches pruned from trees upright in a perennial bed early in the season. The plants grow up through the sticks and cover them with foliage. They should be about 6 inches shorter than the leaves of the plant. We use birch, wild cherry, and maple from our neighboring woods. The name originated in the vegetable garden where this was the method used to hold up pea vines.

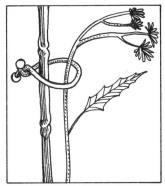

Wire Plant Supports are originally from Scotland and consist of heavy wire rings with five open sections that are held up with three metal legs. The plants grow up through the rings. The supports are neat and reusable for many seasons.

Bamboo or Reed Stakes can be used to support single-stemmed plants. I gather all the stems of my eulalia grasses in late fall and use them with twistems or plastic clips.

Cat's-cradle is the result of putting in four short corner stakes and winding green garden twine across and between.

Container Gardening

Many of the plants described in this book will grow well in containers. This is especially handy for city gardeners who have only a small terrace and for suburbanites with very tiny yards.

A container by definition could be a small clay pot to a sunken soapstone sink to a large raised bed. They all will hold dirt that you will mix to your specifications and can be adjusted far easier than an entire lot of poor soil.

I have an especially fine dwarf redwood (*Sequoia sempervirens* '**Adpressa**') that is much too tender for our winters. Planting it in a terra cotta pot, it becomes an attractive addition to the top of my scree bed in summer and for Christmas is brought into the living room where it's decorated for a living holiday tree.

If the plants in the containers are hardy to your climate they can be left outside for the winter if they are sunk into a trench that is then covered with a thick layer of pine branches or the like, in turn to be topped by snow. When a potted plant is not given protection, the bitter cold winds striking the pot soon kill the plant's roots. If the winds do not do the job, the repeated freezing and thawing of the soil will.

And clay pots soon begin to break from the action of freezing water in the pores.

If you must bring a potted hardy plant indoors for shelter, it must have at least three months of an average temperature of no more than 40° to 45°F. Without meeting this condition, the plant will die. Hardy, outdoor plants from the temperate zones must have a sustained dormancy once a year.

Remember to water on occasion. Since the soil around the roots is not frozen solid, the roots continue to use small amounts of water. The soil should not be allowed to become bone dry.

PLANT PROPAGATION

Propagating Plants: Seeds

When seeds arrive you'll see that most packs are clearly labeled with instructions for sowing. Never open them until you are ready to use them. Until then keep them in a cool spot, never near a radiator. If the seeds need stratification—a period of exposure to cold—before sowing, keep them in the refrigerator for 6 to 8 weeks.

Sow them in a sterile medium, either commercial or of your own make, and use a heating cable to help speed germination. If you are missing information on how deep to sow seeds, use the following: Seeds 1/16 of an inch or larger should be covered by the thickness of one seed; tiny seeds, like begonias, need not be covered at all. Label carefully with species and date. For ease of later transplanting, use individual peat pots for most seeds.

Once seeds are planted, put the pots into larger containers, cover with glass or plastic wrap, and place them in a spot out of the direct sunlight. It need not be completely dark. Keep the wrap away from the surface of the medium; this prevents drops of condensation from swamping the seeds below. Once germination starts, you must never let these containers dry out.

When the first green shoots appear, move the containers into the sun. If you are doing this later in the season some protection like screening should be provided, as the hot rays of a noonday sun can be dangerous to tiny plants.

Pot the plants on as they grow. When frosts are over and the weather settled, move them out to your nursery bed.

Propagating Plants: Cuttings

Late spring or early summer is the best time to start cuttings since at this time the plant has a good supply of food stored in its cells to keep it going until new roots are formed. Most plants will root later in the season but the process seems to be slower. It has also been scientifically demonstrated that the younger the stem, the faster new roots will start.

Take healthy stems, 3 to 5 inches long, using a clean, sharp knife or razor blade. Make the cut slightly below the point where a leaf stalk joins the stem, removing any damaged leaves and those near the bottom of the cutting. Stick the cutting in a peat pot full of moist sand making a hole with a pencil to 3/4 of the pot's depth, making sure that the bottom of the stem touches the medium. Put the whole affair in a plastic bag and seal the opening at top with a twist. The bag holds the moisture that the leaves throw off but cannot replace until new roots form. Make sure the medium is moist but never soggy. After two weeks give it a tug to see if roots are forming. If they are not, pull the stem out and check for rot. If all looks well, try again. You can use the new hormone powders if you wish but I shy away from these. When new roots grow through the peat walls, pot on.

Propagating Plants: Division

Most perennials get larger as they grow. Eventually clumps are formed, and often growth diminishes at the center. The simple thing to do is to lift the clump out of the earth. Then chop it apart with your spade or a hatchet. Make sure a goodly supply of roots is left with each piece. Replant, don't use the woodier center, and give any surplus to gardening friends.

Some plants, especially grasses, produce stolons. These are underground stems that end in a growing tip. If removed from the mother plant, these will root and produce new plants.

AN ALPINE GARDEN

The woman who grew Meconopsis
Was asked to give a synopsis,
How can I she cried,
When all of them died,
Do more than describe their autopsies?

Martha Houghton, at the first meeting of the American Rock Garden
Society, 1934.

My first visit to a true alpine garden was in the spring of 1977
when I met Budd Myers and had the rare opportunity of touring his
hillside domain in northeast Pennsylvania, on the fringes of the
Pocono Mountains. I had seen pictures of other such gardens before
but they always looked like a technicolor world with brilliant dots of
intense but unreal tinting and a great deal of cunningly placed rock,
hence the other name for such plant collections: rock gardens.

Years back when labor was cheap many estate gardeners thought
nothing of moving pieces of granite that weighed tons in an effort to
duplicate the look found when climbing the average mountain. Taking
a clue from photographs returned by globe-trotting explorers and
plant collectors, these major (and minor) captains of industry would
create the Reichenbach Falls—before Sherlock Holmes and Professor
Moriarty plunged over the edge—just as a perfect background for the
rare and ill-fated edelweiss (ill-fated because many gatherers were
thought to have plunged to their deaths while attempting to collect this
rare plant that was thought only to grow at the cliff's edge).

Because most alpine plants are small in stature, Budd was able to
grow some 600 species of unusual and often rare alpines (starting most
of the plants from seed) in an area of about 50 by 50 feet. And by using
the natural terrain of his sloped back yard, and a bulldozer hired for
one day, he created the most fitting environment without resorting to
importing rocks.

I learned much from his garden: how to get the correct soil mix,
the best way to use rocks with the least effort, how many societies
there were in the world that had seed exchanges, and a true apprecia-

Two fine plants for
an alpine garden are
pictured on the opposite
page: an alpine poppy in
bloom, its satiny petals
in direct contrast to the
almost black leaves of
the cultivar 'Arabicus'
belonging to the genus
Ophiopogon.

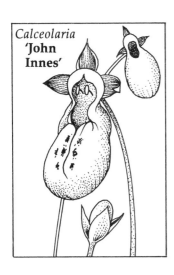

Bletilla striata

Calceolaria **'John Innes'**

tion for the native American alpine. I also learned that it was not necessary to wield a world of rock to have one of these gardens—all that's really needed is good drainage.

And drainage is the key to growing these plants. Whether they come from the Himalayas, the Andes, the high country of New Zealand, the Rocky Mountains or the Appalachians of America, the Alps, the Atlas, or the Urals, first and foremost their roots must never sit in water. Sodden soil is death to them; they want and need water but it must pass quickly over their roots. And even plants that come from the lowlands yet also require perfect drainage to survive, can be at home in an alpine setting. The term alpine covers a multitude of plants.

Thus, if a fledgling gardener had only a flat backyard with a base of clay, then by building a low, self-contained wall of either railroad ties, fieldstone, or any of different types of concrete blocks available, and filling it with the proper soil mix, he or she could grow these plants. And if room was truly at a premium, there is always the trough or container garden.

Then there is the magic of traveling by seed. Walking around Myer's garden I saw the fabled edelweiss from the Alps, blooming cyclamen from the Middle East, dwarf tulips from Central Asia (*Tulipa urumiensis*), Japanese painted fern, the blue Himalayan poppy, *Meconopsis betonicifolia*, and a native prickly pear cactus.

PLANNING AN ALPINE GARDEN

There are a bewildering number of plants suitable for rock gardening. The various rock garden societies sponsor seed exchanges with an average listing of over 1,000 species per year. Making a choice, especially when based on limited experience, is difficult to say the least. And most backyards do not have gentle mountain slopes rising to the distant horizon, nor are they conveniently located within walking—and hauling—distance of picturesque and crumbling stone walls ready to move for the asking.

Rock gardening does not have the sheer bravado of a full scale perennial border: Alpine flowers are usually brilliantly colored but small. Scale is very important here or individual plants can become lost in the vistas.

Therefore the following plan is small. The plot measures 5 by 10 feet and assumes there is a gentle rise somewhere on your property that gets full sun for at least half the day. If you do not have such a place, the plan can be adapted to the instructions for the scree bed on page 10 by just lowering the height of the wall described to between 18 and 24 inches.

After you have chosen the spot, remove the turf and soil to a depth of about 10 inches. It's a good idea to place the excavated soil on a piece of plastic sheeting, especially if you are working on part of your lawn. Use the turf elsewhere or consign it to the compost heap. Break up the remaining soil and make sure there are not weeds or weed roots within. Most alpines cannot fight the vigor of common weeds.

Mixing the Fill

Fill the bottom of the hole with rubble: rocks, stones removed from the soil, pieces of broken crockery, bits of brick, and even broken glass.

Now make a low wall using either pieces of fieldstone salvaged from old walls and foundations, or stones purchased from a dealer who carries a large collection of rock. Common concrete blocks can be used if nothing else is available. I've built low walls of such blocks and then topped them with flat fieldstones picked up from endless walks through fields in the stony Northeast. The drawing shows a

When you are ready to fill the space, mix your leftover soil in a wheelbarrow with some builder's sand (available in bags from the local lumberyard) and some good leaf mold or composted manure. For every full load of soil use a half-load of sand and a half-load of the mold or manure. You can use dampened peat moss if the last two items are not available. To every wheelbarrow load of dirt add a 3 1/2-inch flowerpot full of bone meal.

After half the depth of the bed is filled with the mix, wet it thoroughly with the hose to help settle the soil in the rubble on the bottom. Let it sit overnight before adding the final half of the soil mix. Then let everything sit for a few days more before starting to plant.

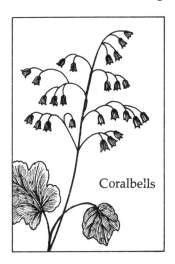

Coralbells

Other Options

If you are lucky enough to know someone with an old soapstone sink—and they are willing to let it go—or you yourself have an old tub or two, you have the makings of a perfect container garden. Keep the drain open, lay a layer of rubble on the bottom and then fill with the mix as described above. Even very small troughs or old-fashioned planters can be used in the same way to make miniature gardens of pure perfection.

Early spring is a great time to put the bed together, after you've ordered plants. Then while you wait for the plants to arrive, construction can proceed.

In my plan I've added a large rock in the upper left corner and a hollowed-out piece of fieldstone at lower right for a tiny reflecting pool. Using a cold chisel on a cool day and just chipping away at a 14 by 18 by 5 inch stone, I was able to pare away enough to hold an inch of water.

Usually the plants are shipped either in small pots or carefully wrapped in aluminum foil. Take care in unpacking so the roots are disturbed as little as possible. Water well and using small pots or folded cardboard, shade the plants from the hot sun for a few days.

Cyclamen hederifolium

The plan for the alpine garden.

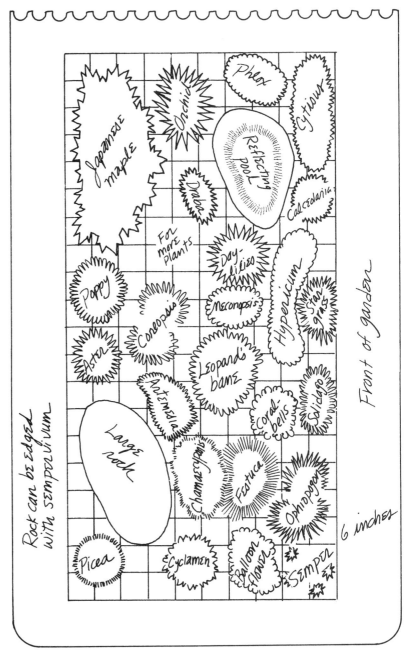

Plants for the Alpine Garden

The following plants are all available from the various nurseries listed in the Appendixes. Nothing is really unusual except for the *Meconopsis,* which I included just for the adventure of it all. In each measurement, the first is the height and the second, the spread of the plant. All have proved to be hardy in our Zone 5.

If while perusing the catalogs you find other plants that pique your interest more than these, simply change the plan. Remember to make a sketch of whatever you propose before beginning to build or to buy.

The Japanese maple (*Acer palmatum*) in my garden was purchased at a garden center when very small. It is now about 10 inches high and spreads about 40 inches. It is an unknown cultivar (on sale because the label was lost) and grows very slowly.

The artemesia (*Artemesia Genipi* or *A. schmidtiana* var. *nana*), 6 by 12 inches, is a small plant that forms a cushion-like mound of beautiful silver-gray foliage. Flowers are small and yellow. This plant is grown primarily as a foil for the other plants in the collection.

The asters are flowers of the fall and *Aster dumosus* **'Niobe'**, 6 by 12 inches, blooms at summer's end with perfect little white daisies. There are other colors, but I think the white with yellow centers are especially attractive.

Everyone loves an orchid, and people are often amazed to find that there is one that blooms without fail (it's usually hardy to 0°F. so this plant is mulched in our garden) every summer. Bletillas (*Bletilla striata*) bear shocking pink flowers resembling miniature cattleyas (the corsage orchid of Senior Proms and Mother's Day), clustering atop an 18-inch stem. Spread is negligible. There is also a white form, **'Alba'**.

The slipper flower (*Calceolaria* **'John Innes'**), 6 by 8 inches, is a miniature of the popular Easter plant. This species bears yellow flowers lightly dotted with red about the lip. They are so tropical in appearance it's difficult to believe their presence when seen in a garden. But without adequate drainage they soon perish, so the alpine garden is a perfect home for them.

Chamaecyparis Lawsoniana **'Minima'**, 20 by 15 inches, is a dwarf conifer that has green fan-shaped foliage and grows at an astounding rate of 1 1/4 inches a year. After 10 years the tree will take on the shape of a round ball, 24 inches in diameter. It needs winter protection from heavy snow or its tender branches will break.

The bluegrass daisy (*Coreopsis auriculata* **'Nana'**), 8 by 6 inches, bears 1 1/2-inch orange flowers. While not truly a rock garden plant, the dainty blossoms are right at home with diminutive cousins. I was introduced to this charming plant by Eleanor Saur of Hillsboro, Ohio. The plant was found by Dr. Lucy Braun near Maysville, Kentucky.

The cyclamens are among the most beautiful flowers in the world. They are beloved flowers for Christmas but an overheated home can quickly lead to their demise. There are, however, hardy specimens and *Cyclamen hederifolium*, 4 by 6 inches, is one. At temperatures below 0°F., this cyclamen will need winter protection. Mine is planted in the shelter of a rock where the bitter west winds blow above its leaf-covered spot.

The brooms can best be described as evergreen whips covered in early summer with pea-like blossoms of pink or yellow. They are spectacular and *Cytisus* × *kewensis*, 8 by 4 inches, is one of the hardiest. These plants do their best when planted in the well-drained soil of a rock garden.

Leopard's-bane

Phlox subulata **'Sneewichen'**

Leopard's-bane (*Doronicum cordatum*), 6 by 10 inches, blooms with bright yellow daisy-like flowers in late spring.

The drabas or Russian mustards (*Draba lasiocarpa*), 4 by 6 inches, are tiny plants from the Arctic circle or the steppes of central Asia. They open four-petaled flowers in very early spring and have a very sweet scent.

Festuca glauca, 8 by 10 inches, is one of the best ornamental grasses for the alpine garden. Its stiff leaves are a silvery blue in color and the plant resembles a small hedgehog balled up at the garden's edge.

The coralbells are mostly from the western part of North America. They prefer a well-drained soil and lots of sun. *Heuchera* **'Red Sentinel'**, 12 by 8 inches, holds many tiny bells atop thin, wiry, stems.

Daylilies are usually thought of as being large and only suitable for a perennial border. *Hemerocallis* **'Good Fairy of Oz'** measures 12 by 6 inches and has rose-colored flowers in perfect scale for the alpine garden.

St. John's wort (*Hypericum olympicum*), 9 by 12 inches, bears many 1 1/2-inch golden blossoms with dozens of sparkling stamens that float above the petals.

Star grass (*Hypoxis hirsuta*), 10 by 6 inches, is an American wildflower that revels in dry soil and bears bright yellow flowers 1/2-inch long.

Meconopsis horridula is included here because I worked three years to get one plant to bloom—but it was well worth the effort. I hope that the reader will allow one blatant adventure and try to grow one species from this usually difficult genus (see page 8).

Ophiopogon planiscapus **'Arabicus'**, 6 by 6 inches, is a member of the lily family but not necessarily grown for flowers; rather, it's the striking dark purple, almost black color of the leaves that makes this plant a fine addition to the alpine bed. It is not reliably hardy north of Zone 6, so be advised.

The alpine poppy (*Papaver nudicaule*, *P. alpinum*, or *P. Burseri*) is one of those flowers that gives joy wherever it grows. It will easily self-sow without becoming a pest. The taproot is long so it does not transplant with ease. Blossoms are white, orange, yellow, or orange-red and have a sweet fragrance.

Every alpine garden should have a few phlox, and *Phlox subulata* **'Sneewichen'**, 3 by 9 inches, is one of the best. While many of its cousins have too-bright colors for a small garden, this one bears tiny, snow-white flowers.

Picea glauca **'Echiniformis'**, 7 by 9 inches, is another dwarf conifer that makes a fine focal point—albeit a small one—in the alpine bed.

The balloon flower of Japan has a small cultivar, *Platycodon grandiflorus* **'Mariesii'** which grows to 12 by 6 inches, with pastel blue flowers.

There are many species of the houseleeks or live-forevers (*Sempervivum* spp.), and all belong in bunches in any alpine garden. There are so many species available that picking just a few is a formidable job. Try *S. arachnoideum* **'Major'** with its purple-green edges, or *S. arachnoideum* **'Raspberry Ice'** with silvery hairs on pink leaves.

The goldenrods have always had a bad press. They are blamed for hayfever every fall when it is really the ragweeds (*Ambrosia* spp.) that stuff up American noses. The English have been working with these flowers for years and now there are miniatures for the alpine garden. *Solidago spathulata* var. *nana*, 6 by 8 inches, originally came from the Far West and looks just like its larger cousins of the field, seen through the wrong end of a telescope.

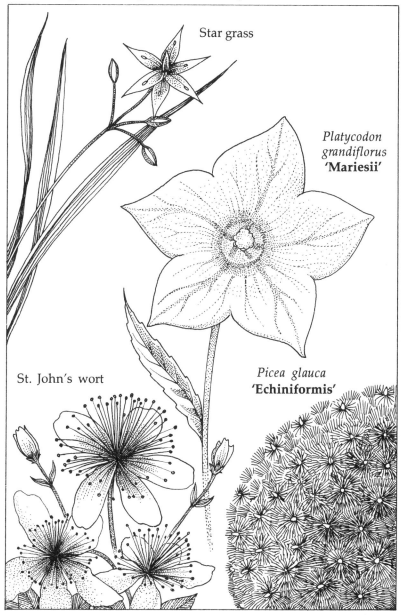

Star grass

Platycodon grandiflorus **'Mariesii'**

St. John's wort

Picea glauca **'Echiniformis'**

MECONOPSIS: A CRUEL AND TANTALIZING RACE

That title is not mine. It was penned by the English garden writer Reginald Farrer, a man who had a profound influence on gardeners of the Edwardian Era just before World War I and who did more to popularize alpine plants than any other. It is said that at elegant and sophisticated dinners where conversation usually dealt with gossip and scandal, everyone turned to talk of alpine wildflowers, drainage, and compost when Mr. Farrer walked into the room. Rock gardens were so popular it's as though the *National Enquirer* would suddenly devote its pages to planting vegetables instead of its usual fare.

When Farrer wrote of *Meconopsis* his thoughts were of a very beautiful flower, a flower that had become, like edelweiss, a legend in its own horticultural time. For these blossoms are four-petaled (sometimes up to ten) poppies with many golden stamens and colors that run the gamut from sky blue to pale blue to deep purple and an occasional lavender. But they are flowers that, unfortunately, could be most politely termed as "difficult to grow."

Every year since starting an alpine garden I've tried to raise a few of these Himalayan poppies, these blue beauties from China and Tibet. Each year germination proceeds until I lose 19 out of 20 seedlings. Then the one survivor is carefully nurtured through a hot summer—

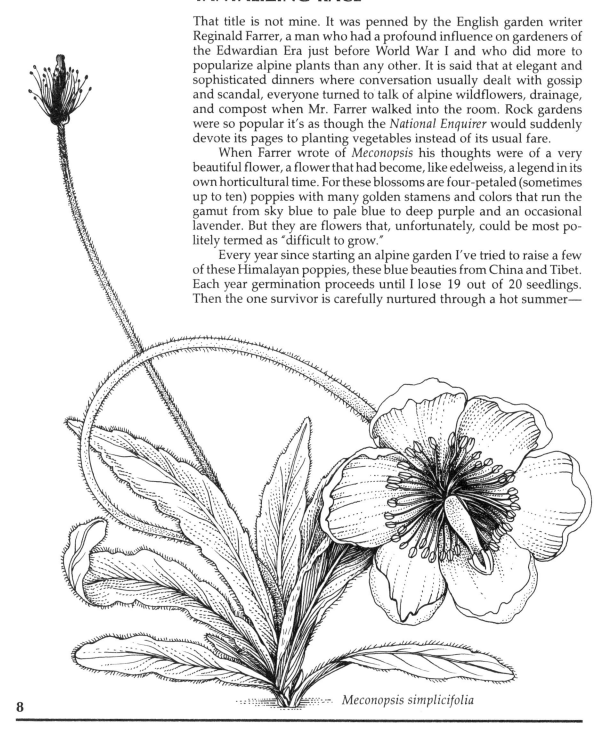

Meconopsis simplicifolia

that it dislikes—and a wet winter without snow—that it detests—
then a fateful spring, one glorious flower, and death. And ironically,
the only species that *has* bloomed in my garden is *M. horridula*, so
called because the stems are covered with spines.

Some books say Himalayan poppies are monocarpic and die after
flowering (just my luck that *M. horridula* is one), others say they are
perennials. But whatever their hold on life, it's tenuous in my backyard.

If you do decide to try growing these fabled flowers follow
Farrer's advice and provide: a cool corner, perfectly drained, but kept
well damped in earth and air alike, a soil compounded of sand,
leafmold, shredded peat, old loam, and charcoal, and a great deal of
hope.

Propagation is by seeds sown in early autumn in sterile sand or
sphagnum moss and then moved on to bigger peat pots when able to
be pricked out. Unfortunately they are also prone to slug damage so
keep a wary eye out for these pests.

There is one alternative. Try growing the only European in the list
of species: *M. cambrica*, the Welsh poppy. Petals are golden-yellow
rather than blue and the plants are tough enough to survive in most
any garden. In fact ours come up every spring and taunt me with their
flaunting flowers that are programmed to remind me of blue.

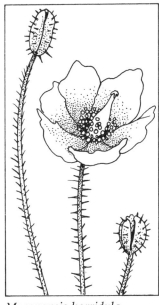

Meconopsis horridula

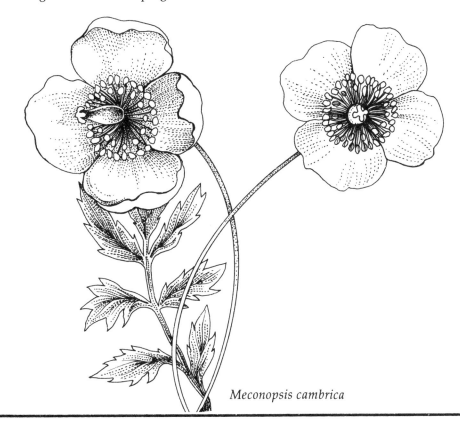

Meconopsis cambrica

BUILDING A SCREE BED

Luckily, when the impulse to install a scree bed on our property came over me a few years ago it was early spring, so by the time I was striding up and down the backyard with a measuring tape, legal pad, and pencil, the snow was gone. I had been rock gardening for well over three years, slowly fortifying the steep bank at the rear boundary of our property with fieldstone barricades; these held the individual clumps of hand-mixed sandy soil with which I had replaced the top foot or so of compacted clay and red shale. The sandy soil helped hasten the replacement of sheep sorrel (*Rumex Acetosella*) and wild carrot (*Daucus Carota*) that occupied the site with various species of *Draba*, a grouping of white potentilla (*Potentilla repestris* **'Alba'**), many cultivars of dwarf ornamental grasses, and a number of small conifers.

I needed room, however, to try some of the difficult mountain flowers, which require absolutely perfect drainage to survive; their roots are so sensitive to standing water that 1 foot of well-drained soil is not enough. The answer to my needs seemed to be what rock gardeners call a scree bed—a pile of crushed stone or gravel through which water would drain before it could harm delicate roots.

The flat part of our backyard that was not devoted to a perennial border was planted in patches of field grasses, perennial rye, and various weeds. Originally I had wanted an English lawn as a frame for the flowers, but after what seemed like decades spent removing that old red shale and clay (and various articles of trash left by two generations of a farming family) I settled for the weedy substitutes.

But the idea of a scree bed continued to intrigue me. If I installed a dry wall of flat fieldstones taken from the many rambling walls that snaked their way about our property—or used some of the old barn foundation from a nearby field—I would have enough rock to build a curved wall some 2 1/2 feet high that would form a semicircle, with the 20-foot straight side running along the back of the bank. And a dry wall held in place by the weight of the stones would allow us to proceed without the bother of mixing and pointing up cement.

If the backyard had been small, or if I had been short of stone, the principle would still have applied: I could have built a bed some 6 feet wide at the base, up to 3 feet high, and as long as possible. But the same problem that occurs with a hobby greenhouse occurs with a scree bed: No matter how large it seems before you start, it always turns out to be too small.

The pluses of a scree bed far outweigh the difficulties of installing it, if you are up to the initial strain of hauling and placing the rocks. Instead of merely dreaming about flowers like lewisias, wild sedums from the mountains of the West, and *Polygonum affine* (which had never yet lived through the winter), I could finally have a chance not only to see such beauties thrive but to enjoy their bloom.

After a few futile attempts at carrying large fieldstones from the walls and foundations over large humps of field grasses in a small wheelbarrow, I enlisted the aid of a neighboring farmer who owned a tractor with a front end loader. This enabled us to drive right up to the

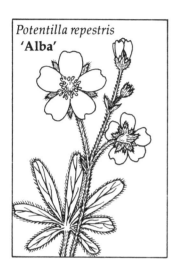

Potentilla repestris
'Alba'

Aster alpinus

stones, load eight or ten on the tractor, and drive back to the site with ease.

We made a single pile, about eight stones high, over which we stretched a string level across the site, parallel to the bank. One of the tricky requirements in laying a stone wall is keeping it level with the terrain, so that one is spared the annoyance of having to look at a crooked wall for the rest of one's life.

There are people who can start at one end of a plot and walk out a perfect curve, but I am not one of them, so to lay out the initial semicircle we set the garden hose in place. The hose was like a thick piece of string that kept its position.

Next, my neighbor and I chose the largest stones, each between 14 and 18 inches wide, 18 to 24 inches long, and 3 to 4 inches thick. After laying each stone along the inside curve of the hose, we removed a bit of soil so that the back edge was about an inch lower than the front. That way the rainwater would flow into the bed along the sloping rocks and reach the roots of plants growing along the face of the wall.

If the soil had been soft, I would have had to excavate at least 18 inches of soil before starting the wall to give it a firm footing. As it was, the clay and shale were solid enough for us to lay stones directly on the ground.

We placed the bottom stones as close together as we could and filled all gaps with a mix of dirt and gravel taken from the truckload of crushed stone we had bought to make up the fill for the bed. Once the initial ring of stones was down, we put the next layer on so that each

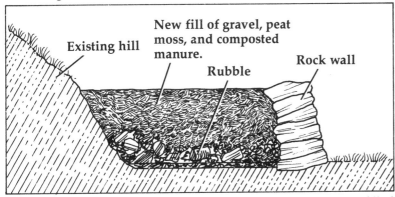

Existing hill

New fill of gravel, peat moss, and composted manure.

Rubble

Rock wall

gap in the first layer was covered by the second, and so on. We filled all the gaps in each level with the soil mix.

We piled layer upon layer in this way until the wall reached a height of 2 1/2 feet. The best-shaped and flattest stones finished off the top. The wall is so strong that one can step on it with nary a wiggle, and at the same time it provides a comfortable place to sit.

Then we began the process of filling in the cavity, throwing into it just about every stone I had gathered during other gardening chores, along with broken pots, bits of broken glass, and other pieces of solid trash. Soon the first foot was full of angular pieces of rubble, but there were many open spaces in between. Only then did I add the planting

List of Plants for a Scree bed:

1. *Cotoneaster horizontalis*
2. *Chiastophyllum oppositifolium*
3. *Erica carnea* **'Winter Beauty'**
4. *Lewisia cotyledon*
5. *Erinus alpinus*
6. Japanese bamboo grass, *Hakonechloa macra* **'Albovariegata'**
7. *Geranium dalmaticum*
8. *Anacyclus depressus*
9. *Caryopteris × clandonensis*
10. *Heuchera cylindrica*
11. Alpine clematis, *Clematis alpina*
12. Alpine columbine, *Aquilegia alpina* var. *alba nana*
13. *Ophiopogon planiscapus* **'Arabicus'**
14. *Hosta Nakaiana*
15. *Abdrosace pyrenaica*
16. Mountain pinks, *Dianthus* spp.
17. Spring-blooming bulbs
18. *Juniperus squamata* **'Blue Star'**
19. For future expansion
20. *Sequoia sempervirens* **'Adpressa'**
21. *Sempervivum* spp.
22. Dwarf grama grass, *Bouteloua gracilis nana*
23. *Dianthus Noeanus*
24. *Aubrieta deltoidea* **'Dr. Miles'**
25. *Allium cyaneaum*
26. Germander, *Teucrium chamaedrys*
27. *Juncus effusus* **'Spiralis'**
28. *Shortia galacifolia*
29. *Draba stellata*
30. Alpine poppy, *Papaver alpinus*
31. *Draba aizoon*
32. *Iris verna*
33. *Aster alpinus*
34. *Sedum nevii*
35. *Tsuga canadensis* **'Jervis'**
36. *Callirhoe involucrata*
37. *Crocus chrysanthus* **'Ruby Giant'** and **'E. A. Bowles'**
38. *Tsuga canadensis* **'Cole'**
39. *Saxifraga longifolia*
40. *Rosularia paniculata*
41. *Cytisus × praecox* **'Luteus'**
42. *Yucca Harrimaniae*
43. *Festuca glauca* **'Sea Urchin'**
44. *Yucca rupicola*
45. *Hesperaloe parviflora*

mix of gravel chips (each chip half an inch or less across), peat moss, and composted cow manure. It took a good deal of material to fill the cavity the full 2 1/2 feet: at least 20 bags of manure, most of the load of gravel, and two to three bales of peat moss.

Although impatient, I could plant nothing until the following winter was over and the mix had settled properly. And sure enough, by next spring the level of the mix had dropped some two inches, so I had to add more.

The real beauty of a scree bed now begins. In the layers of rock and compost towards the bottom of the bed the plants' roots can find air and moisture, but always combined with perfect drainage so that rot is prevented. Plants that would be lost in bad winters if left in a typical garden's soil will survive in a scree. And in a hot summer when rain is in short supply, the garden hose will fill the bill.

I always make sure that plants get shade during their first few days of settling in and plenty of water until their roots begin to grow toward the bottom of the bed. Before inserting plants in the crevices of the wall, I wrap soil and roots in a paper towel. By the time the roots start to grow down into the cracks, the towel has disintegrated.

We are now entering our fourth year with our raised scree bed, and it is beginning to look as though it has been there for many years.

Draba aizoon

Juncus effusus **'Spiralis'**

An alpine clematis (*Clematis alpina*) now climbs up the rock face on a diagonal; a perfect clump of broom (*Cytisus × praecox* **'Luteus'**) flows over the edge at the far right of the semicircle; and some smaller Japanese hosta (*Hosta Nakaiana*) grows along the outside base, sheltered from the afternoon sun.

In early spring the mountain pinks, rock jasmine (*Androsace villosa*), species tulips, miniature daffodils, mountain asters, and various saxifrages are in bloom. By late June the potentillas, *Polygonum affine* **'Donald Lowndes'**, and some dwarf and mat-forming penstemons share space with clumps of free-seeding alpine poppies (often sold under the name of *Papaver alpinum*). The end of July finds large and healthy clumps of *Teucrium Chamadedrys* full of blooms and buzzing with bees.

Along the rear of the bed, snuggled against the rising bank, I've planted a group of dwarf hemlocks (*Tsuga canadensis* **'Cole'**, **'Jervis'**, and **'Gentsch White'**) that share space with clumps of heaths, chiefly *Erica carnea* **'Winter Beauty'**.

And the best part is that the scree bed has just enough room for another year's crop of seedlings gathered from around the world. Then I'll be forced to think of a new place to build another bed.

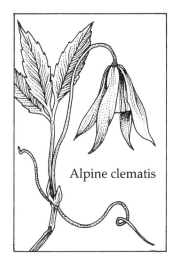

Alpine clematis

Aubrieta deltoidea **'Dr. Miles'**

Sempervivum spp.

Dianthus Noeanus

AN ANNUAL GARDEN

Peonies, roses, I ignore,
Lilies, daffodils, stay away.
But candytuft is sweet and
Morning glories grow upon my cabin door.

W. S. Lecher, *Garden Almanac*

It is September, and an early frost has just come to our new annual garden. It was predicted, and blamed on a Canadian high by the weatherman, but knowing the cause does not blunt the edge of the passing of a summer's work. Today under a warming sun insects chirp and chatter (their din will increase only until cut down by the killing frosts of October), and China asters burn with the glow of Persian miniatures in the front of the garden. Though they are framed by the black and stiffened petals and leaves of rudbeckias, just behind them pink and white spider flowers waft in the wind, and farther back the castor beans have lost only their bottom leaves.

While shoofly plants are decorated with shriveled leaves and ripening soft-brown seedpods, and corncockles show only a bloom or two, the 3-foot spires of basket flowers, admittedly bedraggled, are still bright with pastel colors. And the front edge of the border boasts the orange and satiny petals of star-of-the-veldt daisies, punctuated by the sparkling yellows of the last of the California tidytips.

It's true that the garden is mellower now, but what a show there was a scant three weeks ago!

Last winter my wife and I planned a new garden composed entirely of annuals: plants and flowers that had to sprout, grow, bloom, and set seed within one summer's time, or about 110 days in our region (Zone 5), though every year varies a bit. And the plants we chose had to be different from the familiar crowd; no marigolds, petunias, or common zinnias would flaunt their gaudy blossoms in this garden.

We checked seed catalogs both foreign and domestic, looking for the unusual either in flower, form, or color. In the end we chose some 30 species.

The striking blossoms on the opposite page are those of the spider flower and are always welcome in an annual garden. This particular cultivar is 'Violet Queen' and has petals in a vivid purple.

17

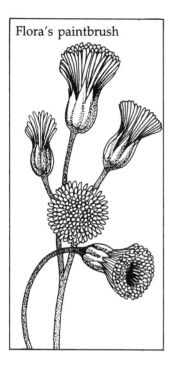

Flora's paintbrush

More About Annuals

An English classification system for annuals, based on the temperatures the seeds need to germinate and grow successfully, divides them into three groups: *hardy, half-hardy,* and *tender.* Many gardeners in the milder sections of the United States think "half-hardy" is superfluous, but I have found that the term is useful to people who have long, cool, rainy springs. Most seed companies use all three.

Hardy annuals (HA) are plants that tolerate a reasonable degree of frost, and even in the colder parts of the country many of their seeds survive a winter outside and germinate in the spring. The alternate freezes and thaws of early spring will not harm them.

Half-hardy annuals (HHA) are usually damaged, set back, or killed by frost, but they stand up to wet and cool weather without rotting.

Tender annuals (TA) come from the warmer parts of the world and need warm soil to germinate. They are killed immediately by frost.

Added to the classification of annuals are perennials, either hardy (usually from a temperate climate) or tender (generally from the tropic parts of the world), that will bloom the first year from seed.

Most seed packets today give full instructions for care and note any special treatment required. Most catalogs do the same.

Planting Out

Since annuals must complete their life cycles in such a short time, they need reasonably good growing conditions. While most produce some flowers even in the poorest of soils, the more friable the ground the better the flower. Applications of fertilizer, compost, and adequate watering will ensure healthy plants and a good show of flowers.

When flowers fade through the season, remove the dying blossoms to prevent seed-set and to force a longer period of bloom. Allow plants to produce seed only as the season winds down. When the seeds are ripe and dry, pick and store for the following year in a cool place away from moisture.

Because our season is so short, we started most of the following plants indoors at the beginning of April, using a heating cable under the seeds to speed germination. At the end of May, after a few days of hardening off in a cold frame, we moved them to permanent positions.

A few plants do not take kindly to transplanting and should be sown directly in the garden and are so noted in the individual descriptions.

THE ANNUAL PLOT

The area in the back garden that we used for the annual border is a five-sided plot about 20 feet long and 8 feet wide at its deepest measurement. It is on a gently rising slope that faces southeast and is surrounded by a lawn—and that term is loosely used, as the greens are more weed than fescue.

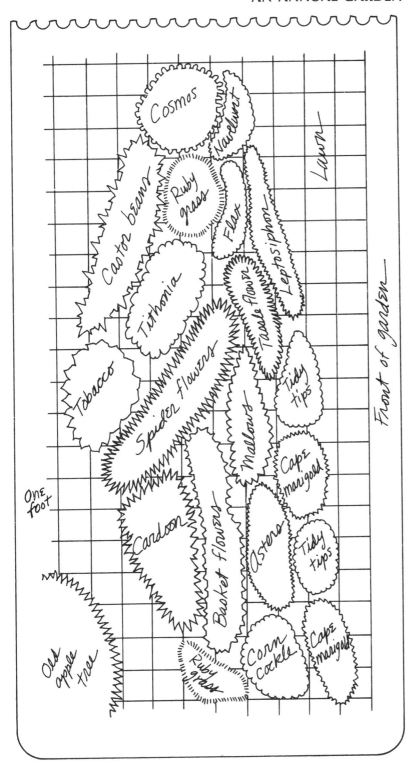

The plan for the annual border.

Corncockle

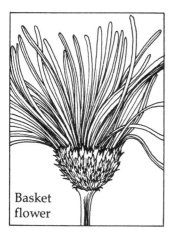

Basket
flower

Plants for an Annual Border

Corncockle (*Agrostemma Githago*), a well-known weed of Mediterranean origin, is called a noxious invader of grain fields by some authorities and passed off as having no horticultural interest by others. In addition, its seeds are said to be poisonous. It would thus seem a back-of-the-border choice at best, especially as plants often reach 3 feet with little care. But the flowers are a soft magenta-rose with satiny overtones, and they deserve better press. Corncockle is beautiful both in the garden and as a cut flower. Each petal is marked with three dotted-to-solid lines that perhaps serve as an insect's guide to the flower center. A cultivar known as **'Milas'** has soft lilac-pink flowers up to 3 inches across. Germination occurs in 12 days, they are hardy annuals, prefer full sun and should be planted in bunches for the best effect. Make a number of sowings over the summer to have flowers for the entire season.

China asters (*Callistephus chinensis*) make a wonderful show in the garden as well as in the house as a cut flower, although once cut, a plant will not rebloom. Originally from China, the one known species has been endlessly cajoled by breeders to produce many cultivars. China asters need good soil and full sun, but will give a reasonable show in partial shade. The particular cultivar in our garden is called **'Giant Princess'** and produces on 2-foot stems a number of mum-like flowers with tightly packed petals of amethyst, ruby red, deep purple, deep pink, pale rose, and a delicate creamy white. Seeds germinate in 10 to 12 days and the plants are tender annuals. Plants should be spaced about 10 inches apart and never planted in the same place twice because they are subject to two fungal diseases that may overwinter in the soil. Make successive sowings over the summer.

One of my favorite annuals is the basket flower (*Centaurea americana*) and it's hard to understand why more fuss isn't made over this plant. This American wildflower is interesting in bud and splendid in bloom. Each flower sits alone on a 4-foot stem and opens to 4 inches across. The color is a light rose, and the flower resembles an open thistle without thorns. The common name refers to the unopened head, which is surrounded by soft, spiny, strawcolored appendages that overlap and give the distinctive appearance of tiny woven baskets. Basket flowers require no special soil but grow best in full sun. They are good at the back of the border because the individual blossoms—which close at night—are large and easily visible from a distance. Germination takes two to three weeks and they are hardy annuals. Set plants 6 inches apart and make successive sowings over the summer.

The cardoon (*Cynara cardunculus*) has made such an impression on my consciousness that it has a special essay on page 26.

Spider flower (*Cleome Hasslerana*) gets its name from the spiderlike (or more truthfully, daddy-longlegs-like) blossoms with many long, waving stamens. Planted in large masses, spider flowers look like blooming shrubbery. The plants like full sun but will take partial shade. They can reach 6 feet in a good growing season. In our annual border I used the following cultivars with the darkest color to the rear: **'Violet Queen'** is a vivid purple; it was followed by **'Cherry Queen'**, a bright carmine rose; next came **'Pink Queen'**;and in the front went **'Helen Campbell'**, a glistening white. Germination takes 10 to 14 days, plants are half-hardy annuals, and should be spaced about a foot apart. They make good cut flowers.

Cosmos daisies (*Cosmos bipinnatus*), have been in every garden that we've ever had. They produce all summer long, make great cut flowers, and even the lacy foliage grows to good effect in the border. Plants are tall and perfect for the back of the border. Look for **'Candystripe'** with white petals edged with crimson or **'Sea Shells'**, the new flower that has petals that curve in on themselves like delicate denizens of the sea. Plants like full sun, are half-hardy annuals, and take about 5 days for germination.

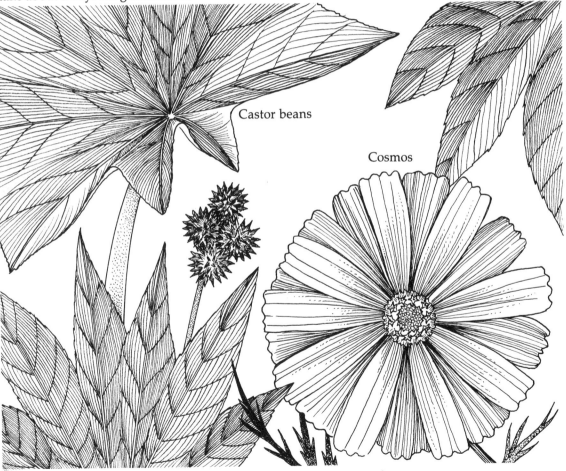

Castor beans

Cosmos

Star-of-the-veldt (*Dimorphotheca sinuata*) is more commonly known as the Cape marigold, a name I hesitate to use, given the number of times that I've been critical of marigolds. This daisy grows about a foot tall and once in flower continues for weeks on end. The

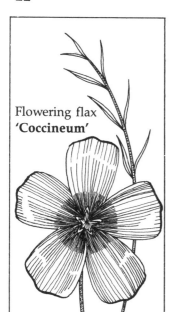

Flowering flax
'Coccineum'

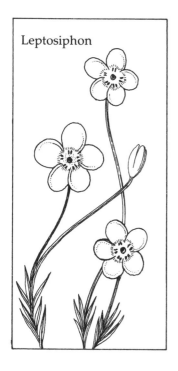

Leptosiphon

species has orange petals and yellow centers, but hybrids are now available in creamy white, salmon, yellow, and pastel colors. Plants prefer full sun and cool nights, and withstand drought conditions with ease. Blossoms close at night and even creep together on cloudy days. Use them in a heavy drift. Germination takes 10 to 15 days; plants are half-hardy annuals and should be spaced 8 inches apart.

The tassel flower, or Flora's paintbrush (*Emilia javanica*), bears bright red-orange flowers, each 1/2 inch in length, on 1 to 2-foot stems. They look exactly like miniatures of the tassels you would find holding drapes in a Victorian living room, or like tiny paintbrushes dipped in scarlet paint. Foliage is neat and gray-green and flowers bloom over a long period. Store seeds away from light. Germination takes 8 to 10 days, plants are half-hardy annuals and should be spaced about 10 inches apart.

Tree mallows (*Lavatera trimestris*) grow to 3 feet or more and are generously covered with hollyhock-like trumpets from mid-July until they are cut down by frost in the fall. But few plants give so many beautiful flowers over so long a season with so little care. Tree mallows prefer good soil in full sun. Remove the flowers as they fade. The cultivar **'Silver Cup'** is usually offered and has petals of bright, shiny rose-pink. All the cultivars make great cut flowers. Because of their growth habit, mallows look more like shrubs than garden annuals and are truly grand in a large grouping. Germination takes 15 to 20 days; the plants are tender annuals and should be planted 2 feet apart.

Tidytips (*Layia platyglossa*) are California wildflowers that I first saw in an English garden catalog. They are as cheerful as their name implies. Their small daisy-like flowers have sunny yellow petals, each with a dainty, white, deckle edge. Blossoms 2 inches across are excellent for cutting. The plants produce such a wealth of flowers, that it's easier to make successive sowings for all-summer blooms than to remove spent flowers from existing plants. Tidytips withstand a temperature of 26°F. Germination is in 12 to 14 days; the plants are hardy annuals and should be spaced 6 inches apart in wide drifts.

Leptosiphon first caught my eye in Gertrude Jekyll's book *Annuals and Biennials,* wherein she refers to them as "pretty little dwarf-growing plants, related to *Gilia*, about 6 inches high." No garden of ours will ever be without them. They come in colors of white, carmine, cream, orange, and yellow, all shining like tiny stars. They may be planted on the spot in areas with long growing seasons, or started indoors. Leptosiphon blooms throughout the summer in self-contained bunches. Unfortunately, its botanical name is not as easy to find as the flowers are to grow. When looking it up in the *Royal Horticultural Society Dictionary,* I was referred to *Gilia*, then to *Gilia × hybrida* or *G. androsacea*, which in *Hortus Third* becomes *Linanthuys androsaceus* (as the leaves are opposite and palmately divided). Catalogs still list the plants as leptosiphon or stardust. Germination time is 10 to 14 days and the plants are hardy annuals.

Flowering flax (*Linum grandiflorum*) grows about 2 feet high in most any soil, withstands dry conditions, and needs full sun. Flowers bloom up to 1 1/2 inches across, with petals that resemble the finest of satin. Three cultivars to look for are **'Coccineum'** with scarlet flowers, **'Roseum'** with rose-pink petals, and bright red **'Rubrum'**. Plants are very strong, holding up in the heaviest of winds and rain. Mass them for the best effect. Common flax (*L. usitatissimum*), Latin for "most useful," is an ancient plant grown for fibers that make linen and seeds that yield linseed oil. Germination takes about two weeks. Plant flax directly in the garden—it is difficult to transplant. The plants are hardy annuals.

Navelwort (*Omphalodes linifolia*) or more properly Venus' navelwort (*wort* is an Old English word for plant), is aptly named. For this sweet flower is surely as charming as the goddess' navel. Individual flowers look like large white forget-me-nots. They bloom in long sprays on gray-green stems and make excellent cut flowers. The inspiration for this plant's common name becomes apparent as seeds develop, four to a flower: They look decidedly like tiny navels. Plants prefer a moist, shady spot, especially in front of a wall. In the plan shown on page 19 they are protected by the tithonia. They grow about a foot high and are hardy annuals.

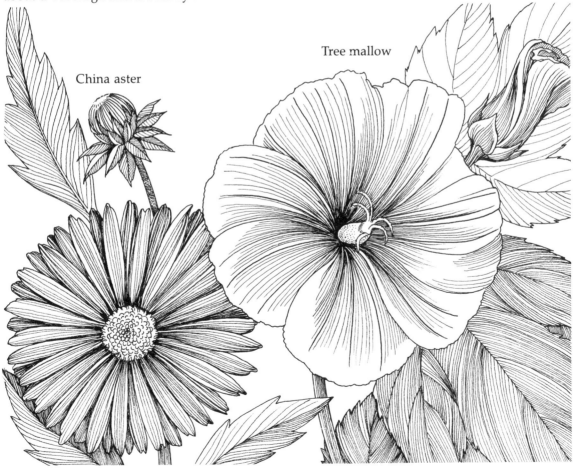

China aster

Tree mallow

Navelwort

Just to make the annual garden look established we used some tobacco plants (*Nicotiana Tabacum*) to the rear of the plot. Most authorities dismiss this plant. They shouldn't. Tobacco plants grow to 7 feet, are covered with blossoms, and are quite beautiful in the garden. In our climate seeds must be started indoors six to eight weeks before the last spring frost. Tobacco is a half-hardy annual. Give plants full sun and watch out for aphids. Though often thought of as being tender, mature plants will withstand a temperature of 26°F.

Ruby grass (*Rhynchelytrum repens*) is a fine ornamental grass that has been used as forage in hot, dry areas and has naturalized in some southern states. The open panicles of bloom are held aloft on 3-foot stems and shimmer with a rosy glow, especially when backlit by the sun. Although the blossoms are said to shatter after they dry, we've kept them in winter bouquets until the weight of the dust caused them to break apart; just treat them with care. They also make an excellent cut flower. Plants begin to bloom in midsummer and will continue until the final frost. Germination takes 25 to 30 days, so in the North start seeds indoors six weeks before the last spring frost. The plants are half-hardy annuals.

Castor beans (*Ricinus communis*) are grown for their leaves, not their flowers, and were once a prominent part of every garden. The plant is the source of castor oil, and the seed is truly poisonous and can easily hurt a child, which may explain why fewer and fewer seed companies carry it. This spectacular plant gives a garden a tropical look, even as far north as Maine. The leaves can often be 3 feet wide, and the plants over 10 feet high. **'Gibsonii'** has dark red leaves with a metallic luster, while **'Red Spire'** has bronzy green leaves on maroon stems. Plants need good drainage and cannot tolerate wet feet. Flowers are small and nondescript, but the developing fruits resemble bunches of small chestnut burrs. Germination takes 15 to 20 days and plants should be set 3 or 4 feet apart. If you are worried that unsuspecting passersby will eat the beans, simply cut off the developing pods before they open and split. Castor beans are tender annuals.

Mexican sunflowers (*Tithonia rotundifolia*) are bright dots of color for the back of the annual bed. The big, 3-inch-wide flowers are ablaze with fiery highlights. These are spectacular plants, reaching to 4 feet in height towards the season's end. Pick off spent blossoms to keep plants pushing out the flowers. And if you use them for cutting, be sure and seal the stem end with a match or gas flame as you would with poppies. A new cultivar **'Goldfinger'**, is a vivid orange-scarlet; the blossoms of **'Yellow Torch'** are bright, bright yellow. Tithonias are half-hardy annuals. To get a full season of bloom, start them indoors about six weeks before the last spring frost.

All summer long the annual garden is full of beautiful flowers. Then in the fall when a bright orange band of light stretches across the western horizon, sandwiched between dark clouds above and the brown earth below, the annual garden is through for another year. But for the work involved and the effort expended, these plants give far more beauty and excitement than a gardener is ever led to expect by the term "annual."

Tobacco

Mexican sunflowers

25

THE CARDOON

Every few years I find a plant that is truly exciting in a very *big* way. I delight in wandering out to the garden to check its progress as the season advances. One such plant is the cardoon (*Cynara cardunculus*), a monumental collection of leaves that is grown as a vegetable in France, questioned by the rest of the world as to why the French eat it, and viewed as a most striking ornamental by all who see it on the spot.

The new leaves are a downy, whitish gray below and a green-gray above and look like the leaves of a thistle without such sharp points. They fan out from a ribbed stem that resembles a stalk of celery. Given good soil and a long growing season cardoons should reach 6 feet by summer's end. One plant can be a focal point standing out with regal splendor from other plants scattered about, and if you have the room, a row of these beauties will make a large and formidable hedge.

To top it off, in mid-August the flowers appear. They look like small artichokes (a very close relation) and are obviously thistles of a sort with many individual purplish blue florets. The spines around the blossoms *are* sharp. Blossoms continue to the end of October and plants withstand frost at least to −28°F.

Although grown as a perennial in southern Europe, we treat the cardoon as an annual here, starting the seeds indoors about 6 weeks before the last spring frost and planting it out at the end of May. At one time any gardener could say, "Plant it out after Memorial Day," but Congress saw fit to tamper even with that holiday date.

These plants need room to grow so allow a 36-inch circle for each one. Full sun is necessary. Soil should be fertile and cardoons will need plenty of water to develop.

Just before the first frosts of autumn, on a bright sunny day when the plants are dry, draw the leaves together around the stem and tie them in place with garden twine. Then take strips of paper about 6 inches wide and starting at the bottom, wind them around the leaves right up to the top. Over this a 3-inch band of hay is tied. Bank up the plants with soil to help with support. Leave for about a month until the blanching is complete. Plants can also be dug up and stored in a cool, dry spot with all the wrappings in place.

But even without blanching, the tender stalks and the root are used in soups. Outer stalks are discarded. Joe Seals of the Country Garden and Lucille Nava of Lava, New York (each of Italian ancestry) have informed me that "carduni" are also cut into pieces 6 inches long, partially boiled, then dipped in seasoned bread crumbs, then pan-fried.

And, Joe added: "Cardoons have also naturalized in parts of three counties in South Carolina, where the flowers are harvested, dried, and sold as 'luck' flowers or cardone puffs, often dyed obnoxious colors."

Cynara cardunculus

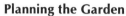

THE CUTTING GARDEN

Janet and Tom are good friends who live in New York City. They visit our country garden in the Catskills every weekend during the season of warmth—a regrettably short time, with usually only 110 days between frosts—and we always send them home to Manhattan with a bouquet of fresh flowers.

You might think that cutting fresh flowers both for friends and for the homefront would quickly deplete our flower garden. Not so. Rather than denude various parts of our permanent flower garden to fill a vase, my wife and I have included an old Victorian idea in our garden plan: a cutting garden. We grow an abundance of annuals for color, plus a few choice perennials, all specifically grown for bouquets.

Planning the Garden

Our garden measures some 20 by 20 feet, but any size that the gardener has the strength and time to tend will do; even a tiny plot can produce an amazing number of blossoms. The cutting garden should be conveniently located, near the house, and near a watering outlet, and if possible, removed from the general view of the home landscape so you never worry about how it looks, especially after you've cut into it. Ours is in the southeast corner of the vegetable patch, where it gets plenty of sun. And since we walk there every day to check on the tomatoes or pick fresh arugula, we always notice the freshest flowers.

Tidytips

Remember that this spot of land is a working garden; any thoughts given to arrangements of planting should revolve around *lebensraum,* or cultural demands, not considerations of form or color. Leave such worries to the more formal garden. For in the cutting garden an accidental contrast of colors, a hot combo that breaks all the rules against placing bright colors next to bright or dull next to dull, could well become a fine addition to the more formal garden plan.

Our layout changes from year to year, but simplicity is the keynote. I place taller plants in the rear, shorter ones up front, and keep the pathways between neat and tidy, so the dots of color resemble a Mondrian painting, a Broadway boogie-woogie of blossoms.

In fact, the cutting garden is often more fun to contemplate than the regular perennial bed or the rock garden. In the formal flower bed, plans are often projected over several years and mistakes are not always evident until it's too late for quick action. But the cutting garden offers no such constraints; in it change can be enjoyed for change's sake, experimentation can be the password.

Our planning begins at year's end when the new catalogs arrive in the mail. We vote for old favorites, choose new varieties, sort seeds on hand, and order fresh seed.

Flowers like the cosmos **'Candy Stripe'** (*Cosmos bipinnatus*) and old-fashioned sweet William (*Dianthus barbatus*) must never beg for room; in fact, we increase their allotted space every year. This particular year we left out the older varieties of marigolds (*Tagetes* spp.) and the bright-orange cockscomb (*Celosia cristata*), deciding that they are not worth the effort involved for the pleasures derived. Finally, after stamping and sealing the orders, we realized we had overlooked that new variety of flowering tobacco (*Nicotiana alata* **'Nicki Rouge'**) and had also forgotten seeds of the Moroccan toadflax (*Linaria maroccana*), a diminutive relative of the snapdragon that trades size for charm.

Planting the Garden

Soils should be well worked and reasonably fertile. Don't overdo: too much fertilizer leads to lush growth and fewer flowers. We solved the problem by building three compost heaps and working the autumn's harvest into the garden's soil every spring before planting. The original clay is now more friable and improves every year. In areas where it was particularly bad, I worked in some leaf litter (gathered in a nearby woods) as well as some moistened peat moss.

If you are starting a garden in virgin soil—especially if it is very poor soil—work in a few bags of dried manure. If you have a source for barnyard manure you can save money by using that instead, but be sure that it's aged at least six months; fresh manure can burn plants.

Try to allot enough space for successive plantings of annuals over the season. There should also be room for a few of the truly weedy flowers; their aspect in a formal garden is one of unintended neglect, but their blossoms look terrific in a pottery bowl. Queen Anne's lace (*Daucus carota* var. *carota*) and the ubiquitous teasel (*Dipsacus sylvestris*) come to mind.

I never like disturbing the formal border for the addition of dahlias (*Dahlia* spp.) or gladiolus (*Gladiolus* × *gandavensis*), and I hate the rush of digging them up on the fall after only the tops are burned by the frost (in my continuing effort to keep the garden orderly). But the informality of the cutting garden allows for the used look of dying leaves, giving us until early November to remove tubers and corms to a box for winter storage.

Sweet peas (*Lathyrus odoratus*) need a trellis of string or wire to ramble over—a casual effect best kept in the cutting garden. Once indoors, their jewel-like aspects shine from a crystal vase and their perfume rides the evening air.

Maintenance

Blooming plants use a great deal of water: All those petals unfurl and expand because of the pressure of water moving through their veins. You should water regularly and always watch for signs of wilting. When you apply water, be sure to soak the soil thoroughly. Most of the water evaporates when you sprinkle lightly. If you are not able to devote daily care to these flower beds, mulch them to conserve water. Leaf litter, peanut husks, pine needles, and even small gravel can be used. Check your garden store for what's available. As mentioned before, cocoa-bean hulls have a smell of chocolate that becomes almost overpowering and definitely detracts from scents of growing plants and flowers.

Common sense should rule your maintenance program. Remove dead or dying leaves, dispose of annuals when they are finished blooming, and remove spent blossoms to encourage the production of new flowers. When seeds form, most plants are chemically triggered to stop blooming. Keep the garden weed-free. Even though this particular kind of garden is not for show, every weed is taking moisture, space, and nutrients from your chosen plants.

A Year in the Cutting Garden

Through careful planning, a cutting garden provides blossoms from April until well after the first frost. Daffodils and narcissus can begin the season;their leaves, left to mature and die naturally, offend no eye. After the last frost you can always hide them with annuals that were started in seed flats in the sunporch or greenhouse. The first of these annuals flower in May along with late-blooming daffodils, poppies (*Papaver* spp.), and armloads of lilacs (*Syringa* spp.) from an old bush at the garden's edge.

June and July are bright with almost too many flowers to contemplate: Bachelor buttons (*Centaurea cyanus*) and coreopsis (*Coreopsis* spp.), larkspur (*Consolida ambigua*) and annual grasses (many too rangy for the garden proper) are cut to combine with our only garden rose—a pink rambler over 100 years old––and a few coleus leaves (*Coleus blumei*) for contrast.

In August we collect sprays of blooming dill (*Anethum graveolens*) from the kitchen herb garden and plunge them into a large bowl with the second crop of corncockles (*Agrostema githago*) and some red and pink zinnias.

In the back of the cutting garden next to the now-burgeoning phlox is a patch of goldenrod (*Solidago* spp.) moved in from the field because of its especially compact mounds of flowers. We picked these and mixed them with Mexican sunflowers (*Tithonia rotundifolia*), large flowers resembling daisies that flow like Incan gold.

September brings glads, dahlias, late-flowering lilies (bought as a naturalizing collection), and the fall-blooming ornamental grasses. This is the month to buy bedding mums at the local nursery for fall planting. We always buy a few extra just for cutting, as they produce new flowers until temperatures plummet to the low 20s. Now too, the flowering kale (*Brassica oleracea* var. *acephala*) begins its climb to glory: Cool nights with a nip of frost turn the filigreed edges to a frothy white with highlights of pink and purple. One head will last in water for days, even continuing to grow.

By mid-fall the nights are markedly colder. The *Hosta plantaginea*, a perennial that I grow for both sweet-smelling flowers and pleated foliage has been hurt once too often. At the shady end only the bunch of rough horsetail (*Equisetum hyemale*) its roots contained by a circle of tin to hold back its wanderings, seems impervious to frost.

When November does arrive and winter hovers just a short distance away, the cutting garden must be straightened up again, this time for the coming months of snow. I pull up the old annuals and their dead roots, rake up dead leaves and litter, and relegate everything to the compost bins. After cutting the last of the dried grasses, I roll the snowfence across the front of the vegetable garden in a vain attempt to keep the deer away from the remaining Brussels sprouts.

On Cutting Fresh Flowers

Always cut fresh flowers early in the morning, when they have had the benefit of night's cooler air. Stems are now tight with water, leaves dappled with dew, and most blossoms have recovered from the excesses of the day before. One school of thought suggests that evening,

Star-of-the-veldt

too, is a good time for cutting, but I would rather confront an awakening butterfly than a journeying slug.

Whenever possible, choose burgeoning buds and flowers just beginning to show pollen rather than older blossoms that have been trod upon by an army of bees.

Take a bucket of tepid, not cold, water into the garden and plunge the cut stems directly into it. (Cold water to a flower has the same effect as a cold shower to a gardener: Shock!) Use a sharp knife or scissors to cut the stems, and take more length than you think you might need to ensure plenty of stem for flower arranging. When cutting, never pull at the stem. This can bruise and damage cell walls, restricting the free movement of water. Cut flowers continue living and need all the water the stems can take in.

Either cut the stems straight across or at a slant. For years there have been proponents of either course of action; stem-cutters claim that the slant exposes more of the stem end to water and at the same time allows more water intake because the stem end doesn't rest against the vase's bottom. I've found no irrefutable evidence to support either method and so opt for the easiest, making sure the cut is clean and neat. Keep buckets of flowers in the shade until you're ready to leave the garden. Back in the kitchen, check again to see that each stem has a clean cut. Experts advise making a second cut, this time under water, although I've never bothered with that extra step. Now remove the bottom leaves. Above the water line, they continue to lose moisture, and when aswim in the vase, they rot and restrict the water flow into stems.

The next step is most important: Use a sparking clean container that has been scrubbed of any growth left over from the previous tenants, and change the water every day if possible, always using tepid water. If the arrangement can stand the alterations, cut about half an inch from the stem ends every few days, especially if wilting is evident.

Adding raw sugar to the water, or pennies, or diet soda does nothing except help the growth of bacteria, thus clogging stems so they cannot take up water. The University of California at Davis conducted an experiment in which a lemon-lime soft drink was added to water (1 part soft drink to 2 parts water) and tests did show that flowers lasted far longer than in plain water. The sugar in the soda apparently feeds the flowers and the acidity inhibits bacterial growth. The same results can be had by mixing 1 tablespoon of corn syrup and 10 drops of bleach in a quart of warm water. (Forgive an old curmudgeon, but that seems like undue effort to keep flowers fresh, with an active cutting garden in the backyard.) Commercial preparations are also available, but I've never tried them.

A few flowers, like poppies, tithonias, and snow-on-the-mountain, contain a milky fluid or sap that will clog stems of other flowers unless it's hardened by a quick pass of a candle flame or lighted match. Or dip the cut end half an inch deep into boiling water for 30 seconds to achieve the same result. Dahlias also survive for a longer time if their stems are singed.

AN AUTUMN GARDEN

'Twas autumn, and the leaves were dry,
And rustled on the ground;
And chilly winds went whistling by
With low and pensive sound.
Seba Smith, *Three Little Graves*

There is a notable lack of silence in the autumn garden. Starting in late July the insects of summer begin their constant trill, building in intensity as the days shorten, and continuing until they are cut short by the killing frosts of late October. During the day the crickets chirp and at night, katydids talk to the harvest moon. Mosquitoes, their senses sharpened with instincts of the coming cold, fly with a louder whine, finding it easier to search for warm-blooded prey on colder nights.

Down at the pond the dragonflies dart to and fro: You can hear their hum long before they come into view. And one lone duck—a young American merganser—waits for colder weather before flying farther south, happy with a good crop of late tadpoles, and quonking to himself every few minutes.

Back in the garden, both honeybees and bumbles buzz about the late blooming annuals and if caught unaware by a quickly fading sky, curl up in the dahlias until warmed again by the morning sun.

Leaves scutter across the lawn and the drying blades of the ornamental grasses rustle in the daily breeze. Chickadees are heard again at the edge of the vegetable garden—they summer in the deeper woods—and the tiny honks of the nuthatch emanate from the big white pine near the garage.

Overhead the geese fly south talking back and forth with louder honks and as evenings cool, you can hear the whistle of the train that winds its way along the Delaware River, miles away from home.

In the older windows of our house, paper wasps noisily build their winter nests, round tiers of cells (each held aloft by a thin stalk), between the storm sashes and the inside frames. In the living room torpid houseflies lose all control and suddenly dive bomb from the ceiling making a vibrant noise as they fall.

The drying flowers of an oak-leaved hydrangea are pictured on the opposite page and are perfect in the autumn garden or within the arrangement of a winter bouquet.

33

Outside vespid wasps construct larger paper nests, some the size of footballs, in what seems to be the eaves of every house around. And they quarrel as they build with an angry sound heard echoed in every backyard.

In fact, the only reasonably silent autumn activities are the workings of the garden spiders as they continue to build and maintain their dew-dropped webs until the final chills of autumn silence all.

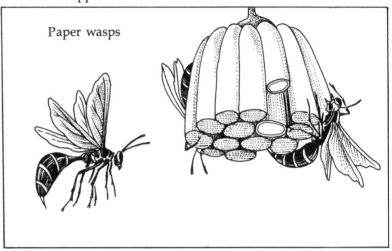

Paper wasps

Plants for an Autumn Garden

Two gardens in this book have no perimeters: The autumn and the winter garden. One reason is that many of the plants involved in each of the collections are bushes or trees that take more land to be adequately sited. The other reason is that the fall, like the winter in many parts of the country, is only a state of mind. My fall has colored leaves, morning mists, hunting season with sometimes a thin layer of snow upon the ground, and crisp, cold nights followed by days of intense blue skies patterned only slightly by clouds.

The flowers, trees, and shrubs in the following list have been chosen from that point of view: The days of late September, October, and most of November in my garden in the Catskill Mountains of upstate New York. They perform in Zone 5 with late-season flowering or brilliant shows of foliage.

So imagine taking a short walk in your backyard, perhaps from the front along the side and then around to the back and passing the following plants:

The New England aster (*Aster novae-angliae*) is a spectacular American wildflower found in old fields and meadows from Quebec to Alberta then south to Maryland, the mountains of North Carolina, and west to Colorado. It is cultivated in England as a Michaelmas daisy and is used by plant breeders to create the colorful varieties of the hardy fall asters that have long been found in gardens. But the New England aster is good enough to stand on its own merits. Growing between 1 and 4 feet tall depending on the soil and the individual character of each plant, the flowers sport many petal-like rays of

New England aster

deep purple. But plants bearing lavender, and even pink or white blossoms are often found in nature. Soil demands are meager so a wild plant will do exceptionally well when moved to good garden soil. Ours bloom into mid-October.

Boltonias (*Boltonia asteroides*) are another genus of asters named after an English botanist, James Bolton. They have common names of false chamomile or the thousand-flowered aster and will grow under

Saw-toothed sunflower

most conditions asking only for full sun. The flowering stems are 3 to 4 feet tall and literally covered with starry flowers. **'Snowbank'** is the cultivar generally found in American nurseries and persists into October and (like the New England aster) does not mind a few light frosts. These plants can be grown as a flowering hedge and are particularly beautiful in a wild garden.

The rockspray cotoneaster (*Cotoneaster horizontalis*) is a hardy shrub (*Cotoneaster* is a Greek word meaning "like a quince" and refers to the leaves in some of the species resembling those of a quince tree) of great garden merit. A young plant will grow against a bank keeping only inches off the ground. Eventually it will carpet the area with overlayered branches of a herringbone pattern each covered with shiny deep green leaves. At this point the plant will start to grow up to a height between 2 and 3 feet. It will also—if trained—grow against a wall without being fixed, or if planted on the edge, pour over like a waterfall. Flowers in June are small, pink, and easily missed but in the fall, the whole shrub is covered with bright red berries that will persist into spring.

Five years ago I placed a cotoneaster plant 2 feet wide against the bank that runs down to our scree bed. I trained it to grow around a stone foo-dog, ramble 2 more feet to the wall's edge, then cascade over, to eventually reach the ground. This fall it's a mass of berries and truly beautiful.

Hay-scented fern (*Dennstaedtia punctilobula*) does not always enjoy good press with some gardeners and suffers from the reputation of being an aggressive and invasive plant. Well, I would never

Boltonias

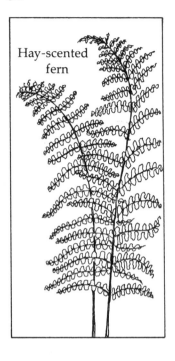

Hay-scented
fern

allow it in a perennial border or a rock garden but for carpeting a bank where little else will grow, it is a superb choice. The fronds are sweet-scented when crushed or when drying. Thoreau said of this, his favorite fern: ". . . . Nature perfumes her garments with this [plant]. She gives it to those who go a-barberrying and on dark autumnal walks. The very scent of it, if you have a decayed frond in your chamber, will take you far up country in a twinkling."

But its true beauty comes in the fall. This fern is very sensitive and withers quickly with frost, turning a wonderful shade of light brown with a golden glow or often a burnt umber. Sometimes in late fall it bleaches to a shade that is almost white, becoming a skeleton of a fern. The fronds grow to 3 feet in height. The hay-scented fern will succeed in partial shade, and plants are not at all particular as to soil.

The burning bush (*Euonymus alata* '**Compacta**') in our garden is a 5-foot-high compact form of the winged euonymus (see The Winter Garden, page 173) and not to be confused with the Wahoo or burning bush, *E. atropurpurea*. This bush does not have as corky a twig as its 8-foot parent, but when it comes to fall, the truly bright scarlet color of the leaves is a traffic stopper. The scale is fine for a small garden and soil requirements are average.

Japanese bamboo grass (*Hakonechlora macra* '**Aureola**') has its place in the rock garden, the grass garden, or even the perennial border, but it's in the autumn garden that it really shines. Plants only grow to, at best, 2 feet tall before the leaves gracefully arch towards the ground. But those leaves—striped with thick and thin lines of green and white—are tinged with a dull magenta when the days get shorter and persist on the plant until well into late fall. Soil should be well-drained and plants need full or at least partial sun.

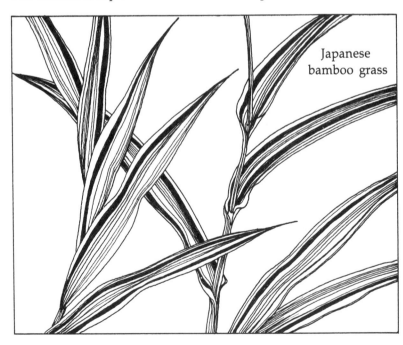

Japanese
bamboo grass

The saw-toothed sunflower (*Helianthus grosseserratus*) is a perennial wildflower relative of the common garden sunflower. Like its annual relative this plant can reach a height of 13 feet when in a happy situation of full sun and average soil. Blossoms are 2 1/2 inches in diameter and up to 20 of them can top the stem. They bloom in early to late October and are easily grown from seed. A clump of these flowers blooms at the bottom of our front garden where the stems wave in the autumn winds, their tips golden in the sun. The leaves are edged with coarse teeth hence the botanical name of *grosseserratus*. Propagate the plants by division.

The sea buckthorns (*Hippophae rhamnoides*) are two species of spiny shrubs or trees with willowlike, silvery leaves. They do well in any soil and even thrive along the seashore in salt air and sand. *H. rhamnoides* will reach 30 feet but can be pruned and kept at 3 or 4 feet and is the species usually offered by nurseries. The other is *H. salicifolia*, a tree reaching 50 feet and only hardy in the South. The flowers are yellow and inconspicuous. But in the fall, bright orange-yellow 1/4-inch berries appear and carpet the stems in color. They persist through the winter. *Hortus Third* notes that the berries are edible but since they are even too sour for birds, nothing bothers the bushes. One wonders why. These plants are *dioecious*, having male and female flowers on different plants so you must have both to have berries.

The hydrangeas are garden war horses but one particular species (*Hydrangea quercifolia*) is perfect for the autumn garden. It was discovered by John Bartram, the pioneer American botanist, in 1791. This handsome shrub with large oak-like leaves usually reaches 6 feet in height and then the branches bend over. Blossoms appear in

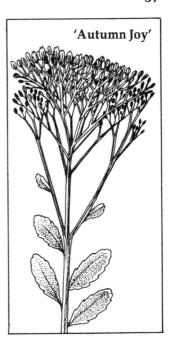

'Autumn Joy'

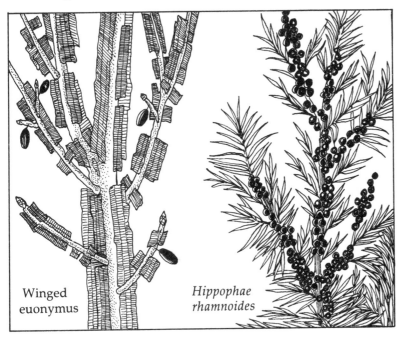

Winged euonymus

Hippophae rhamnoides

Heavenly
bamboo

late summer, lasting throughout the entire fall, and are a rich, pink shade of bronze. They form conical heads of great beauty. Plants will do well in partial shade. My dentist has one of these shrubs on the small lawn in front of his office. There it assumes the shape of a large umbrella and the color is noticeable from way down the block.

To my eye the most desirable of the flowering crabapples (*Malus* **'Red Jade'**) is notable for its fall plumage of glossy red fruits and not the spring crop of flowers. Oh, the flowers, are O.K., and they do brighten up a May morning. But come the fall when the branches are laden with the tiny round crabapples, each hanging like a Christmas ornament, this tree is stunning. Its form is pendulous and it weeps with arching branches touching the ground. **'Red Jade'** will eventually reach a height of 15 feet. Nothing beats this small tree as a specimen plant for a small garden. It was developed at the Brooklyn Botanic Garden and is suitable for planting in a tub or being trained to special forms. Unfortunately the deer enjoy nibbling on the branches so during the winter months I enclose the entire tree in black plastic netting of the type used to protect fruit from birds.

Eulalia grass (*Miscanthus sinensis*) is mentioned in the Grass Garden on page 67 and the Winter Garden on page 185 but is so impressive in the landscape that I had to include it here as well. Reaching 10 feet (possibly 12) in one season and then topped with waving white plumes throughout the fall, this grass is a marvel to witness. Full sun and average soil are the only requirements for healthy growth.

When we first moved to our home in the mountains we found a number of plants left by various gardeners over the years. Some, like the common daylily (*Hemerocallis fulva*) have been mixed blessings at best. But three Japanese roses (*Rosa multiflora*) have been quite beautiful to have. These plants will reach a height of 10 feet, bending over to form a huge mound of spring and summer leaf and in May, clusters of single-flowered white roses loved by bees. It can be invasive and is probably too large for a small yard: One of our bushes is now 20 feet in diameter. Then in the fall the 1/4-inch orange rose hips appear and remain throughout the winter. During very severe winters when temperatures fall well below the teens, canes can be damaged but are easily pruned back and will recover.

Heavenly bamboo (*Nadina domestica*) will reach 8 feet in Zone 7, is root hardy in Zone 6, and is best kept in a pot to be moved indoors in colder areas. Although it's called heavenly and is originally from Japan and China, this plant is not really a bamboo but a member of the barberry family. The canelike stems are a reddish brown, and the leaves are pinkish when new, turning a light, fresh green during summer. In the spring white flowers appear in long panicles, and are followed by red berries. Then in the fall leaves turn to a brilliant red and remain on the plant until the winds blow them away. Light frosts will not harm the plant but only heighten the color.

The staghorn sumac is such a fine tree for autumn it has an essay of its own on page 40.

There is a flower that is colorful in the summer but only achieves its final glory in the fall: It is a sedum (*Sedum Telephium*) cultivar termed **'Autumn Joy'**. The flowers are pink and clustered atop 2-foot stems, appearing in August. Then as the colder nights approach, they turn a fine shade of mahogany, persisting into the coldest months and making fine dried flowers for winter bouquets. They prefer poor soil and full sun. Propagate by division. They are hardy to Zone 3.

Toad lilies (*Tricyrtis hirta*) are unusual plants. Three-foot-high stems bear alternate lance-shaped leaves, eventually forming a clump that is quite attractive but certainly not enough to justify the efforts of planting. Then in October the blossoms appear: Mauve and purple flowers bloom within the leaf axils, each bearing a split pistil that closely resembles the texture of chenille. These plants like a semi-shady spot with moist soil, and it's a good idea to mulch them north of Zone 5. Propagate by division or with seeds.

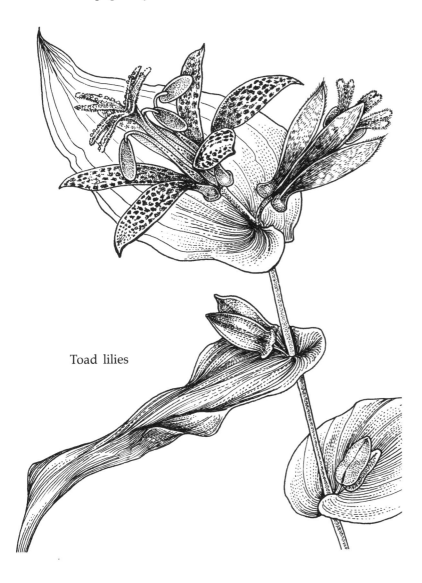

Toad lilies

'Laciniata'

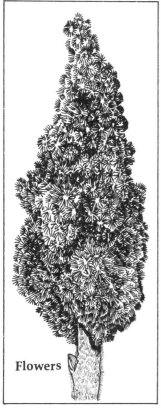

Flowers

THE SUMAC IN THE GARDEN

I wish sometimes for the old days. Not that I am awash in nostalgia or truly believe that life was better years ago than now, but I do feel there was more of a sense of continuity: a remembrance of a past and a sensible wish for a future, in addition to a more stable present. And the feeling of loss always comes when I think of trees and the planting of trees. For putting an oak or a sycamore in the ground today takes a lot of fortitude; you've got to believe that you or yours will be there to see that tree in years to come. In a mobile society where people move from place to place with an ease that is astounding, whether following jobs, dreams, or just warm weather, planting formidable trees in the garden seems to be a practice now at a low ebb.

Oh sure, garden centers stock Japanese maples, a lot of dwarf apples, willows, and such, but the choice does seem to be limited to those trees that offer fairly instant gratification.

So may I suggest a native American, first cultivated in the early 1600s, the staghorn sumac (*Rhus typhina*). It's a tree that has few demands, grows so quickly that gratification gets a good turn, and though short-lived, is quite beautiful for many reasons.

American gardeners and nurserymen usually think poorly of this tree, likening it to a group tagged "trash," and suggesting that it be put in only the poorest of soils and relegated to hillsides and then only when erosion seems to be a problem.

But the English gardeners have a different opinion. They say the sumac offers tropical-type leaves for shade in summer, glorious scarlet foliage in the fall, unusual felted stems when the leaves have gone, and the terminal cones of dark crimson fruits that persist throughout the winter.

William Robinson, who at the turn of the century was instrumental in changing the look of the English border and pioneered the concept of controlled nature in the wild garden, advised using the sumac for its fine autumn color and suggested that it even be grown as a plant rather than a tree by cutting it back every spring and confining the growth to one or two shoots.

The most imaginative use of this tree that I have seen is in the Wild Garden at Wave Hill, a public garden located in the community of Riverdale in the Bronx, New York. There a 50-year-old tree has generated a multitude of smaller trunks and all have been allowed to twist and turn either naturally or by shaping and pruning so they have become a Brazilian bower just above Manhattan.

We, too, have started such a bower at the side of our garden. The largest tree harbors three hanging houseplants during the summer months, giving them the filtered sunlight that they prefer. Underneath is a cool and pleasant place to sit on a hot day. By selectively cutting the suckers that arise throughout June, July, and August, I am able to plan the direction that my living house of shade will pursue.

The young branches of this tree bear many fine hairs and they look like the antlers of a stag when "in velvet." The bark and leaves are rich in tanning and it is said that a black ink can be made from boiling the leaves and fruit. Oliver Medsger reports in his book, *Edible Wild Plants,* that "when the berries are placed in water for a short time, a pleasing and agreeable drink is formed, known to boys as 'Indian lemonade' [and] for this purpose the berries are best in late summer or early autumn."

There is a cultivar available called **'Laciniata'** which has finely cut individual leaflets.

The sumac in the autumn garden.

AN AUTUMN BULB GARDEN

I planned and set out a small bulb bed (really corms and bulbs) this fall and it began to bloom within two weeks of planting—there was no long wait for roots to develop, no months of winter twilight before the flowers appeared! Yet no magic was involved. For the bulbs were six species of colchicum (*Colchicum* spp.), three species of the fall-flowering crocus (*Crocus* spp.), and a clump of *Sternbergia lutea,* all autumn-flowering plants.

The colchicums are fascinating because of the dangerous but beneficent chemicals they secretly hold within each corm; and for the wondrous pictures formed in my mind's eye when I think of their ancient home and the ships that sailed the Black Sea bringing the plants to market in Colchis—the birthplace of Medea and a port then known throughout the world for its poisonous plants. And then from one species of autumn crocus comes saffron, the magic spice worth more than gold. Yet for all their splendid histories these are plants still perfect for the autumn garden.

Unfortunately, to enjoy their qualities the gardener must adhere to a schedule a bit more stringent than most other bulbs require: These flowers are often too impatient, the crocus going into a snit if they stay too long out of soil and the colchicums actually setting forth blossoms while waiting in the shipping box or lying about on a worktable. So orders must be in to suppliers by mid-July and the bulbs shipped for planting in early September.

It's hard to believe how cheering a sight these plants can be when they bloom in October, November, and even December one zone farther south from our garden. The bees love the pollen and gorge themselves to such an extent that many late afternoon visitors remain within the folded petals until the following morning. And garden visitors exclaim that spring is here again!

The Bed's Location

I chose a slightly sloping spot that faces southeast and is sheltered from the worst of the winter winds by a line of pines in the field to the west and is partially shaded by a huge white pine tree that towers above the bed. The colchicums like a bit of shade in the summer so they go to the back of the bed. The crocus and the *Sternbergia* generally like to be baked by the hot sun of July and August as an aid to flowering so they get the front position. All these plants like well-drained soil. Since most of our soil is clay, before planting these bulbs I dug to a depth of 8 inches and worked in leaf litter from the woods and compost from the garden bin.

The bed was watered well after the initial plantings.

Each genus unfortunately has a pest. Colchicums are loved by slugs; I've watched them actually chew open a blossom in minutes. Crocuses are a favorite food of mice. Autumn slugs are, excuse the pun, sluggish and easily removed by hand to be stoned to death. And mice can be controlled by lining the perimeters of the bulb bed with a foot-deep barrier of 1/2-inch wire mesh from the hardware store.

Plants for the Autumn Bulb Bed

Colchicums may be planted out with abandon. No rodent will bother these corms because of the alkaloid colchicine, a poison that has been featured in a number of mystery stories. Edmund Crispen in his novel, *Frequent Hearses,* confounds his detective until the last demise by having the murderer place a lethal dose of this ancient potion in another character's medicine after distilling the poison from a number of the corms of *C. autumnale,* the species with the highest content of the drug.

Chalice-shaped flowers appear on white stem-like funnels that are divided into six petal-like segments. They shoot up directly from the soil without any leaves. The leaves, in turn, usually show up the following spring and then die back like those of other spring bulbs. The long lasting straplike foliage varies in height between 6 to 18 inches depending on the species, so be sure to keep this in mind when choosing a spot. These leaves are rather untidy as they die so be prepared to supply some camouflage with a few bedding annuals next May. Though they resemble crocuses, colchicums are members of the lily family.

Plant all colchicums 3 to 4 inches deep (from the top of the corm) and space them 6 inches apart on center. They should be left alone until such time as the flowers start to diminish due to crowding of the corms; then dig them up, divide, and replant.

They are wonderful when naturalized and planted in the grass, especially in an area that can be left uncut in the autumn for the flowers and in the early spring for the leaves.

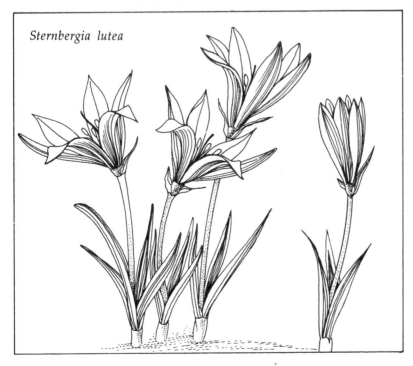

Sternbergia lutea

Colchicum agrippinum is checkered—like the fritillarias—with purple squares on a ground of pink. The flower height is 4 inches and the plants are hardy from Zone 5 south. They bloom in late summer to early autumn. The leaves are 6 inches long.

C. autumnale is called the autumn crocus, meadow saffron, mysteria, naked ladies, and the wonder bulb. The flowers of September and October are between 3 and 4 inches high and the leaves up to a foot long. They are hardy from Zone 4 south. **'Album'** has white flowers; **'Roseum'** has rose-pink flowers; **'Plenum'** has double flowers of a lilac hue.

C. byzantium has rosy lilac flowers, often up to 4 inches across, blooming in September. The plants grow 6 inches tall and the leaves of spring are up to 16 inches long. This species is hardy from Zone 6 south.

C. cilicicum have flowers of a deeper shade of rosy lilac than *C. byzantium*, 5 inches high, and of a greater number. The 12-inch leaves appear directly after flowering. They are hardy from Zone 5 south.

C. speciosum has rose to purple flowers 5 inches high and often 4 inches across. Leaves are 6 inches long. They are hardy from Zone 4 south. **'Album'** has white flowers; **'Atrorubens'** is dark red; the variety *Bornmuelleri* has larger and earlier flowers.

C. **'Waterlily'** is a hybrid with mauve colored, double blossoms that really look like their namesake. Flowers are a stunning 4 inches wide and bloom in early October. If you only have room for one of the colchicums, choose this cultivar. Leaves are 6 inches long. The plants are hardy from Zone 4 south.

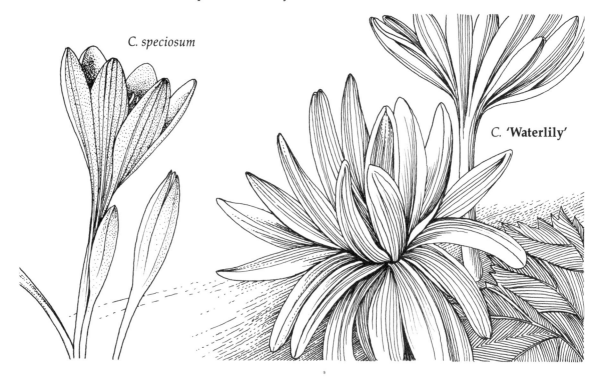

C. speciosum

C. **'Waterlily'**

The fall-flowering crocus are members of the iris family and, like their spring relatives, welcome to the garden scene, especially on a crisp autumn day. They bloom from early September to November. Plant the corms 4 inches deep and 3 inches apart. After three or four years you will note that the corms have come close to—if not reached—the top of the ground. This is because the new corms form on top of the old, just like bricks are added to a wall, and eventually reach the surface. When this happens just dry them off and replant in July.

Remember that the leaves must die naturally in order for the corms to store enough food for the next year's flowering.

Crocus asturicus bears violet-purple flowers about 4 inches long in mid-October. The stamens are orange. 12-inch leaves appear during and following blooming. Louise Beebe Wilder, writing in *Hardy Bulbs,* calls this the Spanish crocus and reports that in its native mountains, it's called *Espanto Pastores,* or "Terror of Shepherds" since it appears just after the autumn rains and presages the coming of winter. It is hardy from Zone 6 south.

C. goulimyi has 4-inch-high globular flowers of pale to deep purple and according to bulb broker Ken McClure, was introduced to gardens by C. N. Goulimis, who found it growing wild in southern Greece in 1954. It only succeeds in Zone 9, where soils never freeze, but is included in this plan to tempt the palate of a southern gardener.

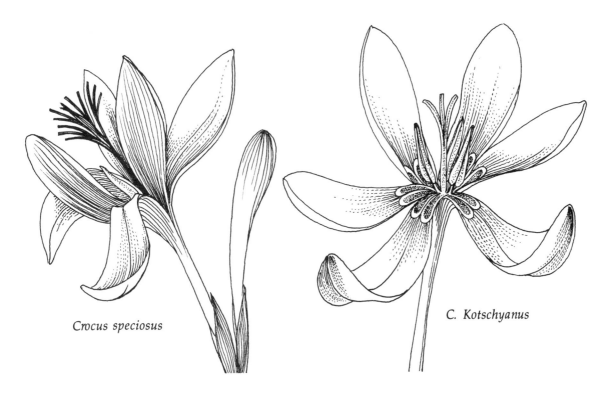

Crocus speciosus

C. Kotschyanus

C. Kotschyanus is a pale rose-lilac, and is originally from the mountains of southern Turkey. It reaches 4 inches in height and blooms in late September and October. It is hardy from Zone 5 south.

C. laevigatus **'Fontenayi'** is the latest blooming autumn crocus, choosing to flower in December. The leaves emerge with the blossoms. Color is lavender feathered with purple, and the flowers exude a delightful scent reminiscent of freesias. Height is 2 1/2 inches and corms are hardy from Zone 6 south. If you are in an area where winters are early but not too cold, try this plant in a sheltered spot.

C. medius blooms with lavender-purple flowers in October. Height is 4 inches and the leaves show up after flowering is finished. It is hardy from Zone 6 south.

C. orhroleucus starts in mid-October and if temperatures are a bit above normal, will continue to November. The flower is a delicate cream color with the throat stained with orange, and compared with other crocuses, the flower seems thin and papery. Where snows come early in the North *C. orhroleucus* will need a sheltered spot, but it's hardy from Zone 5 south.

C. sativus is the saffron crocus, which has been in cultivation since the times of the ancient Hebrews for its value as a spice and coloring agent. Flowers are a rich purple, grow 4 inches high, and appear in October. If you are interested in going into the business of gathering saffron, you will be interested to know that it takes 35,000 flowers to yield 8 ounces of the stuff. The corms are hardy from Zone 6 south.

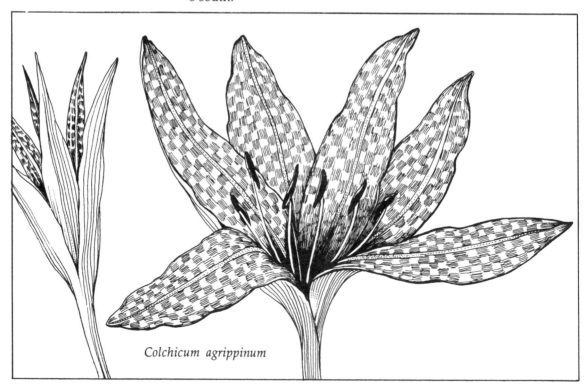

Colchicum agrippinum

C. speciosus is the earliest of the fall bloomers, usually showing up in mid to late September with clear blue flowers. The height is 4 inches. Since the corms increase with ease, this species is great for naturalizing. It is hardy from Zone 5 south. **'Albus'** has white flowers; **'Globosus'** has blue, globular flowers; the variety *Cassiope* has blue flowers with a yellow base and *Pollux* bears the largest flowers of the species, up to 3 inches across.

The final flower choice for a fall garden is *Sternbergia lutea*, called the autumn daffodil because of its yellow color. It is thought that this plant was the original lily-of-the-field in the Bible. The flowers are crocus-like but this time the genus belongs to the lily family and that bulb is really a bulb, not a corm. The petals have a heavier feel than crocus do. The plant's 8-inch leaves are the first to appear, followed in mid-September by the flowers. Plant the bulbs 4 inches deep and 4 inches apart. The plants want a warm garden spot bathed in sun during the summer months. And once ensconced, leave them be. If they ever stop flowering, lift the bulbs, dry them, and then replant with a dash of bonemeal. The plants are hardy from Zone 6 south and will generally keep their leaves over winter.

This year I started my autumn-flowering bed on September 13. The colchicums began to bloom just two days after planting. It is now October 10 and **'Waterlily'** opened this morning, and I still have all the crocuses waiting in the wings.

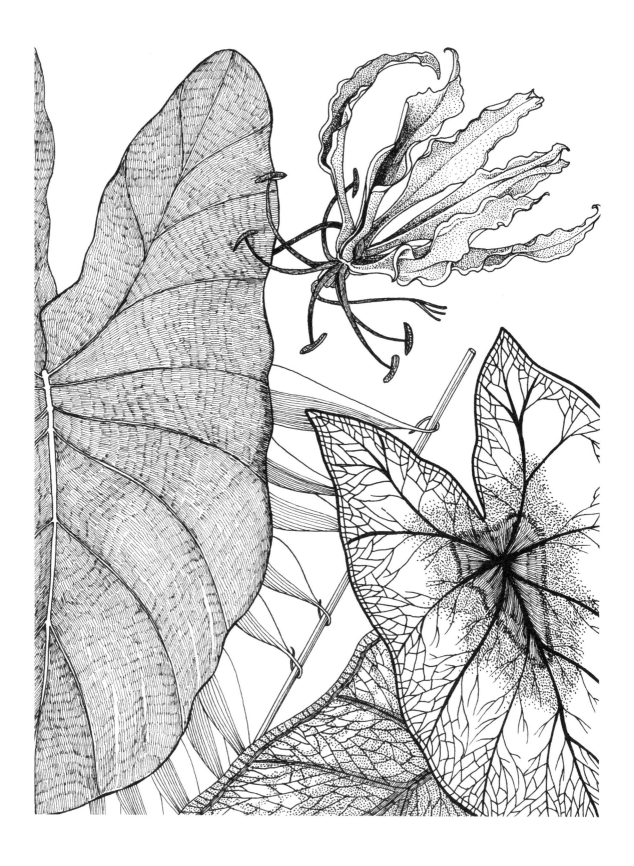

A GARDEN
OF BULBS

Clean and round,
Heavy and sound,
In every bulb a flower.
An old triplet, used by Louise Beebe Wilder

Of all the gardens described in this book, the bulb garden is open to the most interpretation because so much depends on the definition of the bulb. For many years I was a botanical purist and when I used the term bulb, I always meant an underground stem wrapped in a series of leaves that look like scales, forming a rounded shape that if cut open lengthwise will show embryo leaves, a stem and flower, all ready to bloom when the right time comes. Daffodils and onions are bulbs.

I now include corms, tubers, and rhizomes because they too, though much different in structure, contain within themselves a dormant plant along with enough food to keep everything growing during the early weeks of development.

Corms are a series of underground stems wrapped up in a rounded or pear-shaped package, flat on the top and the bottom. Crocus and gladiolus are corms. Unlike bulbs, the current corm usually dries up after flowering but the base of the stem continues to store up food and becomes a new corm.

Tubers are modified underground stems that are swollen with stored food. It is difficult sometimes to tell the difference between corms and tubers. Cyclamen look just like corms but they are really tubers, as are potatoes and begonias.

Rhizomes are perennial stems that are short and thick and give rise to above ground flowering stems. Iris are rhizomatous plants.

The wonderful thing about these plants is the food supply they all carry along. If you buy top quality bulbs from reliable sources, they will usually bloom the first garden year—unless you bury them in concrete. What follows the second season will depend more on the gardener and nature but that first season should be a time of flowers.

There is also an ease of planting where bulbs are concerned: An entire garden can be carried around in a large paper bag while you

Three stellar members of a garden of bulbs are pictured on the opposite page: The blossom is a gloriosa lily, the leaves at the right are caladiums, and the large leaf at the left is an elephant ear.

49

Anemone coronaria

mull over the landscape. And once dormant, they are far easier to move than the majority of garden plants, basically simple to propagate, and many of them take readily to pot culture.

This year in our garden we had a display of spring bulbs that began on April 8 and lasted until the second week of June.

Later in the season came the charming English iris, Japanese iris, the many flowering onions (seven different species), a host of lilies and daylilies, gladiolus of all colors, and for one year at least, the charming hardy cyclamen. And in pots gathered on the terrace and out around the sundial, the awesome devil's tongue, wand flowers from Africa, calla lilies, and a magnificent, white lily-of-the-Nile.

Finally there are late-blooming lilies, autumn crocus (see page 42), and for Christmas, Amaryllis and all the wonderful forced bulbs of winter.

PREPARING THE BULB GARDEN

The garden of bulbs shown in the plan is designed for a space about 8 by 15 feet. There are 20 plant species so something will be in bloom at all times, and by staggering the gladiolus, you'll get these flowers from midsummer on. The asparagus in the pot is a true departure from most bulb gardens, but like the caladiums and elephant ears, the ferny stems are so attractive they belong in the arrangement.

Soil demands are not too great. The one requirement, though, is good drainage. Bulbs will not tolerate a location in wet soil, so be sure to mix in enough sand or locate the garden on a slight slope to make sure water does not stand within the ground. However, during the hot summer months these plants need water as long as they are in active growth, so if rain is short, be sure you provide the water.

The plants in the following descriptions want good light most of the day and need at least six hours of sun.

When preparing the bulb bed, work in about 6 pounds of bone meal per 120 square feet. And when working new soil that needs the addition of organic matter, I've found that a few bags of composted cow manure is an excellent conditioner.

When bulbs do go dormant, their leaves dry, turn yellow, and disappear from sight. The *Allium* species will act this way soon after flowering is over. To cover the bare spots in the garden, move in a few geraniums or some bedding annuals like lobelias, pansies, and the like that you will have kept waiting in the wings.

The bulb garden plan also calls for some flagstones leading to the center of the bed where a pot of begonias, lily-of-the-Nile, and the asparagus reside for the summer. If you have any houseplants that would benefit from a season outdoors in the sun, add them to the group.

Plants for the Bulb Garden

In the following descriptions, the first number represents the height of the plant in bloom (except for those plants grown for foliage), and the second number is the spread. Since some bulbs are tropicals and others will withstand a northern winter, I've also included the Zone.

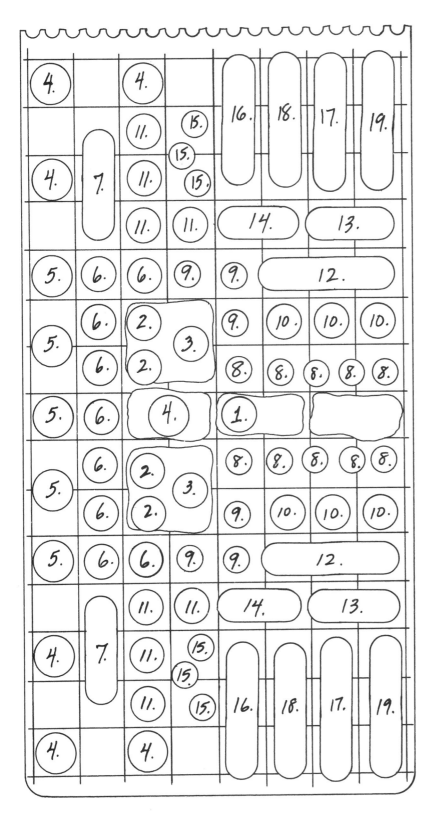

The plan for the garden of bulbs. The numerals represent the following plants:
1. Lily-of-the-Nile,
2. Begonias,
3. Asparagus,
4. Gloriosa lily,
5. Cannas,
6. Caladiums,
7. Peacock orchids,
8. *Allium karataviense,*
9. *A. Christophii,*
10. Four-o'clocks,
11. *Galtonia candicans,*
12. Anemones,
13. *Allium Moly,*
14. Crocosmia,
15. *Lilium forosanum,*
16. Other lillies,
17. Dahlias,
18. Gladiolas,
19. Mexican stars.

Peacock orchids (*Acidanthera bicolor*), 24 by 6 inches, are tender corms from Africa that are closely related to the *Gladiolus*. They bear 30-inch wide flowers of white marked with dark maroon, which are endowed with a wonderful fragrance, especially at night. North of Zone 7 dig them up in the fall. Peacock orchids are great as cut flowers, blooming from the bottom of the stalk upward. If you remove spent blossoms, the plants continue to look remarkably fresh. Since they are somewhat tender and prefer nights above 50°F., I often start them in late spring using 3-inch peat pots. By planting new corms every two weeks (cover them with 3 to 4 inches of soil) you can guarantee a long season of bloom. Save the corms after the leaves dry in the fall and use them year after year.

Lily-of-the-Nile (*Agapanthus africanus*), 20 by 12 inches, is a tropical plant with thick rhizomes. It is year-round only in Zone 9 and south. These plants flower best when rootbound in large pots or tubs (use wood, as the roots can break clay pots). They can spend northern winters indoors in the greenhouse or any spot where temperatures stay above freezing. Flowers are many (blue or white depending on the cultivar) and bloom for at least a month or more atop long, straight stems. The seedpods remain interesting and the long, straplike leaves are also attractive. Fertilize with a balanced houseplant fertilizer (see Bibliography) once a month while the plants are in active growth. When plants become too large for easy removal, divide them and repot.

The stars-of-Persia (*Allium Christophii*), 18 to 30 by 10 inches, Zone 4, provide round balls of blossom up to 8 inches in diameter.

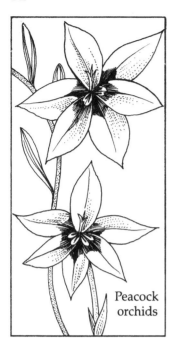

Peacock orchids

Allium karataviense

Each flower head is made up of individual metallic pink stars with green centers. (These ornamental alliums are members of the onion family; they have an onion-like odor when leaves are broken or the bulbs are scratched.) Star-of-Persia flowers are even attractive when dry. The leaves become untidy, so the plants look better when placed behind other plants. Plant three times the depth of the bulb. The bulbs may be left alone for years; just work in some good garden compost early in the spring.

Allium karataviense, 8 by 8 inches, Zone 4, has no common name. Beautiful straplike leaves enfold burgeoning balls of starry flowers of a greenish white. These bulbs will also do very well when forced in a pot indoors for late winter flowering. Plant as for *A. Christophii.*

The golden garlic (or lily leek) is another *Allium* (*A. Moly*), 12 by 4 inches, Zone 4, producing golden yellow flowers in June and July. Plant as for *A. Christophii.*

The windflower (*Anemone coronaria*), 10 by 5 inches, is often seen in fine restaurants, where its red, purple, blue or white petaled flowers look so elegant in a plain crystal vase. Plant the tubers outdoors in early spring, covering with 2 inches of soil after soaking them overnight in tepid water. North of Zone 7 dig up the tubers in the fall and store them in a warm spot (55°F.) in dry peat moss.

Asparagus officinalis var. *pseudoscaber* is a graceful variety of the common garden asparagus that hails originally from Rumania. It has rhizomatous roots, tiny, green bell-like flowers, and wonderful drifts of green branchlets (not true leaves) on stems that can reach 4 feet in

*Begonia ×
tuberhybrida*

*Asparagus officinalis
var. pseudoscaber*

Dahlias

length. The burgeoning spears are miniature, too small to be used as food. These are cool and inviting plants in the garden. They grow easily from seed and are quite happy in a 6-inch clay pot to be taken indoors in winter, or planted directly in the ground (where they need a mulch north of Zone 6).

Tuberous-rooted begonias (*Begonia × tuberhybrida*), 16 by 12 inches, must be dug up in the fall. These plants produce vast numbers of spectacular flowers with satiny petals all summer long. Tubers may be planted—hollow side up—directly in the soil or placed in 5- or 6-inch pots (or treefern baskets) with a soil mix composed of 2 parts loam, 2 parts peat moss, and 1 part of composted cow manure. Cover the tubers with less than 1/2 inch of soil. To get a jump on flowering, start them at least eight weeks before nighttime temperatures drop down to about 50°F. Store at 50°F. in dry peat moss over the winter months.

Fancy-leaved caladiums (*Caladium × hortulanum*), 24 by 12 inches, are tubers from South America that may go directly outdoors only in Zone 8 and above. Their thin, colorful leaves are often too tropical to be believed and they make a marvelous show all summer long. Plant 1 inch deep in the same soil mix recommended for the begonias, and only when the daytime temperatures are 70°F. or above. Start early, about eight weeks before warm days are due, placing the tubers 1 inch deep in damp peat moss. Place the pots in a warm spot, where temperature is 75°F. When leaves appear move the plants to 4-inch pots. In the fall, when the first frost kills the leaves, tubers should be dug and stored over winter in a warm (60-65°F.) and dry spot. These plants need plenty of water in a typical summer.

The cannas (*Canna × generalis*), 24 to 60 by 18 inches, are hardy only in Zone 7 and above. Flowers come in yellow, red, orange, and white, with 4 to 5-inch spreads. These showy tropical tubers were very popular in Victorian parks and even today can still be overdone by municipal gardeners. But when held within bounds, they are beautiful summer stars. Like the other tropicals, cannas resent cold so start them in 3-inch peat pots about eight weeks before the 50-60°F. nights begin. Outdoors plant them with a covering of 2 inches of soil. They do well in pots in a mix of peat moss, potting soil, and sand, 1/3 each. Keep the soil moist, and fertilize once a month during the summer with the fertilizer you use for houseplants. Always keep the pots above freezing.

Elephant ears (*Colocasia esculenta*), 48 to 60 by 24 to 36 inches, are only hardy in Zone 10. Everywhere else they dislike nights below 60°F. so treat them like the cannas but start individual tubers in 6-inch pots.

Montebretias (*Crocosmia × crocosmiiflora*), 36 by 3 inches, are hardy with protection in Zone 6, and without in warmer spots. These are cormous herbs that belong to the iris family. Brilliantly orange, funnel-shaped flowers are spectacular in bloom and today, many cultivars are available. Plant them out in early spring, 3 inches apart and cover with 2 inches of soil. Dig up and store the corms in a dry place over the winter where temperatures average 40°F.

Dahlias (*Dahlia* × *hybridia*), 12 to 30 by 10 inches, are tender tubers and outside of Zone 10, must be dug up in the fall or treated like annuals and let go. There are so many kinds of dahlias that a special code has been devised to describe the many variations. This garden plan only uses the so-called dwarf dahlias, which never top 30 inches yet bear up to 4-inch-wide flowers of great beauty and many colors. Buy tubers at your local garden center, covering the sweet-potato-like roots with 6 inches of soil on top. Or start the plants from seed beginning indoors eight weeks before the last spring frost. Yes, dahlias easily bloom from seed the first summer. If you find a type that really pleases you, keep the tuber over the winter in dry peat moss at a temperature of 40°F. When using dahlias as cut flowers, singe the cut end of the stem in a flame before putting in a vase of water.

Summer hyacinths (*Galtonia candicans*), 40 by 12 inches, are hardy with a mulch in Zones 6 and warmer. These lovely flowers are bulbs that produce straplike leaves up to 3 feet long and tall stems of pendulous, bell-shaped flowers of white with a touch of green at the base. Plant bulbs 6 inches deep and between 12 and 15 inches apart. Summer hyacinths need adequate water during dry spells. If you dig them up in the fall, store them where the temperature is about 50°F.

Lily-of-the-Nile

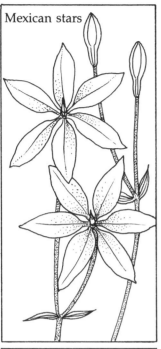

Mexican stars

Montebretias

Gladiolus (*Gladiolus × hortulanus*), 24 by 60 inches, are tender corms from Africa. They are available in a bewildering variety of colors and sizes. To follow this garden plan, shop for gladiolus that reach about 3 feet in height when in bloom. Plant the corms 6 inches apart and 6 inches deep at intervals of 15 days, starting with the last spring frost. This will give you all-summer bloom and plenty of flowers to cut. Today's plants are top-heavy with flowers and easily fall over with only a minor disturbance. When plants are about a foot tall, hill a little earth around the stems to hold them up, or put in a network of stakes. Store corms over winter in a temperature of 40-50°F. after pulling up the plants, cutting off the tops, and drying the corms for a few weeks.

Gloriosa lilies (*Gloriosa Rothschildiana*), 36 to 48 by 6 inches, are tender tubers that can live outdoors only in Zone 3 and above. They climb by hooking their leaf ends around a support or string. Flowers are up to 4 inches wide with curved orange petals turning yellow at the center. Put plants out after the last spring frost or keep them in pots, allowing the tubers to become dormant from late fall to mid-February. Use the same soil mix as for cannas.

True lilies (*Lilium* spp.) are a gigantic genus and like dahlias, quite overwhelming in variety. For this garden use a mixture of the Asiatic hybrids **'Mid-Century'** (bright oranges, reds, and some pastels) for flowers in June and July. Follow with the **'Black-Dragon'** (white with maroon ribs on the outside) for July and August, then *Lilium speciosum* **'Rubrum'** (white and crimson) or **'Roseum'** (rose colored blossoms) for August to September. But these are only suggestions; you might find other colors you prefer. Bulbs should be planted out as soon as you receive them: Lily bulbs never go into a true dormant period. Plant them 4 to 8 inches deep and 10 to 18 inches apart, depending on the ultimate height, putting a teaspoon full of bonemeal in the bottom of each hole.

If you have the room, try one of the numerous lily naturalizing mixtures offered by many nurseries. For a very reasonable amount, you can buy 30-inch-tall, blooming-size seedlings, in colors of red, orange, yellow, white, cream, or pink.

For bloom in mid- to late September use the fine *Lilium formosanum* with its elegant, 6-inch-long white atop 4 to 6 foot stems. Or try *L. formosanum* **'Little Snow White'**, a cultivar from Taiwan with the same size flower but on a 9-inch stem. If grown from seed sown in September, this lily will bloom the following summer. It also makes an excellent pot plant.

Mexican stars (*Milla biflora*), 16 by 4 inches, are hardy from Zone 8 south. Plant bulbs out in mid-spring under 3 inches of soil, 3 inches apart. They bloom on and off all summer, producing six-petalled white flowers with a sweet fragrance. The leaves are grass-like. Dig up the bulbs in the fall and store them over the winter between 45-50°F.

Also included in the bulb garden plan are two lines of four-o'clocks (*Mirabilis Jalapa*). These plants grow from tubers, and I like them because they produce flowers all summer long, until frost. See the Night Garden for cultural information.

Lilium formosanum

Summer
hyacinths

57

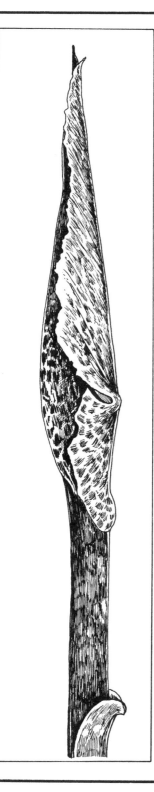

THE DEVIL'S TONGUE

Ever since I was entertained in the '40s with Saturday afternoon matinees featuring the thuggee of India, temples with one-eyed idols, and the cannibal plants and giant spiders of "Tarzan's Desert Mystery," I've been singularly fascinated by unusual and frankly bizarre flowering plants. Memories of fingery white blooms clawing at spiraling mists and loathsome floral interiors livid in jungle light continually walk along the edge of my consciousness. Oh sure, I like roses and daisies as well as the next person, but something happens to my psyche when confronted with growing and flowering the strange.

A case in point is the plant known as the devil's tongue (*Amorphophallus Rivieri*): I first read of this and other horrors in a used copy of *Plants with Personality* by Patrick M. Synge (Lindsay Drummond Ltd., London, n.d.) that I found in a bookstore in the mid-70s. After mentioning stapeliads in the chapter entitled "Fly-Pollenated Plants," Synge speaks of one of the largest flowering plants in the known world, *Amorphophallus titanum*, a ". . . gigantic and monstrous aroid [that] grows at an incredible rate, sometimes six inches a day until it opens at a height of eight and a half feet. The mature inflorescence is said to give off an offensive scent, resembling the smell of decayed fish. The inflorescence," (note the writer never says flower), "consists of a gigantic fleshy spike pale-green in color, with touches of white. This spike emerges from the centre of a spathe, a sheath, which at first surrounds it and then opens like a rococo sea-shell with a fringed edge, displaying a rich maroon or liver-coloured inside . . . There is also a smaller species of *Amorphophallus*, *A. Rivieri*, sometimes called devil's tongue, which has a dark red spathe about three feet long."

At that time I found no sources for either the huge *A. titanum* or the smaller devil's tongue and all passed from the conscious mind.

Then in his fascinating book, *In for a Penny: A Prospect of Kew Gardens,* by Wilfred Blunt (Hamish Hamilton, London, 1978), again I found mention of the clan.

Blunt, in describing the Orangery at Kew, refers to a life-sized drawing of *A. titanum*, 18 feet long and some 15 feet wide that was presented to the gardens by an Italian named Beccari who discovered the flower in Sumatra in 1878. "If Puritans contrived its removal," muses Blunt, "surely in this permissive age it could be reinstated . . ." and in the same volume appears the following description of the first flowering at Kew and the plant's initial discovery:

". . . [T]his obscene-looking plant was discovered . . . in the mountains of Sumatra, where it grows to a height of seventeen feet and makes a load for a dozen porters." (This description proved to me that the larger plant was beyond my grasp.) "The plant, which flowered at Kew in 1890 and was 'one of the sensations of the London season' was a mere dwarf, less than seven feet tall; but its stench—'a mixture of rotten fish and burnt sugar'—soon drove the curious out of the Orchid House and into the fresh air."

I should have taken my cue from this description of its scent and gone on to better things, but in the spring of 1980 I found a source for the devil's tongue and immediately sent for the largest tuber I could procure.

Upon arrival it was planted in a 10-inch Rivera self-watering pot (the first scientific name of this plant was *Hydrosme* referring to its love of water) with a mix of composted manure, potting soil, and sand, one-third each, whereupon it sent up a rather attractive leaf that grew some 3 feet across and lasted well into fall. I then took a hint from the cultural instructions in *Hortus III* and allowed the earth to dry, the leaf to shrivel. I stored the pot with the tuber in a sheltered spot in the greenhouse at a winter temperature of 50°F.

Early the next spring I added water to the pot and set it in a sunny spot in the greenhouse. Activity began within two weeks and a sheathed and speckled shaft burst through the dirt and continued to grow—it seemed—inches a day until on May 22, a 20-inch spathe began to open about a taller spadix, all standing on a 3-foot stem. A massive invasion of flies began, while a pervasive odor wafted through the wall between the greenhouse and our living room.

"You just can't leave it there," said my wife. "I'm trying to be fair but this is too much."

"But I'm afraid to take it outside since the next few nights will be in the low 30s."

"Heaven provides," she said.

I compromised by setting the flower in the rock garden during the day and moving it to the garage at night. This did cause a bit of a problem in the morning necessitated by opening the door and all that such an act implies.

Visitors to the garden did not know quite what to say about the giant maroon and leathery appurtenance set amid the blooming plants of the rock garden so they avoided all mention, which is fairly hard to do with a plant now 4 feet high and surmounted by buzzing flies.

By now it was the end of May and the flower began to shrivel, then slowly dissolve into a gelatinous mass, which in turn dried. The entire plant above the dirt was gone by June 5.

On July 5, the first leaf began to poke through the soil, a normal routine for this plant.

I'm now in a bit of a quandary: It was a most interesting plant but the experience of flowering the devil's tongue would seem to be one of those once-in-a-lifetime experiences that is so beautifully expressed by the old proverb, "Once bitten, twice shy!" There's a gardening friend one town over who is going to get a present very soon.

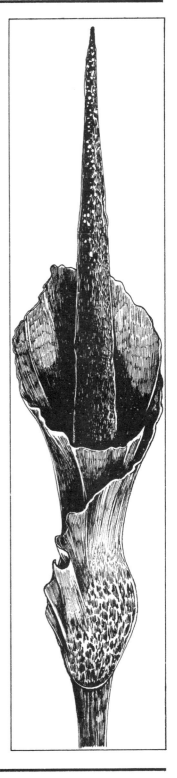

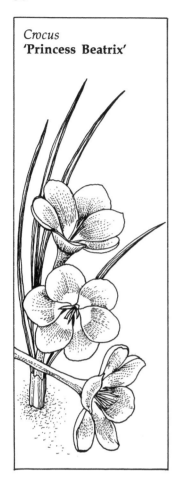

Crocus **'Princess Beatrix'**

A SPRING BULB BED

Last July we made plans for a new bulb bed on the side of the hill that begins its rise just to the rear of our perennial border. The flowers chosen to grow would be taken from a list including daffodils, narcissus, a few of the lesser known spring bulbs, and one species of tulip (I'm not too fond of tulips).

But like everything in our garden, the initial planning and work takes its toll in energy expended. Our soil bank consists of a thin layer of acid topsoil deftly scattered over a layer of red shale which in turn rests on a granite shelf that extends on either side of our land for miles.

Thus the first step was to build a retaining wall of fieldstone (I'm not too fond of railroad ties or layers of old newspapers, either) that was lugged by hand from an old wall in our nearby woods. By hauling exactly 72 stones, small, medium, and large, I built up a rectangular terrace that was even with the hill at the rear, 20 inches above the original soil at the front and measured 16 by 8 feet. I might add that the hauling began in late September when the days began to cool off but giving me plenty of time to complete construction before mid-October, when the bulbs were scheduled to arrive.

After the stones were in place, larger at the bottom and these tilted slightly towards the rear for stability, I spaded up the original soil, turning the hunks of turf over, roots up. Next I proceeded to add ten bags of top soil (on sale at the nearby garden center), four bags of composted cow manure (also on sale), mixed it thoroughly and left it all to settle until the bulbs turned up on our doorstep.

When we prepared our list of wanted bulbs, one of the considerations was when they bloomed and for how long. We hoped to have flowers from the beginning of April (about the time our mountain snows truly melt) at least until the end of May. We also wanted a permanent arrangement that would produce for a number of years without a great deal of care. True, the leaves of the past-blooming plants would have to remain as the bulbs ripened but by that time we knew we could scatter annuals about for camouflage. And, too, the perennial border and the other flower beds in the garden would detract from the browning leaves.

We began with crocuses choosing *Crocus chrysanthus* **'Princess Beatrix'**, a clear lobelia-like blue with a golden yellow base, and *C. sieberi* **'Firefly'** that opens to a rich lilac with a yellow base. Both bloom as the snows disappear.

Next we picked glory of the snow, *Chionodoxa lucilae* **'Pink Giant'**, a cultivar that bears eight to ten rose-pink flowers on every stem. And two charming fritillarias, *Fritillaria meleagris* **'Artemis'** with a checkered pattern of purple and green, and **'Poseidon'** gleaming white with purple checks.

Since we have a number of species tulips (small and charming) in the rock garden and scree bed, we decided on just one for blatant color, *Tulip eichleri,* a wild type that is truly brilliant with scarlet petals and a bright yellow center.

A few grape hyacinths, both rather exotic for the genus, were chosen for the front of the bed: *Muscari burtryoides* var. *album,* the

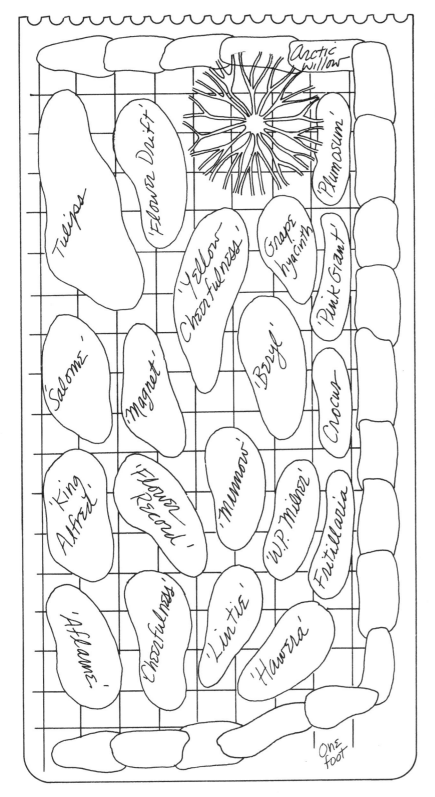

The plan for an autumn bulb bed.

'Arctic willow'

'Plumosum'

'Flower Drift'

Tulips

'Yellow Cheerfulness'

'Grape hyacinth'

'Pink Giant'

'Salome'

'Magnet'

'Beryl'

Crocus

'King Alfred'

'Flower Record'

'Minnow'

'W.P. Milner'

Fritillaria

'Aflame'

'Cheerfulness'

'Lintie'

'Hawera'

One foot

white variety, and *M. comosum* **'Plumosum'**, a form introduced from the Mediterranean region in 1612. The flower looks like a feathered plume from under the sea as each petal has been cut into fine shreds.

Finally came the daffodils. We carefully picked 13 varieties, some short, some tall, some dainty, like *Narcissus triandrus* **'Hawera'** (a flower so captivating that even hardened garden haters had to ask what that beautiful flower was), and some frankly close to jumbo, like the old war horse, Narcissus **'King Alfred'**. Time of bloom was most important here: We wanted some blooming early in April, some at month's end, and a few flowering well into mid-May.

The bulbs arrived at the end of October.

We had worked out a master plan of bulb distribution on notepaper assigning a number for each kind. Then that number was marked on the individual bulb bags and we began to work.

The daffodils were planted at a depth of 6 inches for the larger bulbs and 4 inches for the smaller. We placed them between 4 and 6 inches apart.

The crocus and other smaller bulbs were usually placed 4 inches deep. We used approximately 12 bulbs of each of the larger daffodil variety and 24 of the smaller. The total number of bulbs planted numbered about 400. As we placed each bulb we added just a bit of bulb fertilizer—never use non-organic types next to bulbs—just for an extra bit of food to help in the years ahead.

Finally, in the right of the bed on an open area I transplanted a small arctic willow (*Salix purpurea* **'Nana'**) that grows about 3 feet high, 3 feet wide, and can be pruned if it gets out of hand. This tiny tree would add interest to the bed during all the months of the year.

Next we watered the bed well and looked forward to spring flowers in five months' time.

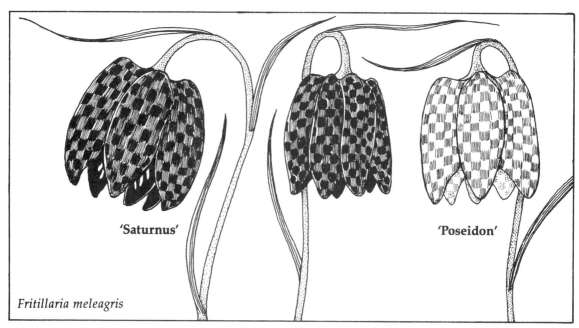

'Saturnus'   'Poseidon'

Fritillaria meleagris

Spring in the mountains was ushered in by a major sleet storm, followed by another massive attack on March 30. But on April 8 the crocuses began to bloom. Then on April 9 the temperature at night plummeted to 18°F. The crocuses closed and well they did for the next night saw 16°F. But on the eleventh, they opened again to a bright spring sun. On the day that income taxes are due, the *Chionodoxa* **'Pink Giant'** saw the light of day. And on April 24 the fritillarias and the tulips started their display. Meanwhile seven patches of daffodils were acting out the Wordsworth poem by "fluttering and dancing in the breeze."

By May 14 a few late frits were still nodding their blossoms while four patches of late-blooming daffodils were wide open and the tulips were finished. At the end of May a bunch of *Narcissus jonquilla* **'Lintie'** were still hanging on. And the tulip leaves turned a beautiful shade of burnt sienna as they dried, adding another touch of color. As seed pots formed on the various plants I carefully cut them off, thus guaranteeing extra strength to next year's show.

The night of June 3 saw a final spring frost, one of the latest in years. On the next day I seeded some tender annuals in amongst the bulbs, moved out other plants from the greenhouse and when the last of the bulb leaves died back, moved in a host of geraniums.

The bulb bed had lived up to advance notices giving color and a light heart to the gardeners far longer than most other flower beds.

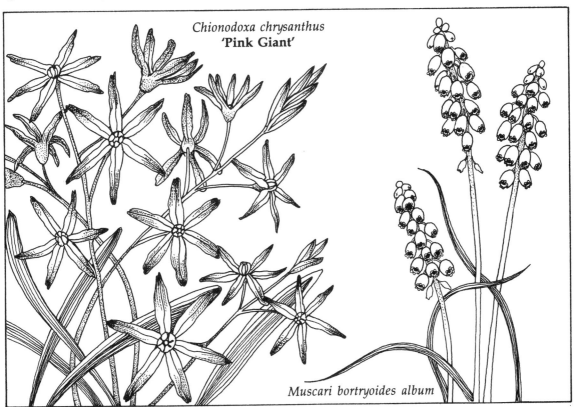

Chionodoxa chrysanthus
'Pink Giant'

Muscari bortryoides album

(1)

(2)

(3)

(4)

(6)

(5)

(7)

A List of the Bulbs Used in the Bulb Bed

VE = very early; E = early; M = middle; L = late blooming; H = height

(1) Trumpet daffodils; (2) Long-cupped daffodils; (3) Short-cupped daffodils; (4) Double daffodils; (5) Triandrus daffodils; (6) Cyclamineus daffodils; (7) Jonquilla daffodils; (8) Tazetta daffodils.

Narcissus **'Aflame'**; H: 17"; E; (3); White petals with a small red cup with an orange eye.

N. **'Magnet'**; H: 14"; E; (1); White petals around a yellow trumpet.

N. **'Beryl'**; H: 10"; E; (6); Primrose yellow with a globular orange cup.

N. **'W. P. Milner'**; H: 7"; E; (1); A miniature warm white trumpet.

N. **'Flower Record'**; H: 16"; E/M; (2); White with an orange, red-rimmed cup.

N, **'King Alfred'**; H: 16"; M; (1); Large yellow trumpet.

N. **'Flower Drift'**; H: 14"; M; (4); Double white flower with small tufts of orange between the petals.

N. **'Minnow'**; H: 7"; M; (8); Miniature with white petals and a yellow cup.

N. **'Salome'**; H: 18"; M/L; (2); White petals with a coral-pink cup.

N. **'Hawera'**; H: 8"; M/L; (5); Three to five lemon-yellow flowers on each stem.

N. **'Cheerfulness'**; H: 15"; L; (4); White with a creamy yellow center.

N. **'Yellow Cheerfulness'**; H: 14"; L; (4); Primrose yellow flowers.

N. **'Lintie'**; H: 7"; L; (7); Yellow with a flat orange crown.

Crocus chrysanthus **'Princess Beatrix'**; H: 3"; VE; Lobelia-blue with a golden yellow base.

C. sieberi **'Firefly'**; H: 2 1/2"; E; Lilac with a yellow base.

Chionodoxa chrysanthus **'Pink Giant'**; H: 5" to 8"; E; Rose-pink flowers.

Fritillaria meleagris **'Poseidon'**; H: 10"; M; White flowers checkered with purple.

F. meleagris **'Saturnus'**; H: 10"; M; Red-violet flowers.

Tulipa eichleri; H: 8"; E; Scarlet petals with a yellow-margined center.

Muscari bortryoides album; H: 8"; M; White form of the grape hyacinth.

M. comosum **'Plumosum'**; H: 8"; L; Feather-like grape hyacinth.

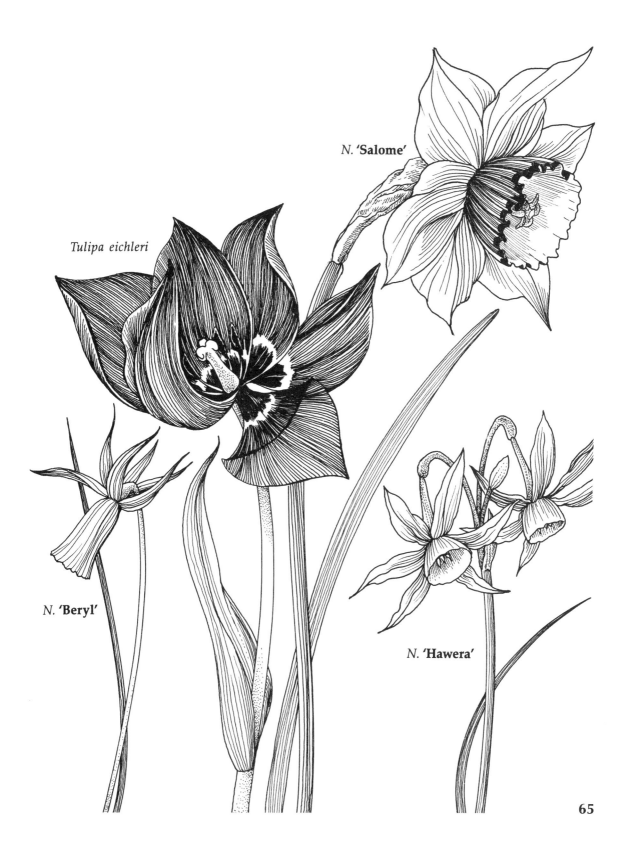

N. **'Salome'**

Tulipa eichleri

N. **'Beryl'**

N. **'Hawera'**

65

A GARDEN
OF GRASSES

Here in the country's heart
Where the grass is green,
Life is the same sweet life
As it e'er hath been.
Norman Gale, *The Country Faith*

The present is mere grass, quick-mown away —
Eugene Lee-Hamilton

I've been growing ornamental grasses in the garden for over eight years. By the end of August, eulalia grass is often over 10 feet tall, reed grass reaches to 15, Japanese blood grass is turning deep red, golden top shimmers with silken gilt, blue fescue forms 18-inch clumps of steely blue, and spike rush is 1 inch tall. They are all beautiful.

Unfortunately, at the same time that the garden is a graceful jumble of abstract lines, the lawn is a scraggly 2 inches higher than it should be and badly needs a trim.

It's difficult to realize that they all belong to the same family, the *Graminaeae,* a group of friends and foes that probably represent the single most important group of plants in the world.

For rice, wheat, oats, corn, bamboo, barley, rye, sorghum, and sugar are all close plant relations. In their seeds and foliage are stored the starches, sugars, and vitamins needed to keep humanity alive and healthy.

And it's also the family that brings you crabgrass and 274 other species with 274 different common names that have been in commerce—or backyards—at one time or another.

The annual ornamental grasses are usually grown for their seed panicles—flowers are there but they are minute and hardly noticeable—many of which dry beautifully for winter bouquets. Leaves of these grasses are usually not too showy.

The perennials have magnificent and varied foliage, with all shades of green, blue, and variegations of cream, white, gold, or a host of tans, in addition to notable seed heads.

On the opposite page is Ravenna grass, one of the stars in the grass garden and magnificent even in a northern garden.

Bamboo

With their plant sizes running the gamut from tiny to huge, they belong in every garden and if you have the room, they make an impressive garden all their own.

Included in this garden are a few plants that are usually thought of as grasses but really belong to closely allied but more primitive families: The sedges and the rushes.

A GARDEN OF PERENNIAL GRASSES

This garden of grasses is planned for a plot measuring 10 by 20 feet. It features 15 species or cultivars of the perennial grasses (including two tropical varieties), one bamboo, and one sedge, for a total of 17 different plants. You might think this is a small number of plants for such a large piece of ground. It isn't! The grasses take a lot of room. I went out today with a measuring tape just to make sure the height and the breadth given in the plan was correct.

If you want to get some of the feeling of walking through a jungle, plant a thicket using just eulalia grass or ravenna grass. By summer's end you will be amazed at the size of the grasses. Remember to allow at least three years of active growth before these plants will begin to approach their ultimate size.

Soil for this garden need not be better than average. Remove the turf, then try to turn the earth to a depth of 1 foot. Add a mix of clean garden soil and some composted manure to make up for the lost earth. Plants do best (except for sea oats) in full sun.

The only real chore in dealing with grasses is the annual pruning of the larger types in early spring. Then you will cut the dead stems and leaves to within 6 inches of the ground, before new growth begins.

The larger clump-forming grasses grow from the inside out, and you may notice the plants are dead in the center after a few years. That is the time to divide the clumps with an ax, and pass on extra plants to other gardeners. These plants are not fragile.

Plants for the Grass Garden

In the following descriptions, the height given is that of the plant in bloom, when the plumes usually stand above the leaves. Except for the tropicals, they are all hardy in Zone 5. Those that can live in Zone 4 are so marked. In the measurements, the first is the height and the second the spread of the plant, in inches.

At Wave Hill, a beautiful formal garden in the Bronx, New York, there is a specimen of Ravenna grass that required blasting to a depth of 2 1/2 feet in solid rock in order to provide the needed hole for planting. The effort was worthwhile: The grass, both in leaf and in bloom, is spectacular! That grass is the center of the planting with others grouped—according to height—around it. The plan also includes a short path of stone that would be an ideal place for a sundial or a spot to summer out the tropical grasses.

The first grass is a bamboo (*Arundinaria viridistriata*), that is hardy with protection in Zone 5, where it is not invasive. Farther south is another matter and care should be taken in planting to

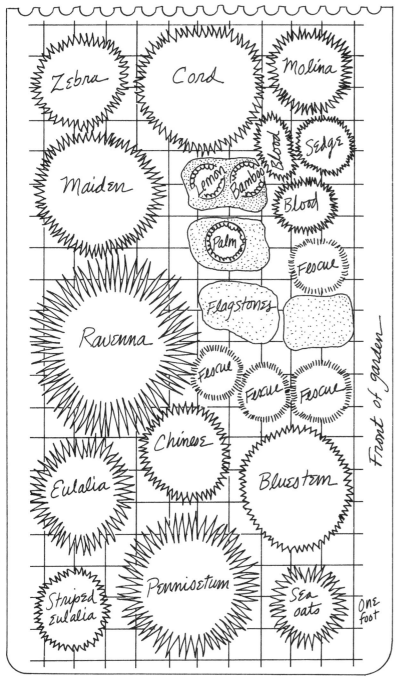

The plan for a perennial grass garden.

prevent unwanted spread. This bamboo is a true beauty: The leaves have a velvety look when new and are a rich combination of gold and green that glows in the distance. The stems reach a height of 2 1/2 feet. It likes partial shade and I find it does best when grown in a 12-inch pot.

Japanese sedge grass (*Carex Morrowii* var. *expallida*), 18 by 8 inches, is hardy in Zone 5 but should be given a cover of evergreen branches or other loose mulch when real winter comes. It also likes some shade from the noonday sun in summer. The gracefully arched leaves are striped with creamy white and green with strange flowers in the spring, flowers that resemble camel's-hair brushes dipped in yellow powder.

Northern sea oats (*Chasmanthium latifolium*) 36 by 24 inches, will also survive in some shade. It is still listed as *Uniola latifolia* in many catalogs. This is a beautiful plant with flat panicles of drooping flowers that are green at first but turn a golden brown after a severe frost. If started from seed sea oats will not grow with gusto until the second year.

Lemon grass (*Cymbopogon citratus*), 36 by 12 inches, is only hardy in Zone 10, but it does well in a pot up north. It will rarely exceed 3 feet when grown indoors but can top 6 feet in the tropics. The flower, if it blooms, is nondescript, but the plant is very attractive with its arching leaves of light green. It makes a great conversation piece, for lemon grass is the commercial source of lemon oil, and a crushed leaf sends forth a wonderful smell. Soil should be light, with plenty of sand for good drainage. You will also see this grass on the spice rack in large supermarkets where it's used in flavoring many Southeast Asian recipes. In the garden of grasses it sits outside all summer surrounded by its hardier cousins.

Ravenna grass (*Erianthus ravennae*), 10 to 11 by 5 feet, is the highpoint of this garden and some thought should go into its placement especially when used along in a perennial border: It has a

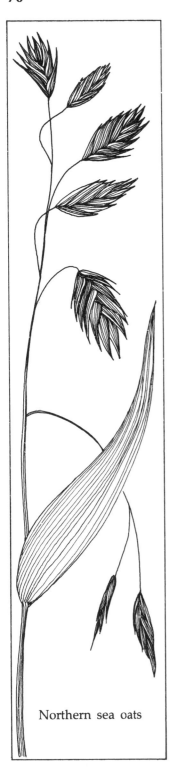

Northern sea oats

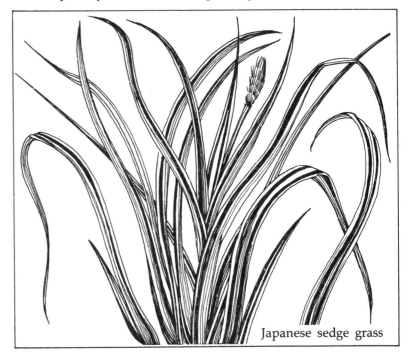

Japanese sedge grass

tendency to dominate almost any setting. The leaves form a fountain of green that changes to a rich brown in early autumn. Then its silvery beige plumes appear. Soil should be better than average so give this plant an extra shot of composted manure when planting. Remember not to stint on space.

Blue fescue (*Festuca ovina* var. *glauca*), 18 by 10 inches, is hardy in Zone 4. It is a variety of sheeps' fescue grass and has a bluish bloom, which is actually a powder that covers the leaf-blade surfaces and will easily rub off. The name is derived from the Celtic word *fest*, meaning pasture. Plant these grasses in clusters and fill up any vacant spots in the plan with their attractive leaves. The clumps are easily split when they become too large. The flowers are rather small; the color and shape of the leaves is the chief reason for cultivation.

Japanese blood grass (*Imperata cylindrica rubra*), 18 by 12 inches, is hardy to Zone 5 with winter protection from freezing winter winds. I solved the problem of exposure by placing the plants in front of a low wall. In the plan an uneven space with a 3-foot diameter is set aside for this grass. The reason for cultivating this grass is the color: A rich, blood-red that starts about midway on the grass blade and reaches to the tip. Japanese blood grass is fairly new to this country, but two sources in the Appendixes keep it in stock. It has never flowered for me: I think the season just isn't long enough.

Chinese silver grass (*Miscanthus floridulis*), 8 by 3 feet, sits next to eulalia grass in the plan as it's the shorter of the two. They are alike, except for stature.

Eulalia grass (*M. sinensis*), 10 by 3 feet, is a genus of ornamental grasses extensively cultivated throughout the world. They grow very

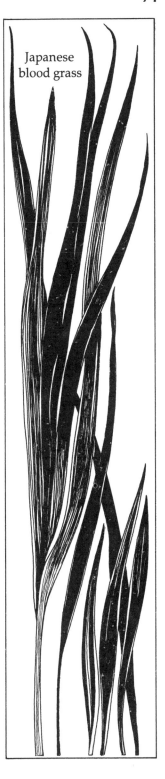

Japanese blood grass

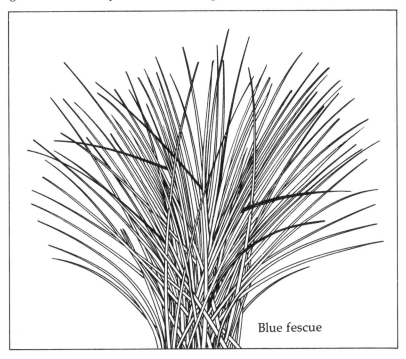

Blue fescue

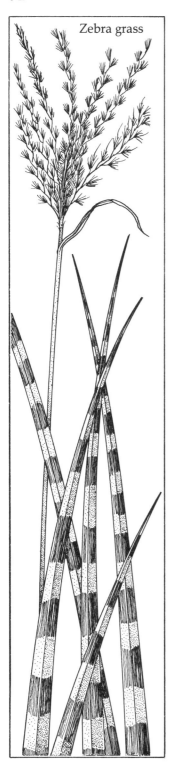

Zebra grass

tall and produce magnificent plumes of silvery spikelets with a purple sheen and are much like the feathers carried by Egyptian slaves to fan Cleopatra. As the summer progresses, the bottom leaves die back, and by tearing them off you reveal more of the handsome stems. These stems become very dark and hard with age and exposure to weather. After the growing season is over, the stems can be cut off and will take a beautiful polish. In ancient Japan they were used to form many implements: brush handles, kitchen utensils, and tools for print making. If your growing season is less than 90 days eulalia grass may not flower for you, but it's worth growing for the leaves alone.

Maiden grass (*M. sinensis* **'Gracillimus'**), 6 by 4 feet, is aptly named—both its common and cultivar names—since the plant reflects the charm of a graceful maiden. Leaves are long and narrow, and lightly curved at the tips. Color is light green, and the mid-rib is white.

Zebra grass (*M. sinensis* **'Zebrinus'**), 6 by 3 feet, is another close favorite of mine: It's a delight to any gardener who suffers through a northern winter. One is hard put to believe that any grass with such a tropical look could succeed in a land of plummeting temperatures. Individual leaves are not striped but dashed with horizontal bands of a light golden brown. A clump can become massive over many years and look like a sparkling fountain. Zebra grass, like others of the *Miscanthus* tribe, grows in damp soil so it's excellent for the poolside.

Striped eulalia grass (*M. sinensis* **'Variegatus'**), 5 by 3 feet, is the variegated form and its leaves are heavily stripped with white.

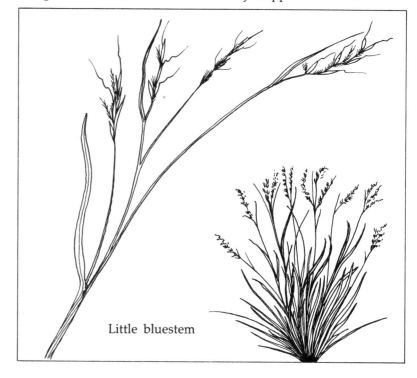

Little bluestem

Purple moor grass is such a beauty that it has an essay of its own on page 74.

Fountain grass (*Pennisetum alopecuroides*), 3 by 4 1/2 feet, has a very wide spread—its leaves and flowering stems arch toward the ground. The blossoms are especially beautiful when covered with dew and lit by the morning sun. Fountain grass is effective when placed next to a planting of little bluestem, for the reddish stems of the second plant echo the russet tones of the first. Leave enough room for the plant's spread.

Little bluestem (*Schizachyrium scoparium*), 4 by 4 feet, is still listed in many catalogs as *Andropogon scoparius*. It's the state grass of Nebraska. The flowering stems turn a golden reddish brown in the fall sparked with tiny white tufted blossoms along their edge.

Palm grass (*Setaria palmifolia*) is a slender tropical grass that reaches 6 feet in a warm climate. The plaited leaves are 2 feet long and 3 inches wide, and of a deep emerald green. The plants do well in containers but need full sun outdoors in summer to thrive. I grow palm grass in a 14-inch pot.

Cord grass (*Spartina pectinata* var. *aurea variegata*), 5 by 4 feet, has many common names: bull grass, tall marsh grass, slough grass (*slough* is an old Anglo-Saxon word meaning a wet or marshy place), freshwater cord grass, and Upland Creek grass. American pioneers used this grass to thatch roofs and protect haystacks against the weather. This variegated form of the common grass is quite graceful in the landscape, with gracefully bending leaves striped with light tan. As its many names suggest, cord grass does well in a damp spot.

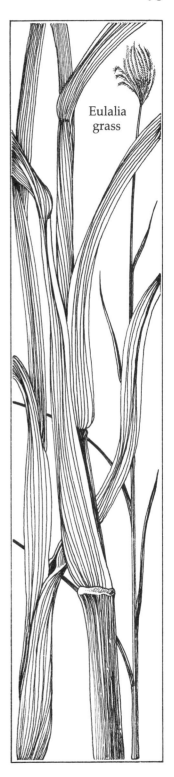

Eulalia grass

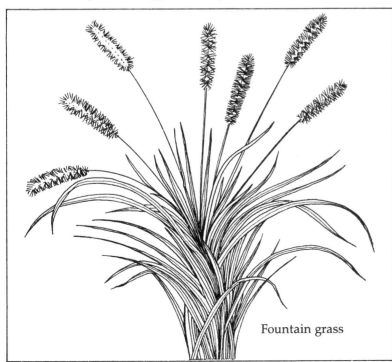

Fountain grass

PURPLE MOOR GRASS

The *Dictionary of Gardening* compiled by the Royal Horticultural Society (of England) has the following entry for purple moor grass:

> **Molinia** (in honor of Juan Ignacio Molina, 1740–1829, writer on the natural history of Chile). Fam. *Gramineae.* A genus of perhaps two species, one spread over Europe, Asia Minor, and N. Asia, the other Japanese. Perennial densely tufted grass with slender leaves. . . . A grass of bleak, wet moorlands, the variegated form of which is a good bedding plant; propagated by division.

"Bleak, wet moorlands" and "a good bedding plant" are such telling phrases and so English; such understatement for a grass that should be in every garden and especially interesting since it's one of the few grasses where actual outdoor observations have been carried out documenting the early stages of germination.

In 1915, T. A. Jefferies, wrote the following in *The Journal of Ecology:*

> On the moors about Huddersfield . . . little peat hollows, sometimes only about two square feet in area, are common; these become pools in wet weather, but are robbed of their surface water by a few days' drought. Bright sunshine and a strong wind playing on the unprotected surface of such a hollow, cause the formation of a network of cracks. Into these the seeds of *Molinia [caerulea]* are blown, and are sheltered there from the wind. When the water has disappeared in the early summer, lines of crowded seedlings appear, marking out the meshwork of last season's cracks like miniature green hedgerows.

Later, Jefferies points out that *Molinia* is particularly notable for the firmness of its root system, which makes the plant difficult to pull up from the ground. It is also noted that the swollen nodes at the base of the plant were often used as pipe cleaners and toothpicks while the dried stems went into local broom manufacture.

While I cannot testify to the germination of *Molina,* I can note its tenacious hold upon the soil, and also attest to the beauty of the variegated form.

We have had the variegated form (*M. caerulea* **'Variegata'**) in the garden since 1978. Every year the fountain of rather rigid leaves, each banded with white stripes and gently curving towards the ground, becomes a little larger and more impressive. The panicles occur atop curving stems and reach 3 feet in height; they are striped like the leaves, but tinged with violet and greenish highlights.

Unlike most grasses, *Molinia* will accept some partial shade, and because of its ancestry, prefers an acid soil and will tolerate some dampness. And that fibrous and tough root system makes it an excellent plant for banks, and steep hillsides.

If you are forced to choose among a dozen ornamental grasses, choose this plant.

Goldentop

The vase on the opposite page contains (reading from the left): Hare's-tail grass, black sorghum, quaking oats, bearded wheat, foxtail grass, brome grass, and canary grass.

ANNUAL GRASSES FOR BOUQUETS

Purple masses of New England aster, the restrained but elegant flowers of grasses and great yellow drifts of goldenrod are all just outside my studio window. The view is not of a northern meadow in the fall, but of our front garden where I have planted three types of field asters, fourteen species of annual grasses, and five varieties of goldenrod grown from English seed (we Americans still mistakenly believe this beautiful plant causes hayfever).

Of all the garden flowers, the annual grasses are still favorites of mine. As a group, they are rarely grown for their foliage, which, except for the ornamental corns, looks weedy at best. Instead grasses are grown for the endless variety of their flowers and seed heads. Whether we plant them to relieve our dependence on the typical bedding annuals or to gather and dry them for winter decorations, these plants deserve a place in many more gardens.

As a general rule, these plants need a position with full summer sun for adequate growth and flowering, but they are not too fussy about soil conditions. As long as the soil drains and is capable of supporting a good crop of weeds, the annual grasses should do well.

My wife and I usually start most of our seeds indoors in early spring because our local growing season only really guarantees 110 days between frosts. In warmer climates, the seeds can go directly into the ground as soon as the weather settles.

When you plant these grasses in your garden, prepare and mark the seedbed with care. The new little plants look for all the world like any other grassy weed, which can lead to confusion and dismay. I was careless one year and lost much of the hare's-tail grass I had planted. It was squeezed out by crabgrass before I realized what was happening.

As the seedlings grow to 1 and 2 inches tall, thin them to 6 or 12 inches between each plant, depending on their ultimate height. Wild oats, for example, should be about 12 inches apart, while the hare's-tail only needs a 6-inch space. Also, be generous with seed—the smaller grasses look better when planted in substantial groupings of the same species.

Remember to collect seed for future gardens. Store in carefully marked packages (stamp and coin envelopes are excellent) in a cool, dry place.

Foxtail millet (*Setaria italica*) grows between 2 and 4 feet tall and looks exactly like the foxtail that was tied on the rumble seats of Fords in the 1930s. The dense panicles are often up to a foot in length and bow towards the earth with the weight of the seeds. While the plants are tolerant to some lack of water, they perish quickly under drought conditions. This grass was cultivated in Ancient China (2700 B.C.), reached Europe during the Middle Ages and in 1849 entered the United States, where it has become an important fodder crop. The seed is harvested for bird feed. A bowl of these panicles can make a striking addition to a room and will last as long as you have patience to dust them.

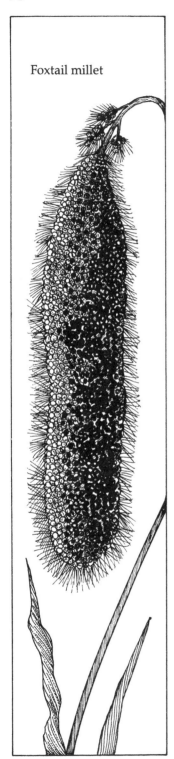

Foxtail millet

Variegated corn (*Zea mays* var. *gracillima* **'Variegata'**) grows up to 6 feet tall, but usually hovers between 3 and 4 feet. Unlike the other annual grasses, it is grown for its beautifully shaded leaves that are striped with green and pure white. The cobs never grow very large, and the silk just adds interest to the plants. Corn is a heavy feeder, so always plant it in fertile soil, add fertilizer at monthly intervals, and never skimp on water. Try growing variegated corn in 8-inch pots, and group a few for an effective outdoor terrace decoration.

Z. mays var. *japonica* has the added beauty of a touch of red and pink along with the green and white variegations. There are other varieties that are grown for their ears of many-colored kernels.

Goldentop (*Lamarckia aurea*) will grow to 20 inches in good soil. Named after J. B. Lamarck, the French naturalist who lost out to Darwin in the evolutionary sweepstakes (Lamarck thought that giraffes got long necks from reaching for food in trees), this is a favorite grass. The one-sided panicles have a shimmering look when fresh and become a tarnished silver-green with age. By midsummer the plants are turning brown, so a second crop should be prepared. The flowers shatter easily when dry, so be sure to pick them before they mature. Goldentop is found growing as a weed in the southeastern United States.

Quaking grass (*Briza maxima*) reaches 3 feet in height during a good summer season. A native of southern Europe, this grass has been in cultivation as a garden ornament for well over 200 years. The spikelets quiver and shake with every gentle motion of the breeze, and they are faintly striped with purple, making it a most attractive addition to any bouquet. Quaking grass should be limited to the cutting garden—it is a bit too ungainly for a prominent place elsewhere. The panicles should be picked before they open.

Brome grass (*Bromus madritensis*) will reach 2 feet in height. It is one of a number of species in this genus eminently qualified for both garden and vase. The flowers retain all their grace when dried, and the grass tips of the species illustrated become tinged with auburn as they ripen. Most seed catalogs that carry annual grasses list two or three types of this grass.

Hare's-tail grass (*Lagurus ovatus*) grows between 18 and 20 inches tall and has been cultivated for centuries. The foliage is light green, and both stems and leaves are soft with down. The plant produces numerous terminal spikes until the first killer frost does it in, and it is a favorite for winter bouquets because the flower heads do not shatter with age. However, their very durability has led to unending mistreatment by people who die them outrageous colors, and place them in plastic vases for sale at highway rest-stops.

Champagne grass (*Rhynchelytrum repens*) will form large clumps of leaves up to 4 feet tall. It is often listed as *Rhynchelytrum roseaum* or *Tricholaena rosea* in seed catalogs and is also called ruby or Natal grass. It's an annual in the North, but becomes a perennial where temperatures stay above freezing. Floridians should beware: This plant can become a pesky weed! It blooms over a long season but is stopped by the slightest frost. The reddish-pink plumes turn a soft silver with age and are great cut flowers. They can be dried for winter bouquets, but with care—they shatter easily. When gathering, pull the stems rather than breaking or cutting them.

Canary grass (*Phalaris canariensis*) grows to 3 feet tall. It is a native of the Canary Islands and southern Europe and is grown as birdseed for both wild and domesticated canaries. The flower heads are a variegated green and yellowish white at the top of long, slender stems, but the plant itself is not at all attractive and should be kept in the cutting garden. Because the refuse from bird cages often goes to landfills, canary grass is sometimes seen at the local dump.

Feathertop grass (*Pennisetum villosum*) grows between 2 and 3 feet tall and is an annual in the North, perennial in the South. It's often termed *Pennisetum longistylum* in catalogs. The grass is rather sloppy in appearance, for the magnificent flowers become quite heavy. If picked before they open entirely they can be dried but they shatter with the slightest bump. They do make beautiful fresh flowers.

Bearded wheat (*Triticum turgidum*) will grow to 4 feet. The tradition of cultivating this hardy cereal annual reaches far back in time. Its seeds are ground to become durum flour, which is used with great popularity for pastas. Grown in most arid regions of the world because of its resistance to drought, the long seeds that appear to be bearded are unlike any others in the grass kingdom. The flowering stalks are a decorator's delight.

Black sorghum (*Sorghum bicolor* var. *technicus*) will top 6 feet over the summer. The sorghums have been used since prehistoric times, and man has approached the species with an inventive mind. The sweet sap of some varieties is used for molasses, a second variety is used for making flour, a third is grown for silage and cattle fodder, and a fourth for making brooms. The shiny black seeds immediately spruce up floral arrangements, and even the cornlike leaves with their light green color lightly spattered with brown can be very effective when added to a vase of cut flowers. This is a very tender plant and should not be planted out until all danger of frost is past.

Foxtail grass (*Setaria lutescens*) will grow to 2 feet in height. It is a relative of foxtail millet and was originally a common weed in Europe. Since its introduction into the United States, it has also become invasive here, but the yellow-orange bristles of the seed heads are attractive and retain their color after drying. In fact, a massive arrangement of 50 to 60 stems (and with any luck that is not a lot to gather) could cause even the most sophisticated guest to ask where they are found and how much they cost.

Job's tears (*Coix Lacryma-Jobi*) is a close relative of corn and can grow to 4 feet. Since ancient times this grass has been in cultivation as an especially sweet-tasting cereal flour but it also has the distinction of being the oldest ornamental grass in cultivation—it was grown in the fourteenth century in monastery gardens. The seeds fall readily from the plant at maturity and are extremely hard, colored with streaks of gray and black on white.

For years the seeds have been utilized in the manufacture of jewelry, especially rosaries, and in Italy are known as Lachryma Christi or often St. Mary's-tears. In Assam they are crow's-jewel

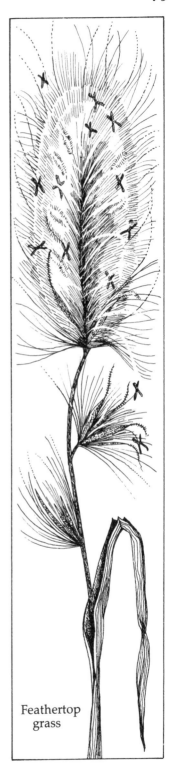

Feathertop grass

Job's tears

Champagne grass

while the Arabs term them David's-tears. The women of certain Burmese tribes use these seeds in combination with silver, beetles' wings, and squirrels' tails to embroider fanciful designs on cloth. Plants are often found growing wild in the southern United States. Job's tears will tolerate some shade and prefers a damp spot in the garden. In colder climates start the seeds indoors. Old gardening books list a variegated form called *C. Lacryma-Jobi* var. *zebrina*, but I've yet to find a source.

Wild oats (*Avena fatua*) grows to 4 feet tall and is considered by most eastern farmers to be nothing but a troublesome weed. It can be found growing along the roadside in high summer. Even for a grass the plant looks straggly, but the flowers dry to a beautiful shade of light brown. A more civilized species called animated oats (*A. sterilis*) has a larger flower that looks like wild oats held under a magnifying glass. It is termed animated because the needlelike spike (or awn) that protrudes from the seed heads moves about as the humidity in the air changes.

Gathering the Grasses

If you wish to gather some grasses for winter bouquets, pick the stems on a dry and sunny day after the dews of morning have evaporated. Pick flowers that have not yet completely opened and cut the stems as long as you can—they can always be trimmed later. Strip off any excess leaves, tie small bunches of stems tightly together and hang them upside down on wire coat hangers, leaving plenty of air space between each bunch. Hang the hangers well apart in a cool, dry, airy room. Check the bundles every few days. The stems will shrink as they dry, and some could fall to the floor and shatter. It should take about three weeks for the drying process.

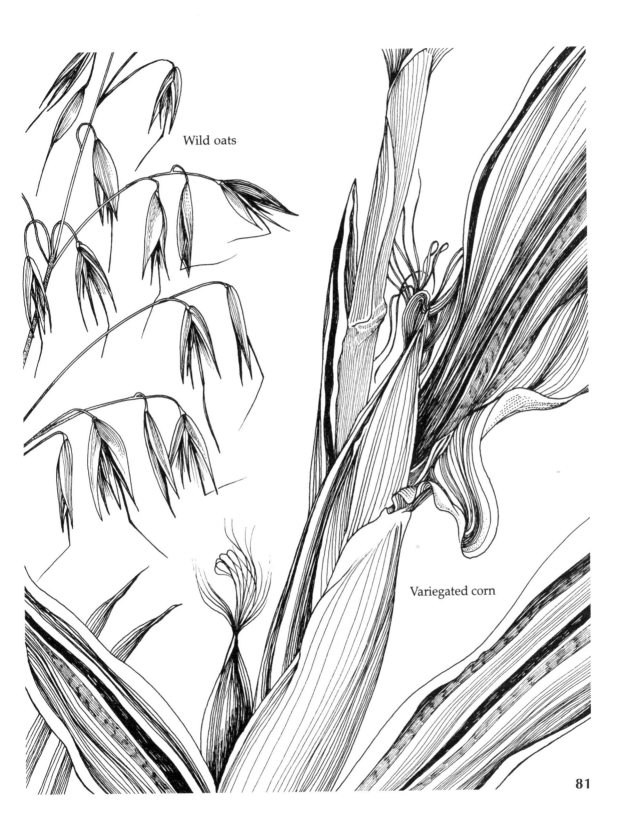

Wild oats

Variegated corn

81

THE NIGHT GARDEN

Even a man who is pure at heart
And says his prayers by night,
Can become a wolf when the wolfbane blooms
And the autumn moon is bright.
The Wolf Man, 1941
Universal Pictures

The idea of a garden that bloomed at night first crossed my thoughts when I was an editor/reporter for a small weekly newspaper. Newspapers start to function very early in the morning, and fingers must fly over typewriter (or computer) keys while many suburbanites are just spooning sugar on their cornflakes. So by the late afternoon when I arrived home there was little time or energy to work in the garden and the time that was spent went into weeding, watering, and general upkeep. Then, before exhaustion could take over, it was too dark for more.

The desire to make the evening hours more productive merged with an active memory of the horror movies of my youth, wonderful movies where Sherlock Holmes battled the Spider Woman (who grew night-blooming plants in a dank basement south of Soho to feed poison-producing spiders) or the Werewolf of London (clean shaven by day but hirsute by night), a man bathing pale white blossoms of a cryptic plant under the light of an artificial moon in a vain search for an antidote to prevent the overt effects of lycanthropy.

My first child of the night was the moonflower, a tropical perennial that will bloom so soon after germination that in the North it's treated as an annual. Easily grown as a vine in any sunny window in a 6-inch pot, it can also be planted out in the garden, where it needs only a set of strings or a trellis to slither up into the evening. The flowers are so fragrant that night moths quickly fly to the opening buds.

Next came the night-blooming daylily, a conflict of terms that works. These hybrids of the genus *Hemerocallis* have names like **'Golden Trinkets'** or **'Ida Miles'** and unfold their unusually fragrant flowers at dusk and stay open until the following morning, unlike others of their tribe.

On the opposite page a giant silk moth visits the blossoms of the night-blooming daylily under a full moon.

83

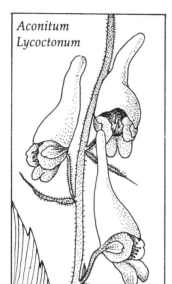

Aconitum Lycoctonum

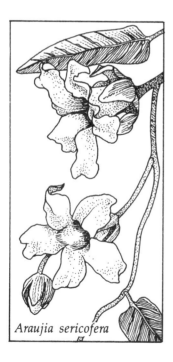

Araujia sericofera

Soon I succeeded in finding a host of other plants: Annuals, perennials, or biennials that will open their flowers in late afternoon, at dusk, or in the full dark of night. There were elegant evening primroses; four-o'clocks, flowers of grandmother's garden; and for adding perfume to the night air, night jasmine and other exotic types of flowers that are only fragrant after dark.

Then I discovered a wonderful book entitled *Old Time Gardens* by Alice Morse Earle, first published in 1901. Chapter XX described a moonlight garden, a garden of all white flowers—first designed by the parents of one Hon. Ben. Perley Poore of Newburyport, Massachusetts—that Miss Earle thought was radiant in the sunshine but glorious when bathed by silvery moonlight. The plan for a moonlight garden in this chapter is a mite smaller than Poore's but the thought is still there. It is dedicated to the memory of Miss Earle.

Since the light of the moon isn't available every evening, the next step in creating the night garden is to provide enough light to mimic the moon or otherwise bathe the garden path with a gentle glow so the night visitor can enjoy the sights, sounds, and odors without tripping or stubbing a toe against a low rock wall. And almost in answer to a night gardener's prayer, the concept of low-voltage lighting has become available to the mass-market and ceased to be a luxury available only to those in the higher income brackets. Even local hardware stores are known to stock for a very low price a complete garden-lighting kit that anyone can install in an afternoon.

The following pages give a general plan for a garden of the night that includes both hardy and tender plants (including some houseplants) and could easily be adapted to a city terrace; a moonlight garden in homage to Miss Earle; a list of all the plants involved; a section on garden lighting and some comments on the creatures of the night.

And yes, there really is a plant called wolfsbane. But note that Curt Siodmak, the scriptwriter at Universal who made up the entire wolfman legend, incorrectly called it wolfbane. It's a member of the monkshood family, in which many species are poisonous and used in the manufacture of drugs. The scientific name is *Aconitum Lycoctonum*.

A Place for the Night Garden

The night garden is planned for an area around a terrace, either close by or attached to a house or apartment. This location is for two reasons: First, a source of electricity is needed for the outdoor lighting and second, it's much nicer to sit on stone or gravel to watch the fireflies than dew-besotted grass. Nights are romantic, but in the Northeast, decidedly damp.

The terrace shown in the plan measures 10 by 15 feet (and could easily be smaller in scale) and is decorated with tropical night-blooming plants that can spend summer outside but must come in for the winter in most of the United States. The terrace garden includes a few pots of the moonvine, nightblooming cereus, Angel's trumpet, cruel plant, a night-blooming gladiolus, and night jessamine.

Around the terrace are the annuals for night fragrance, a trellis

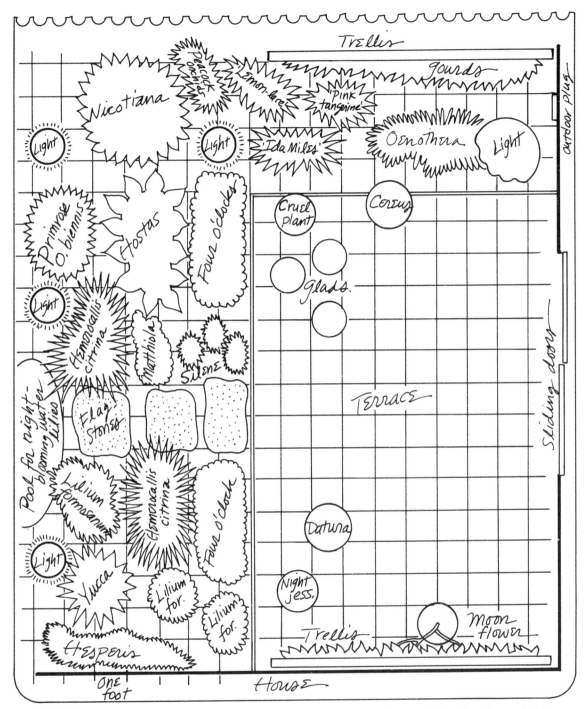

The plan for a night garden.

with the white-flowering gourds, and scattered about, the other flowers of the night. A fieldstone path leads to the backyard, where low-voltage lighting illuminates a tree and powers three garden lights for atmosphere—and provides for easier walking when there is no moon.

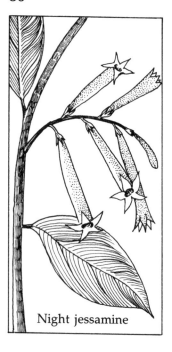

Night jessamine

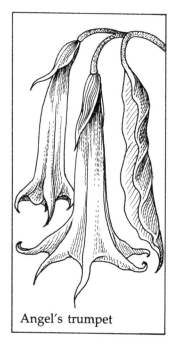

Angel's trumpet

Plants for the Night Garden

Peacock orchids (*Acidanthera bicolor*) have a wonderful and sweet fragrance which is present all day and then intensifies at night. They are described in the bulb garden on page 52.

The cruel plant (*Araujia sericofera*) comes from Brazil and Argentina and is hardy only from Zone 9 and south. Everywhere else it does well in a 10-inch pot filled with a mix of good potting soil and composted manure, 2/3 to 1/3. Pots should contain a trellis or be near one, for *Araujia* is a climber. Seed germination takes three to six weeks and seedlings will bloom about ten months later. And it's the bloom that is the most interesting feature of this unusual plant. Starry, creamy white, 1 1/2-inch flowers use their sweet scent to attract the nocturnal moths from the garden. Once lured to the flowers the moths are trapped in the sticky pollen.

But the cruel plant is not as cruel as you think: The plant is at least sure of being pollinated, and when the morning sun dries the pollen the moths escape.

The angel's trumpet (*Brugmansia suaveolens*) is a tropical plant from southern Mexico and blooms in mid- to late summer with huge white flowers than can reach a length of 12 inches. Many books still list this plant as *Datura*. These pendant trumpets are sweetly fragrant at night and a well-grown specimen is a breathtaking sight. The plants are hardy only from Zone 9 south and elsewhere must spend their life in a heavy 12-inch pot where the strong trunk often stands about 6 feet tall. Use the same soil as with *Araujia*.

Night jessamine (*Cestrum nocturnum*) grows to a 12-foot shrub in its native West Indies but in a 12-inch pot (which is where gardeners in temperate zones must grow it) the plant rarely reaches 6 feet. As a shrub it's not much to speak about but when its tubular green flowers open to the night air, it produces a perfume that is intensely fragrant. Jessamine should be pruned either after blooming or in early spring. Plants generally bloom all summer and into autumn. Night jessamine is hardy from Zone 9 south but it does very well in post. If the plant is burned by a slight frost it will recover. Use the same soil as with *Araujia*.

There are at least five genera of cactus that contain plants called night-blooming cereus: *Epiphyllum*, *Hylocereus*, *Nyctocereus*, *Peniocereus*, and *Selenicereus*. The best one for a houseplant is *Epiphyllum oxypetalum*, the queen of the night. This plant prefers warmth (temperatures between 60° to 80°F.), partial shade in the hottest months of the summer, and a humus-rich soil that is kept evenly moist (cut back on water during the winter months). In winter, plants must be kept above freezing.

When grown indoors, epiphyllums will be about 6 feet high and at a certain point need staking. Flower buds develop (plants must be at least three years old) every year from April through September and when they are ready to bloom—believe me, you will know—call your friends and tell them to follow the fragrance to where you keep the plant during the summer. Blossoms open like a very slow Walt Disney nature film and are spectacular! They last only for the night.

The night gladiolus (*Gladiolus tristis*) has fragrant, cream-yellow blossoms that rise above very unusual leaves with a most peculiar structure: They look like a pinwheel when cut in half. The flowers are very fragrant at night and the plants do quite well in a 6-inch pot. Allow the corms to completely dry by withholding water after flowers and leaves fade. Let the plants rest for about three months.

The night-blooming daylilies belong in every garden. Unlike others in the clan, these flowers open at dusk and remain fresh throughout the night. In our garden buds begin to swell about 6:00 P.M. and are wide open by 7:30. *Hemerocallis citrina* is the best of them all. Its 3 1/2-foot-long leaves are lightly crinkled along the edge, and gracefully bend to form a fountain of green. Many lemon-yellow flowers, most 6 inches long, bloom on 4-foot stalks. The fragrance is very sweet. The sphinx moths that delight in the dark visit these flowers night after night and the hummingbirds follow in the morning until the blossoms fade about 10:00 A.M. Plants produce blossoms over a period of three to four weeks starting at the end of July.

Sweet rocket

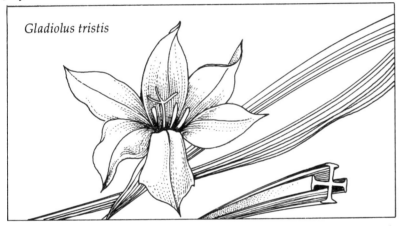

Gladiolus tristis

There are cultivars, too. *Hemerocallis* **'Golden Trinkets'** is yellow, and grows 20 to 24 inches tall; **'Ida Miles'** is ivory-yellow, and grows to 30 inches; and **'Pink Tangerine'** is melon in tone, and grows 34 inches. These three cultivars all bloom at the end of June. **'Lemon Lace'** is lemon yellow, 32 inches tall, and blooms in mid-June. All are hardy in Zone 4.

Sweet rocket (*Hesperis matronalis*) is a fragrant nighttime flower that is variously a perennial, a biennial, or an annual depending on luck and well-drained garden soil. It performs best as a biennial. Lilac, purple, and violet flowers cluster on 2-foot stems, releasing a beautiful perfume as twilight falls. The botanical name comes from the Greek *hesperis,* for the evening star.

The fragrant plantain lily (*Hosta plantaginea*) grows with lush, ribbed leaves, 10 inches long. In late summer to early autumn, 5-inch-long, white, very fragrant tubular flowers appear on 2-foot stems. At night the petals seem to spread and the perfume of honey fills the air. They are hardy in Zone 5 but may need a light covering

Evening stock

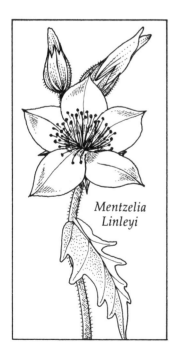

Mentzelia
Linleyi

on very frosty nights to protect the delicate blossoms. They make an excellent cut flower, lasting for days in a vase.

The moon flower has an entry all to itself on page 96.

The vesper iris (*Iris dichotoma*) came to me from The Fragrant Path. The plant produces flowers on 3-foot stems during August and September. Originally from Siberia and Northern China, it's the only iris that I know of that begins to bloom at vespers, or about 6:00 in the evening. Flowers are small and mauve in color. They are hardy in Zone 5.

The bottle gourds (*Lagenaria siceraria*) deserve a spot in the night garden and the reason has nothing to do with their fruit (see page 110). The fragile looking flowers with their sweet perfume demand their inclusion here. Night moths visit each blossom, and even their light weight will cause the tissue-paper-thin petals to bend. The plan shows a trellis to contain the long-reaching vines where dozens of buds will slowly open on warm summer nights.

Lilium formosanum blossom from mid- to late September with 6-inch flowers of white on 4- to 6-foot stems. Although open and fragrant during the day, their perfume is stronger at night. They are described in the Bulb Garden on page 56.

Evening stock (*Matthiola longipetala*) is a straggly, hardy annual that either falls along the ground or stands up to 12 inches. In spring sow the seeds directly where you want the plants—they are also fine in pots—and about six weeks later be prepared for a big surprise. These flowers, uninspiring by day, open to pink or purple four petalled stars at dusk. Their sweet vanilla-like odor is so strong that it would seem only a much larger flower could scent the night so much.

Mentzelia Linleyi was to occupy this spot in the lineup. All references say that it opens at night. For three years I searched for viable seed and finally this summer managed to grow three plants that were promptly moved, after frost danger was past, to the night garden. Buds swelled . . . I waited. Then one morning in early July, they bloomed. Note, one morning. Day after day I waited for just one flower to open at dusk, or even in the late afternoon. No luck. The books are wrong. Well, not all the books. William Robinson, in his classic *The English Flower Garden and Home Grounds*, just calls it "A showy golden-flowered hardy annual."

Four-o'clocks or the marvel-of-Peru (*Mirabilis Jalapa*) are one of my all-time favorite flowers. First, they fit perfectly within the concept of the night garden opening as they do with fresh, sweetly scented flowers in the late afternoon, always later than 4:00 unless plants are situated in some shade. Next, the bright tubular blossoms, up to 2 inches long and 1 inch wide, flower freely in shades of yellow, pink, red, vivid crimson, or even striped orange on yellow, persisting until cut down by frost. Finally, though they are tender perennials originally from the Peruvian Andes, their long, black tubers can be dug up in fall and stored for the following spring. In fact, this is the best way to get the finer colors, saving only those plants with appeal. Keep the tubers in a dry place. I place them in an open box in the greenhouse comfortably pillowed with shredded peat moss. In the spring when tubers start into growth and the ground is past freezing, they go back to the garden. You will get very big plants this way.

Four o'clocks need a good soil, deeply prepared (at least 8 inches), and mixed with sand and garden compost. Plants also benefit from an occasional watering with a liquid manure during the summer months and they do like plenty of water. *Mirabilis* will do well on the terrace when grown in 12-inch (or bigger) pots. Plants will also flower the first year from seed. Start them six weeks before the last spring frost in your area.

Flowering tobacco plants come in both day-flowering species, including the very large tobacco plant (*Nicotiana Tabacum*) of the annual garden (see page 24) and the following night-bloomers for the evening garden.

All are treated as annuals with seeds started indoors six weeks before the last spring frost. Plants like a good garden soil liberally laced with compost or manure, and a location either in full sun or partial shade. Set them 1 foot apart. All do well when grown in 12-inch pots on the terrace, as long as they get plenty of water. Space plants 1 foot apart in the garden.

Nicotiana alata originally came from southern Brazil, and its flowers once opened about 6:00 P.M. But hybridizers have been busy and the flowers now stay open most of the day. Yet it is at night that the sweet fragrance makes its mark. Two cultivars are especially recommended: **'Grandiflora Alata'** growing 3 feet high, with large white flowers often 2 inches across; and **'Lime Green'** reaching 30 inches in height, with flowers the shade of lime sherbert.

N. suaveolens comes from Australia and grows some 2 1/2 feet tall. Leaves are somewhat sticky. The 2-inch-long and 1-inch-wide flowers are cream-colored tinged with green on the outside and white within. These plants like partial shade, are especially fragrant at night, and are beloved by moths.

Night-blooming tropical water lilies(*Nymphaea* spp.) are a bit too large to grow in a whiskey barrel (see page 148), but there are a few species that will do well in a small plastic pool set into the ground. And what could be a more elegant pastime than sitting about the terrace at twilight waiting for the lilies to open?

These flowers do best when planted in a polyethylene utility tub that holds 16 quarts (1/2 bushel) of good garden soil, preferably soil with some clay. Never use commercial potting mixes for these plants, or anything remotely connected with herbicides or insecticides. Mix the soil 3 parts to 1 with well-rotted cow manure.

The lilies are set out only when water temperatures will stay above 70°F. A layer of gravel is spread on top of the soil so the water will not be muddied when the tub is eased carefully into the pool. Unless you have a frost-free place to store the tubers over winter, treat the lilies as annuals. Water depth should be 18 inches. Here are three favorite cultivars:

Nymphaea **'Juno'** has large white flowers, needs at least five hours of direct sun daily, and has a spread of 8 to 10 square feet.

N. **'Texas Shell Pink'** is a glowing light pink, needs five hours of sun, and has a spread of 10 square feet.

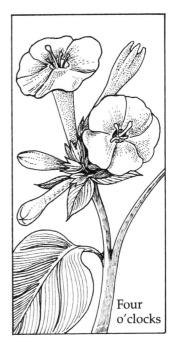

Four o'clocks

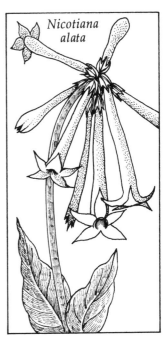

Nicotiana alata

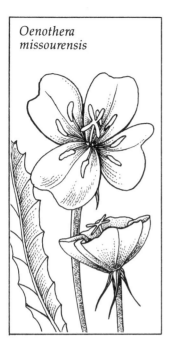

Oenothera missourensis

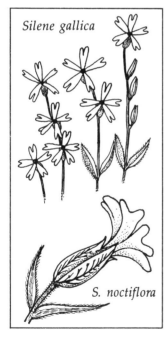

Silene gallica

S. noctiflora

N. **'Emily G. Hutchings'** has petals of rose-red, needs five hours of sun, and has a spread of 8 square feet.

There are two types of *Oenotheras*: the day-blooming species called sundrops, and the night bloomers or evening primroses. These plants have been in cultivation for centuries. Their usually yellow or white flowers are large and beautiful, they are never fussy about soil, and all including the perennial types flower the first year from seed. Except for the somewhat tender *O. rosea*, even in our cold climate the only problem that I've ever had with these plants is their dislike of wet soils in the winter. I plant them in ground that is well-drained. Start seeds inside six weeks before the last spring frost.

O. biennis is the wild evening primrose of North America. It is a biennial that will often reach 6 feet the first year and bloom with large, 2-inch-wide lemon yellow flowers on reddish stems. This is a big plant so leave a circle with a 3-foot diameter for its spread.

O. erythrosepala, long called Lamarckiana, is a biennial with sweetly scented, yellow, 3-inch flowers. Height is about 3 to 4 feet. Plant 2 feet apart.

O. caespitosa bears 3-inch-wide flowers that start out white but slowly turn to pink. Plants are almost prostrate and crawl along the ground. Flowers have a faint perfume. Space plants 1 foot apart. This species is reliably hardy only to Zone 6.

O. missourensis, the Missouri primrose, is usually a prostrate plant, but sometimes will grow upright to 1 foot high. A perennial, it will make a large clump over time. In Zone 5 and north plants benefit from a winter mulch if snow is lacking. Flowers are yellow and 4 or more inches across.

O. rosea is unusual in that the 2/3-inch-wide flowers are rose colored instead of yellow. Plants grow about 14 inches high and should be spaced 9 inches apart. This species is not hardy north of Zone 7 but grows readily from seed.

The catchflies (*Silene* spp.) have three family members that open at night. Two are weedy and should go on the outer fringes of the garden, and the third is little-known and charming. They are all treated as annuals and have no special demands as to soil. Plants prefer full sun.

Silene alba is the white campion, growing to 3 feet high with small, white flowers of five forked petals. The flowers arise from oval, inflated pods. They have a light perfume and are favored by moths. Plants have few leaves at the bottom of the stem so plant them a scant 6 inches apart.

S. noctiflora is called the night-flowering catchfly and is often confused with *alba*. This flower, however, arises from a pod or tiny balloon that is prettily marked with a tracing of green branches joined with fine green lines.

S. gallica is a pretty plant and not weedy at all. Flowers are small, 3/8 inch long, white, and starlike. They form a one-sided row running down an 18-inch stem, and open slowly at dusk, just like twinkling stars on the horizon. Space plants 6 inches apart and plant them five or six to a group.

The yuccas are stately plants and are especially strange when seen in a snowy, northern landscape. The plant usually found in Zone 5 is *Yucca filamentosa*, often called Adam's needle. Its touch leaves are up to 2 1/2 feet long, with very sharp points and threads along the edge. Allow a 2-foot circle of ground for each plant. Since they are not easy to transplant—a tap root will extend many feet into the soil—either raise them from seed (a slow process) or buy plants in containers from a nursery. Yuccas like full sun and tolerate most any kind of soil including pure sand.

Flowers are greenish white and bell-like, nodding on short stems from a central stalk that can grow up to 10 feet in height. Although blossoms often open during the day, as dusk approaches they turn up to the night air and release a sweet perfume to attract the moths they need for pollination.

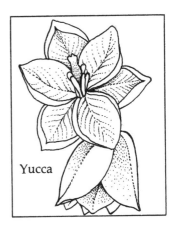

Yucca

Epiphyllum oxypetalum

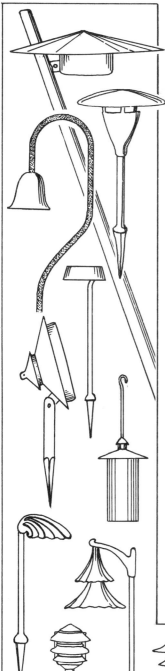

Lighting the Night Garden

The night garden is a fascinating place to be, especially when a full moon is riding high. But having to stumble around in the dark on evenings when the moon is down is hardly practical for either the walker or the plants. Flashlights are not exactly the solution, either. Luckily for gardeners, outdoor lighting has appeared on the scene. Summer or winter, the garden can become a dramatic place at night.

Low-voltage lighting is the result of using a special transformer to reduce the regular household current of 120 volts down to a safe 12 volts. And it's truly safe. Even if you grasp a bare wire or cut through a cable with a chain saw, you will not get a shock! You need not worry about children or pets and the cables can be buried in the garden by hand using a common trowel. Before low-voltage lighting was introduced to the market, it was an expensive proposition to lay electric wires within metal pipes, completely waterproofed, and carefully buried for safety.

Costs are reasonable, too. We've had a system of outdoor lights in the garden for two years, and I doubt if the average three hours of light a night we use there has raised our electric bill more than a few dollars a month.

Basically you need an outdoor 120-volt convenience outlet on the side of your house near the terrace. Once this is installed—preferably by a local electrician who knows the housing codes in your area—the rest of the job can be done by you.

Basic lighting kits usually contain a transformer, with more expensive models featuring a timer, plus 50 or 100 feet of insulated cable and four or six lights. Low voltage lamps are either bulbs that fit within a fixture, or floodlights. To install them you merely walk through the garden laying the cable behind you (total cable length for each transformer should not exceed 100 feet), attach the light fixtures where you want them, and bury the cable. This is one of the few home embellishments that is as easy to do as the instructions say. You'll be done in time to sit back and enjoy the night.

Lamp and Fixture Styles

A number of different styles are available. The first type are usually divided into lamps affixed to short posts or mounted on the ground and meant to light a pathway. The second group are fixtures to shine a beam of light on a favorite plant or garden object, including up- or down-lighting a tree. A few different lamps are illustrated in the drawing below.

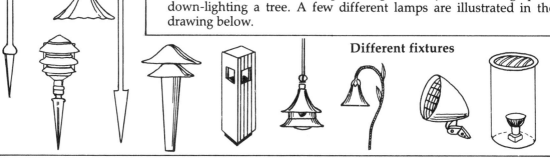

Different fixtures

Lighting Styles

Down-lighting refers to flood lamps set high in a tree and aimed towards the ground below. They produce a magical effect. If placed high enough in a tree and somewhat shielded by the leaves, they mimic the light of a moon where no moon shone before: in summer the lights dance through the waving leaves; in winter, they silhouette the starkness of the trunk and branches.

Up-lighting means lighting the scene from the ground and is very dramatic. Leaves and branches spring into view and the backyard becomes a stage.

Diffused lighting is achieved by locating the fixtures behind a screen, or behind a grouping of plants, and is especially pleasant when installed in an outdoor dining area.

Spotlighting should be used with care. After all the aim of lighting the garden is to see the shadows. But sometimes there is an object or sculpture that enters a new visual dimension when a light shines directly upon its structure.

Shadowing is achieved by silhouetting an object's shadow on a wall or the side of a house or garage.

The Sky's the Limit

Entering the world of outdoor lighting is a bit like buying stereo equipment or becoming involved with cameras. Once you start there is no way out. You will find the simplest of systems consisting of just wire, transformer, and plainly styled fixtures, to the most complex and sophisticated equipment on the market, which has remote control timers that allow you to play a symphony with the lights.

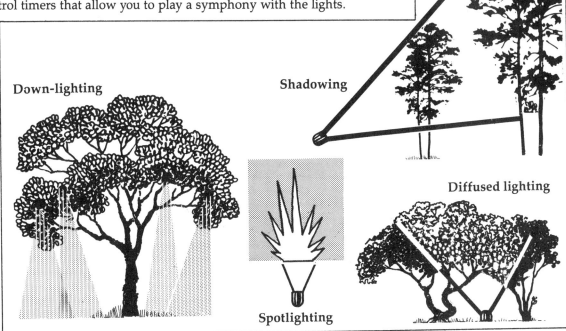

Up-lighting

Down-lighting

Shadowing

Diffused lighting

Spotlighting

CREATURES OF THE NIGHT

When twilight falls in our garden and the edge of the woods is already deeply dark, we sometimes go out to watch the bats—yes, the bats. With an effort born of instinct they swoop and glide, fluttering bits of brown against a darkening sky. And with every dive another insect enemy is gone; the garden can breathe free another day.

Everyone knows the visitors to the daytime garden: Birds, bees, and bugs, they are all familiar to gardeners. But just as there's a nightlife in every city, there's a nightlife in the garden, too.

Instead of the hummingbird, at night it's the hawk or sphinx moth that hovers on invisible but noisy wings and dips its tongue into the open flowers, gathering nectar, and mixing pollen. As caterpillars some of the members of this insect family are pests of tomatoes, tobacco, and other garden plants. But when they mature, they hum through the night, valuable pollinators and garden companions in the dark.

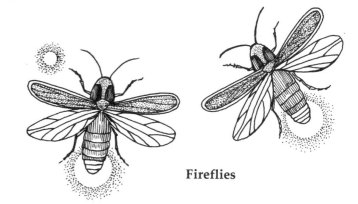

Fireflies

We always know when high summer has arrived in our night garden for the fireflies start to flash their mating lights. From mid-June to mid-August every bush and cranny twinkles with the firefly morse code. Each beetle has its own light organ containing 7,000 cells, packed with minuscule granules of chemicals and a catalyst called *luciferin.* When the granules and luciferin meet oxygen, cold light is emitted and the courtship lamp is lit. Only 10 percent of that energy reaction is heat, 90 percent is cold light. By comparison, electric lights are 5 percent light and 95 percent heat.

Later on in mid-September the lights are seen again, only this time among the drops of dew on the grass. For the larvae of the firefly have their own set of lamps. The youngsters live on the ground, taking two years to mature, and while not hibernating, they hunt for snails and slugs, a noteworthy occupation.

Bats glide through the night and replace flycatchers and robins, for most birds are fast asleep at night. Toads prowl the garden walkways and crickets chirp (count the number of chirps in 15 seconds and add 40, and you have the approximate temperature in degrees Fahrenheit). In the distance there is the hoot of an owl.

The Bat House

Elizabeth Erdman is an American conservationist and a champion of the bat. She is out to tell the world what many people already know but many more do not, that the bat is a valuable predator, harmless to people, having a relatively low incidence of rabies, and suffering from the mindless fantasies of publicity agents and overactive imaginations.

Miss Erdman and Bat Conservation International (Milwaukee Public Museum, Milwaukee, Wisconsin 53233) warns everyone that the bat is in danger and her facts are backed up by the United States Department of the Interior. According to their publications, bats are being killed by people, insecticides, and habitat destruction at an alarming rate.

"People are needlessly afraid of bats," she writes. "This is primarily due to use of bat-type wings [in horror cartoons] and other art depicting such things as demons and dragons. Then, of course, there is the legend of Dracula and the rumors of bats attacking people.

"They are gentle, warm-blooded mammals that keep to themselves and [are] an integral part of our ecological system and vital to natural insect control."

My wife and I both believe her. So we installed a bat box 15 feet above the ground in the white pine tree that stands between the garden's edge and the woods. The box is made in Germany of precast concrete with a metal handle and hook. It is unobtrusive and it was occupied by the first family of bats by mid-May.

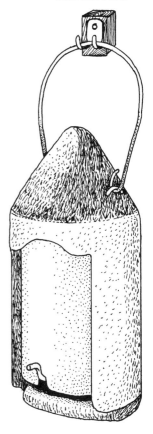

Brown bats

THE MOONFLOWER

Moonflower seedpod

Moonflowers are perennials in the tropics or a warm greenhouse but are treated as annuals up north. Their current botanical name is *Ipomoea alba* but they have been known as *I. grandiflora, I. noctiflora, I. Bona-Nox,* and *Calonyction aculeatum* (in Greek *kalos* meant beautiful and *nyktos,* night). The plant is a vine that will grow up to 10 feet in a good summer season but up to 40 feet at the jungle's edge. The flowers are white, very showy, and look like large morning glories that have mistaken the hour.

They are highlights of the night garden for they bloom in the early evening, unfolding their long twisted buds like flowers opening in a nature film featuring slow-motion photography. Within a few minutes sweet-scented, salver-shaped blossoms up to 6 inches across hover before your eyes and will persist until touched by the first rays of the morning sun, whereupon they quickly close.

In subtropic climates the moonflower will often flower within six weeks of sowing but in most of the United States expect eight weeks to pass. To help in germination the seeds should be nicked or soaked in warm water overnight. They need at least eight hours of sun for reliable bloom.

These flowers are so attractive and unusual that they easily can become the center of a party or gathering as guests gather in the evening hours to watch the buds unfold.

If insects and moths of the night neglect to pollinate the flowers, use a cotton swab to dust the flower's stigma with a bit of pollen. The developing seed pods are unique and interesting to watch.

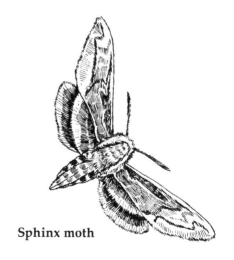

Sphinx moth

Abeliophyllum distichum

THE MOONLIGHT GARDEN

In 1904 Alice Morse Earle published a book called *Old Time Gardens.* Among the gardens she describes is one to be enjoyed not only during the day but especially by moonlight. It was designed in 1833 and maintained at the home of the Hon. Ben. Perley Poore of Newburyport, Massachusetts. There Poore's parents filled twin flower borders with all-white flowering plants, borders that were 700 feet long and 28 feet wide with a path 4 feet wide through the center.

"It do swallow no end of plants," the gardener is quoted as saying.

"I want you to see and feel this moonlight garden," wrote Miss Earle, "as did Emily Dickinson her garden by moonlight:

And still within the summer's night
A something so transporting bright
I clap my hands to see."

But why all white flowers for a moon garden?

J. E. Purkinje (1787–1869) was born in what is now Czechoslovakia and was a versatile genius who made discoveries in many fields, notably ophthalmology and embryology. In fact, he coined the word *protoplasm.* He also described the *Purkinje effect.*

If you look at bright red geraniums in a flower border against a background of dark green leaves, in daylight the reds dominate. In twilight and later in the evening the contrast is reversed and the flowers almost disappear, appearing darker than the leaves. This is the *Purkinje effect.*

It's because in normal light our eyes see with the cells in the retina called *cones,* and use the other cells called *rods* for weak illumination. The former are sensitive to yellow, the latter to blue-green.

Now moonlight is so weak that only the rods in the eye are at work and colors in a landscape are no longer visible: We are, for all practical purposes, colorblind, and see only a blue-green landscape.

But our eyes are still capable of discerning brightness and can easily see white light. So white by contrast seems to glow under moonlight, and white flowers are readily observed. An all-white garden can even be seen by starlight.

I've pared down the Poore's borders to a reasonable rectangle 15 feet long and 6 feet wide. If you feel happier with a free-form shape, no matter, since the flowers are so beautiful they will adapt to most any pattern you choose.

Spring nights are often damp and chilly here in the northeast—and short until Daylight Saving Time begins—so the peak of flowering will be in late July and on into August. In fact, the bed will be at its brightest under an August moon.

The largest feature of the bed is a white forsythia (*Abeliophyllum distichum*). If you start with a good-sized plant, it should reach 6 by 4 feet in about three years, and can be easily pruned if it becomes too large. Blooming occurs in the first few weeks of spring when four-petaled flowers cover the bush and sweetly smell of honey, under an

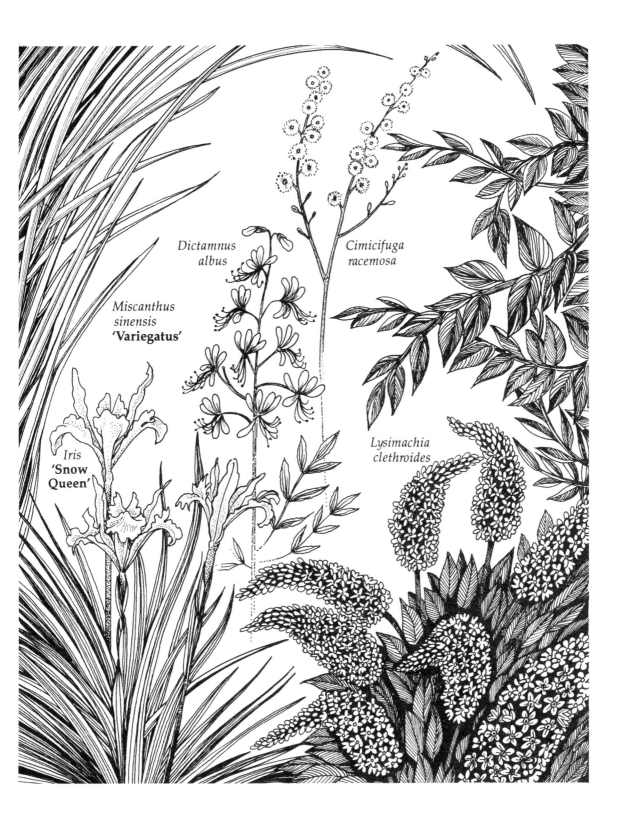

*Dictamnus
albus*

*Cimicifuga
racemosa*

*Miscanthus
sinensis*
'Variegatus'

Iris
**'Snow
Queen'**

*Lysimachia
clethroides*

Campanula
**'Grandiflora
Alba'**

April moon. Later in the season the leaves will act as a background for many of the other flowers.

Another feature that will last throughout the entire season is the variegated maiden grass (*Miscanthus sinensis* **'Variegatus'**) with its white-edged leaves.

As spring progresses white columbine (*Aquilegia canadensis* **'Silver Queen'**), is followed by white Siberian iris (*Iris sibirica* **'Snow Queen'**), especially fine as its grassy foliage looks good all summer long, and yucca (*Yucca filamentosa*) with its soft-white bells on 6-foot spikes.

Then the white gas plant (*Dictamnus albus*) spends the month of June covered with its attractive spikes of unusual flowers. It's called the gas plant because rumor has it that a match held close to the leaves on a still summer night will cause a puff of gas, emitted by the leaves, to burn and quickly glow. It's never worked for me. Planning is needed with this particular plant, for it dislikes being moved and once in place should be left alone.

By July the white campanula sends forth its bell-shaped flowers (*Campanula persicifolia* **'Grandiflora Alba'**) and will continue blooming into August.

The black snakeroot (*Cimicifuga racemosa*) also starts blooming in July. The white flower wands are over 6 feet high. The rhizomes were once used medicinally to treat St. Vitus's Dance of children and are still employed by the drug industry for an astringent and diuretic.

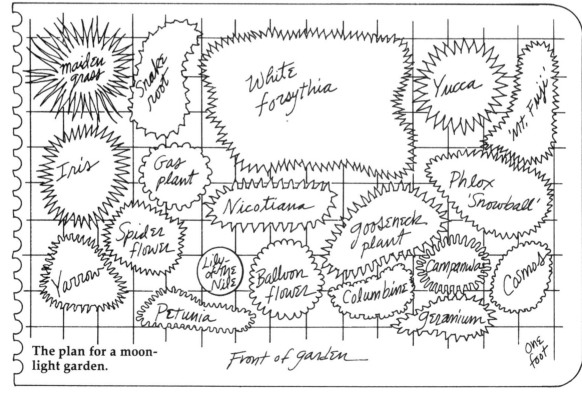

The plan for a moonlight garden.

And then by late July and on into August the gooseneck plant (*Lysimachia clethroides*), the white balloon flower (*Platycodon grandiflorus* **'Album'**), the phlox (*Phlox decussata*) either **'Mt. Fuji'** at 40 inches or **'Snowball'** at 30 inches—and wait until you see the moths that visit these flowers every night—and the yarrow (*Achillea ptarmica* **'The Pearl'**) are all at their best and will continue so into September.

Also for late July into August a pot containing one blooming lily-of-the-Nile (*Agapanthus africanus* **'Albus'**) should be moved about for the best effect. This plant is only hardy above Zone 8 and should spend winters in a greenhouse or a cool north window.

Among the annuals used for the moonlight garden are white geraniums (*Pelaragonium × hortorum*), white petunias (*Petunia × hybrida*), white nicotiana (*Nicotiana alata* **'Grandiflora'**), white cosmos (*Cosmos bipinnatus* **'Purity'**), white spider flower (*Cleome Hasslerana* **'Alba'** or **'Snow Queen'**), and for a final round of color under a Harvest Moon, some white bedding mums (*Chrysanthemum × morifolium*).

I've left out white Madonna or Easter lilies only because I personally find their evening fragrance just a bit too overpowering for my tastes but they, too, make a fine addition to the moonlight garden.

If you have more room try adding a white poppy (*Papaver orientale* **'Barr's White'**), some 30 inches in height. When it goes dormant at the end of July interplant with more cosmos or cleome.

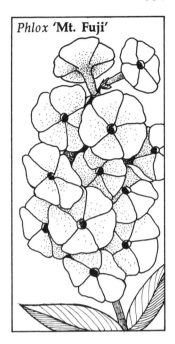

Phlox **'Mt. Fuji'**

Papaver **'Barr's White'**

A GARDEN OF
SEEDS AND PODS

*And one class of plants, the Gourd tribe, can be
used in many beautiful ways, for covering any unsightly
bank or mound, or to make a temporary screen, or to
train over the roofs of low sheds. These plants may be
either the Vegetable Marrows, or any of the many
ornamented Gourds, great or small.*

Gertrude Jekyll, *Home and Garden*

*Collecting pods is a year-round pastime. It almost
becomes a game to be on the lookout for new pods . . .*

Jane Embertson, *Pods*

A garden is usually a happy place to be. But flowers are usually not
thought of as being fun. Their beauty is often so ethereal or so bold
as to overwhelm the senses and at best they are rewarded with epi-
thets containing the words cute, delightful, or charming. But many
pods, seeds, and especially gourds are *fun!*

Every afternoon from mid-July until frost, I've walked out to a
part of the garden that is trellised, tepee-ed, and criss-crossed with
horizontal poles and strings, to see what's new with the annual
gourd patch. And I've yet to be disappointed. Out of 15 some varieties, there is almost always a new gourd growing and rounding out,
lengthening or slimming down, all caricatures of people or animals
and all fun to see.

And pods are the same. They've lost the look and feel of flowers.
Their stems are now dried and often contorted—in a painless way—
and the fanciful shells that hold next year's seeds become pixies,
elves, and yes, clowns.

Who would not smile at a penguin gourd (*Lagenaria siceraria*),
needing only paddle feet and an arctic ice floe to complete the scene,
or silently chuckle at the nodding pods of the bladder campion (*Silene vulgaris*) as they whisper to each other in the winter wind?

In addition to their talent to amuse, the gourds will cover a
multitude of sins with their rambling vines and large, attractive leaves.

**The flower on the top of
the opposite page is the
bloom of the snake gourd.
The vine on the bottom is
a striped pear gourd.**

103

As Gertrude Jekyll advises, they are "great for covering any unsightly bank or mound."

Finally there are the everlasting flowers or *immortelles*. These blossoms with petals that shine like satin and feel like straw will dry with the qualities of rag paper and last for years without ever becoming brittle or growing old. Their colors are white, off-white, reds, oranges, blues, and myriad shades between. And flowers picked in the August sun will shine in a northern window as the snows of February blow about.

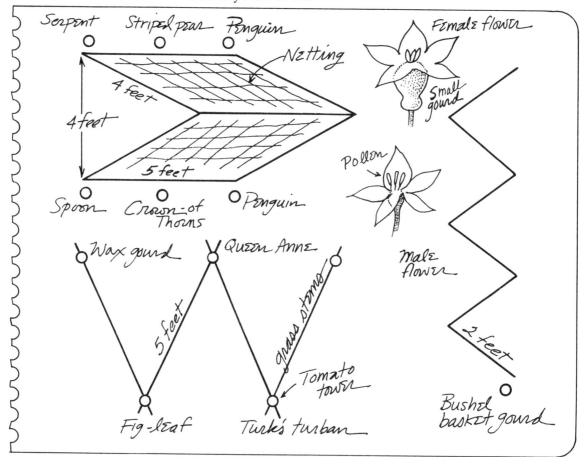

A GLUT OF GOURDS

I've just come back from the garden on a warm, muggy morning in late August. Before writing this particular piece, I thought I would measure the plots of land that were set aside for the gourds. It's a good thing I picked today because tomorrow would certainly be too late: The vines are everywhere. And they are making for the tomato and the bean patches with deliberate speed. I felt that if I stood in one place too long, my ankle would be bound with vine; by noon I would be in flower!

There are three patches of ground in this part of the garden, each 10 feet long and 5 feet wide. The first patch contains a tent made of five aluminum poles with nylon netting in place of canvas, each side measuring 4 by 5 feet. The second plot contains an expandable trellis with eight sections, each 2 by 2 feet. The third holds five 5-foot-high tomato towers each joined with 5-foot-long poles made from the stems of my eulalia grasses. The poles are poked through the towers and would seem to form a large "W" if you were to look down upon the structure from above. Each side of the "W" is a bit less than 5 by 5 feet.

It's probably a good thing that I limited my gourd selection to 11 varieties from 5 genera.

The Gourd Groups

There are three main groups of the gourds:

1. The hard-shell and durable gourds with large, day-blooming yellow or cream-yellow, squash-like flowers. In this group are *Cucurbita Pepo* var. *ovifera* or most of the common ornamentals, and *C. maxima* **'Turbaniformis'**, the Turk's turban.
2. The soft-shell or disposable gourds with day-blooming yellow flowers. This includes *Cucurbita ficifolia* and *C. Melo*, Dudaim Group.
3. The night-blooming, white flowered gourds of which some are durable and some will perish. These are the *Lagenaria* species or bottle gourds.

I also grew two more vines that fall outside the previous categories: *Benincasa hispida*, the wax gourd and *Trichosanthes Anguina*, the snake gourd.

Starting from Seed

Even in an area with a short growing season you can start the gourds from Groups 1 and 2 directly outdoors after the last spring frost. They need a location with full sun and close to a water spigot, because the vines use lots of water both during their early development and when they are setting fruit. Soil should be reasonably rich, mixed with humus, and have good drainage. Plant five seeds in a little hill of soil, each hill at least 5 feet apart. This is important because all seeds will not be of the same quality. If you have any well-rotted manure, put a shovelfull underneath each hill before planting.

When the plants are 3 or 4 inches tall, pick out all but the strongest three. Soon they will be reaching up for support and on their way.

The gourds from Group 3 need a much longer growing season and might take up to six months to develop mature fruit. And add to these both *Trichosanthes* and *Benincasa*. In colder areas start them indoors six to eight weeks before the last frost, in individual 3-inch pots. Soak seed for 24 hours and keep soil temperatures at 70°F. In the fall make sure they get covered on nights when temperatures fall into the low 50s.

Queen Anne's
pocket melon

Harvesting the Gourds

Group 1 gourds should be picked as they become hard to the touch. They should not be subjected to a heavy frost so it's a good idea to cut them all after the first frost in autumn. Leave 1-inch of stem on each gourd and handle them carefully to prevent bruising. Dry them in a spot with low humidity and keep them apart, placing them on racks or old window screens to allow adequate air circulation. The gourds are completely dry when seeds rattle inside. You may wash them with a liquid wax but don't use varnish.

Group 3 gourds will mature on the vine when grown in the southern states, changing in shade from yellow to brown. In the North they are usually picked when still green but should remain on the vine as long as it's alive. When harvesting leave 2 inches of stem on the fruit. To cure these gourds place them on racks in a dry place with good air circulation. They can also be left on layers of newspaper but must be turned periodically. Seeds will rattle inside when the gourds are finally dry.

According to the American Gourd Society (see Appendix 201), gourds will "often mold but seldom rot." They suggest wiping off any excess mold that grows, and point out that the growth of mold leads to interesting designs on the surface of the gourd. If gourds shrivel, it usually means rotting and they should be thrown out.

Although the *Lagenaria* species will not cross-pollinate with the other ornamental gourds, they will do so with each other. If you are growing more than one species, keep the plants a good 25 feet apart.

If the heavier gourds rest upon the ground, place a piece of plastic wrap between the gourd's skin and the ground to prevent discoloring and perhaps decay.

You need not make decorative lamps or smiling clowns out of your gourds. They are really attractive just hanging on the vines in the garden or placed in a large wooden bowl for the Thanksgiving holidays.

The Gourds Themselves

The wax gourd (*Benincasa hispida*) is a native of tropical Asia and named after Count Benincasa, an Italian botanist who died in 1596. The vines are strong with 6-inch rounded leaves and reach 10 to 12 feet in length. The 3-inch flowers are yellow. The fruits are cylindrical in shape, 8 to 10 inches long and about 2 inches wide. Fruits are whitish with a wax cover, hence the common name. Both the R.H.S. *Dictionary of Gardening* and the Thompson & Morgan catalog mention that the fruit is used to prepare either preserves or curries but I can find no recipes at this date.

Queen Anne's pocket melon (*Cucumis Melo,* Dudaim Group) is a smaller vine not growing more than 6 feet and it bears smaller fruit. The flowers are yellow and 3/4 inch wide. The rounded leaves are 3 inches wide. The oval fruits are green at first but turn to yellow stripes on brown when ripe. The best reason to grow this vine is the sweet perfume of the ripened fruit. It is said that good Queen Anne

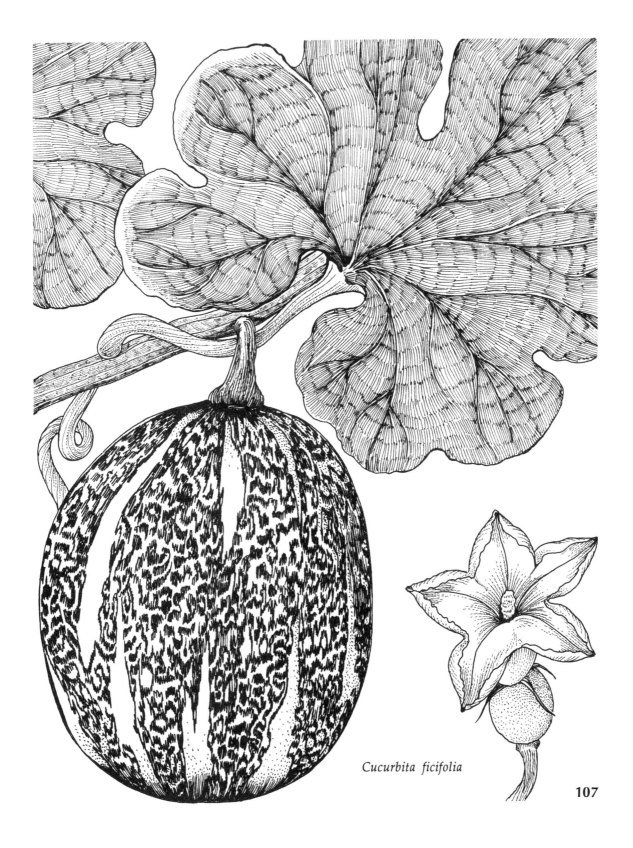

Cucurbita ficifolia

107

would carry this melon in her reticule as she walked the palace halls, inhaling its fragrance now and then to be revived from the odors that permeated the castle.

The fig-leaf of Malabar gourd (*Cucurbita ficifolia*) is a giant among vines. Here is an ornamental to use if you wish to screen an entire barn. The large leaves (*ficifolia* means fig-leafed) look like their namesakes, being a healthy 9 inches wide. L. H. Bailey in his book, *A Garden of Gourds,* called the fig-leaf gourd the most vigorous species he ever grew. He measured the length of the main stem and branches of one plant that totaled 825 feet, and this in Ithaca, New York. The fruits are almost round, about 6 inches in diameter. They are beautifully marked with streaks of white on a dark green background. The fruit is said to be eaten in tropical countries.

The Turk's turban (*Cucurbita maxima* **'Turbaniformis'**) is an ornamental member of the squash family. Vines grow to 8 feet and produce quite interesting gourds with bright orange, white, and green colorations. And it does look like a turban. Grow this one for holiday decorations.

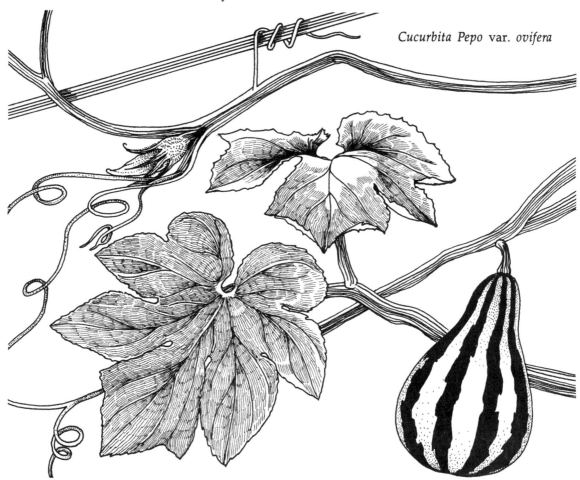

Cucurbita Pepo var. *ovifera*

The crown of thorns or finger gourd, the striped pear, and the spoon gourds (*Cucurbita Pepo* var. *ovifera*) are all members of the same genus yet look different enough to be families apart. And there are more members: the white pear gourd, the goose-egg, the miniature gourd, the broad striped, the ladle or scoop gourd, the warty hardhead, the bell, and the big bell. The flowers of all are yellow, and the vines grow up to 12 feet long.

The finger gourd is small and white—an ovoid of 5-inch height and 4-inch diameter—more strange than anything else. This is not a beauty and the comments that it will elicit (and it will) are usually: "My goodness, what is this?"

The striped pear gourd sports white stripes on a dark speckled green, and is about the same size but decidedly nicer in aspect. This gourd is nice on the vine or in a decorative group on the mantle.

The spoon gourds are yellow, green, two-toned, and cute from every aspect. Usually when decorative gourds are thought of, this is the type that first springs to mind.

Crown of thorns

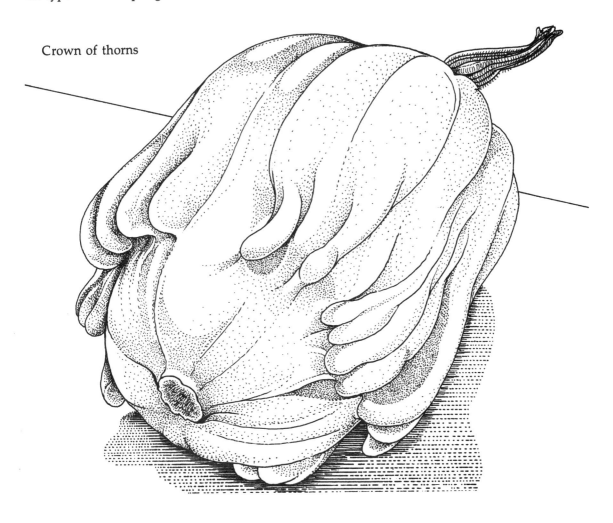

The bottle gourds, bushel basket gourds, and powder horn or penguin gourds (*Lagenaria siceraria*) are all variations within one species. The flowers are large, sometimes up to 5 inches across, with white paper-thin petals. They are sweet-smelling, and bloom at night or on gloomy late afternoons. Vines can reach up to 25 feet in a good growing season. Leaves can measure a foot across. I have in the garden at this time a powder horn of light, pastel green that is hanging down 15 inches from the vine above its head, a bottle gourd 8 inches wide at the bottom and 10 inches high, and a bushel basket gourd that is meant to be the size of its namesake and weigh about 100 pounds. With our climate and luck, the bushel basket will never make it to maturity.

The snake gourd (*Trichosanthes Anguina*) is unusual. The flowers are small, little over an inch wide, with petals that are incredibly fringed. The fruit grows like a snake, long and coiled, and the warmer the climate the longer the serpent. In *Handbook of Tropical Gardening* (published in Ceylon), H. F. Macmillan writes:

> A quick-growing climbing gourd, bearing long cylindrical, green (sometimes greenish-white) fruits, which not unfrequently reach the length of five to six feet. In an unripe state these pod-like fruits are sliced and cooked in the manner of French beans being also rarely used as a curry vegetable in the low-country. Seeds are sown in the monsoons [and] it is customary to suspend a small stone at the end of each fruit whilst growing, so as to weight it down and induce it to grow straighter, and perhaps longer, than it would otherwise do.

Frankly I've become fascinated with gourds and pods after doing this book. Next spring I have the feeling that the garden is going to expand again. And one summer not too far from now, the searching vines might even make it to the next farm.

Benincasa hispida

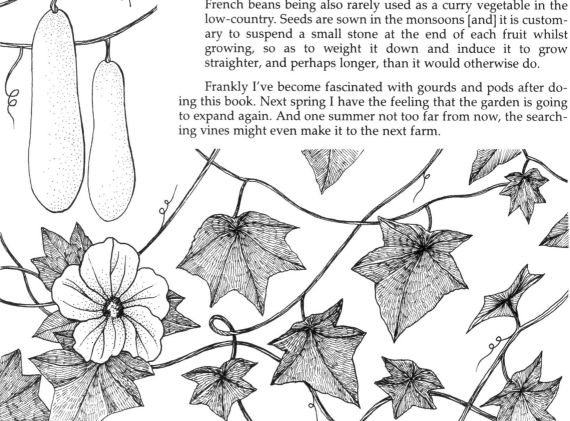

Lagenaria siceraria

LOVE-IN-A-PUFF

I've mentioned that I find gourds to be fun. Now, love-in-a-puff is too demure to be fun but it certainly is charming. The botanical name is *Cardiospermum Halicacabum* (*kardia*, heart, *sperma*, seed) and refers to each of the three ripened black seeds that reside within an inflated green pod and have a heart-shaped white spot near their point of attachment.

This plant is a quick-growing vine, perennial in India and Africa but treated as an annual in most of the United States. It has naturalized in parts of the country below New Jersey. The common names are love-in-a-puff, heart-seed, and heart-pea (referring to the mark on the seed) and balloon vine because of the six segmented puffs that begin to cover the vine shortly after flowering begins. In medieval times the Doctrine of Signatures ascribed powers of healing a damaged heart to this plant because of the mark on the seed. The seed is still used medicinally and the leaves are often taken as a salad green in India.

The flowers are very small, 1/4 inch across, with four tiny white petals and four even smaller sepals. But under a lens they look like exquisite orchids. By late summer there are so many flowers, each on a delicate stem, hovering over the slender-pointed, deeply toothed leaves, that the vine looks as though it's wrapped in lace.

And the balloons, each 1 1/2 inches across when mature, float like dozens of different sized light green bubbles just below the mass of blossoms. The puffs are so strong that you have to squeeze with your fingers before they break.

The vines will grow up to 10 feet in one summer season and should be provided with a support, either a trellis or strings. They need full sun and average soil. A number of plants (spaced 12 inches apart) along a wall or open porch make a fine summer screen.

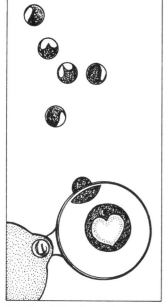

Seeds of the love-in-a-puff.

Love-lies-bleeding

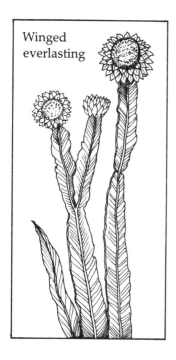

Winged
everlasting

A GARDEN OF EVERLASTINGS

The garden plot for the everlasting flowers is roughly 15 feet long and 12 feet wide. It's located in front of the vegetable garden, in rather heavy soil that is rototilled every spring after the addition of a small amount of compost from our own pile. The plot faces southwest and gets sun all through the day.

The plants chosen are mostly annuals, plus one hardy biennial, and two hardy perennials, all of which will bloom the first year if seeds are started early indoors. In fact the majority of these plants will benefit from an early start indoors thus guaranteeing enough flowers in areas with short growing seasons.

While most of the flowers in the garden of everlastings are fine for cut flowers in water, they are best when used in dried arrangements. And they are especially beautiful in the garden right where they grow.

For information on drying these flowers for winter bouquets follow the instructions in *Gathering the Grasses* on page 80.

The Plants for an Everlasting Garden

Love-lies-bleeding (*Amaranthus caudatus*) had to have been named by a Victorian poet in the throes of an unhappy love affair, for its long chains of tiny blood red blossoms do bend and then flow along the ground. Each can reach 2 feet in length. Plants in bloom are fascinating in the garden, keep their looks as cut flowers, and when picked and carefully dried become theatrical statements in winter arrangements. If you are looking for an effective pot plant try this in a 6-inch pot with average houseplant soil. The cultivar **'Viridis'** bears chartreuse flowers. Plants themselves grow between 3 and 5 feet in height, should be spaced 24 inches apart, and are half-hardy annuals. Wait for warm nights before planting them outside.

Winged everlasting (*Ammobium alatum*) is a perennial in its native Australia but is grown as an annual in most of the northern hemisphere. *Ammobium* means "living in sand" and comes from the plant's native habitat. The popular name refers to the form of the stem, which looks like a 3-foot-long paper-covered wire "twistem" from a plastic trash bag. The flowers are up to 2 inches wide, white, with yellow centers. Plant 8 inches apart. These should be treated like half-hardy annuals and not planted out until nights are warm—above 50°F.

The walking stick cabbage (*Brassica oleracea* var. *ramosa* or *longata*) is indeed a conversation piece. It's a perennial form of the common vegetable that grows up to 7 feet tall in the Channel Islands, the English islands off the French coast. There the stems are dried, given hand grips, and sold as walking sticks. The plants look like ungraceful palm trees and need to be propped up, for they become top-heavy and can easily blow over in a summer storm. But at the back of the border the walking stick cabbage exhibits a tropical look that is fine as a foil for other plants. If your climate is mild enough, the plants continue to grow and could reach 20 feet. They are hardy annuals.

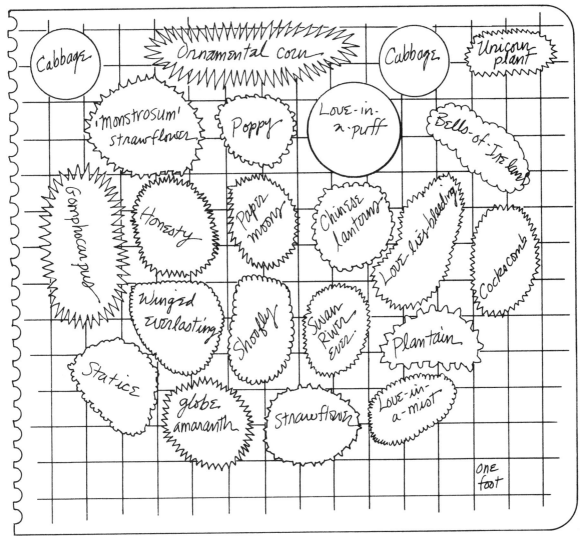

The labels within the garden plan read:

Cabbage — Ornamental corn — Cabbage — Unicorn plant

'Monstrosum' strawflower — Poppy — Love-in-a-puff — Bells-of-Ireland

Gomphocarpus — Honesty — Paper moons — Chinese lanterns — Love-lies-bleeding — Cockscomb

Winged everlasting — Shoofly — Swan River Ever. — Plantain

Statice — Globe amaranth — Strawflower — Love-in-a-mist

one foot

Love-in-a-puff grows nicely on a wire circle of rabbit fencing, 4 feet high and 2 feet in diameter. It's treated as a half-hardy annual and is so interesting that it has a separate essay on page 112.

Cockscomb (*Celosia cristata*) or the woolflower, has flowers too small for individual interest. But when hundreds bloom in a featherlike cluster, or others twist like coral branches (or cock's combs), they become fantastic in the garden. The colors are truly blatant—brilliant oranges, red, purples, and yellow—and too many cockscombs can detract from every other flower in the garden. Cockscombs are useful fresh-cut or when dried. They were great favorites in Victorian parlors, massed like ostrich plumes in heavily decorated vases. Look for the cultivar **'Apricot Brandy'** with rich color and a short stature, some 8 inches in height. Place plants 9 inches apart in the garden. They need full sun and are half-hardy annuals.

The plan for a garden of everlastings.

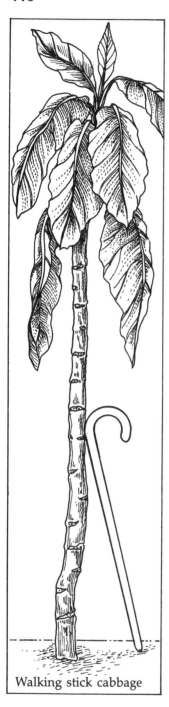

Walking stick cabbage

The globe amaranth (*Gomphrena globosa*) is a tropical everlasting flower with clover-like blossoms in shimmering iridescent colors. The flowers will keep their color for a long time and are fine for both border and vase. Globe amaranth also makes an excellent pot plant. Colors include orange, purple, pink, dark blue, and white. The plants like full sun, are about a foot high, and should be spaced 8 inches apart. They are half-hardy annuals.

Strawflowers, everlastings, or immortelles (*Helichrysum bracteatum*) are Australian natives of great beauty. The genus name means "golden sun." Daisy-like flowers have bright yellow-orange centers surrounded by stiff petals of red, orange, white, or yellow up to 2 1/2 inches wide. This summer some of our plants grew over 5 feet high so make sure you put yours at the back of the border. Space plants 8 inches apart. **'Monstrosum'** is the giant cultivar, and there is also a dwarf form available for gardeners with limited space. Treat these as half-hardy annuals. They will withstand frost to 26°F.

Swan River everlastings (*Helipterum Manglesii*) also come from Australia. This time the genus name means "winged sun," and refers again to the bright centers. These centers are the true flowers, the petals being modified leaves. Blossoms bend over on thin stems. Plants should be spaced 8 inches apart and reach 2 feet in height. They do not transplant well so be sure if starting early to use individual peat pots so roots will not be disturbed. They like full sun, do well in dry soil, and are half-hardy annuals. Colors are white, off-white, and pink. Make successive sowings of this plant for blooms all summer.

Limoniums (*Limonium* spp.) are a large family of plants (usually called sea lavenders) from the Mediterranean regions. Florist's statice (*L. Bonduellii* or *L. sinuatum*) comes from North Africa (*Limonium* means "meadow" in Greek and refers to the salt meadows where many of these plants are found) and produces 2-foot stems with clusters of tiny flowers each surrounded with bright, papery wraps. They are fine either fresh or dried. The plants have basal rosettes of scalloped leaves and need to be spaced 8 inches apart. Many cultivars are available. Treat as half-hardy annuals. They will withstand frost to 26°F.

Honesty (*Lunaria annua*) is a hardy biennial that will flower and seed in the first year when started early in the season. The purple- or white-flowering plants are used in formal beds all over England. Other popular names for honesty are money plant, moonwort, or satin flower and all refer to the nearly round, silvery white *replum,* a parchment-like disk about 1 1/2 inches wide that holds the seeds. Honesty has been in cultivation for over 400 years and a vase of the disk-topped branches is still beautiful. Plants grow to 2 1/2 feet. There is a form with variegated leaves. These plants are quite hardy and should self-seed in your garden. Space them about a foot apart in full sun.

Bells-of-Ireland (*Moluccella laevis*) are named in honor of their cone-shaped green blossoms—really modified leaves that wrap around tiny white flowers—and are attractive growing in the border and when dried in arrangements. *Moluccella* is from Molucca, which refers to the Spice Islands where one species is supposed to have originated. Flowering stems reach 2 to 3 feet and plants should be spaced about a foot apart. They do not transplant well so either plant them outdoors when frost danger is past or start indoors in individual peat pots. They need light for germination and can take 10 to 20 days.

I'm not sure that the shoofly plant (*Nicandra Physalodes*) truly possesses all the qualities attributed to it. If it really lived up to its name, every garden would boast 20 or 30 plants because whiteflies are believed to eschew the foliage and stay away from any garden containing the plant. Shooflies grow to a height of 3 feet. The light green ovate leaves have a toothed edge. Flowers are small and bell shaped, violet with a white throat, and open only for a few hours at midday. The developing fruits, each enclosed by sharply defined papery sheaths, are the most interesting aspect of the plant. They are shaped like either the headdress on Ming the Merciless' daughter in *Flash Gordon,* or the shoulder pads on a medieval Japanese knight. Germination takes 15 to 20 days. Plant 18 inches apart. Shooflies are hardy annuals.

Love-in-a-mist (*Nigella damascena*) is also known as the fennel flower and is another plant that has been in cultivation for over 400 years. The name refers to the pastel-colored blooms that hover just above a tangle of light green, fern-like foliage. Plants are especially attractive when massed in the front of the border. **'Persian Jewels'** gives flowers of rose-pink, light blue, or white. Its ripening seedpods inflate like balloons crowned with jester's caps. Love-in-a-mist do not transplant well and should be sown directly in the garden or started in individual peat pots. Plant 8 inches apart and use successive sowings to have flowers all summer long.

Most poppies belong in the more formal garden but the particular species in this everlasting garden is both attractive in flower and effective in pod. It's grown to produce seed for poppy-seed rolls and is called *Papaver Rhoeas* **'Hungarian Blue'**. *Papaver* is an ancient Latin word said to be derived from the sound made when the seeds are chewed. The pods are at first covered with a bloom and are a beautiful blue-green, turning brown as they dry. They become their own seed shakers. Plants grow to 3 feet in height and will do well in a very dry but sunny spot. Flowers, if cut, should have their stem-ends seared over a flame. These poppies are hardy annuals.

Chinese lanterns (*Physalis Alkekengi*) are old-fashioned flowers whose orange, inflated pods are often seen in paintings on old tea trays from the '20s. They are hardy perennials but will bloom from seed the first year if started early. Put plants about 2 feet apart.

Great plantain and hoary plaintain (*Plantago major* and *P. media*) are variations on a common lawn weed. Both are hardy perennials that will produce seed the first year. I grow the cultivar **'Atropurpurea'** for its rosy bronze leaves and tall stems topped with brown seeds. Hoary plaintain is a wildflower in England and produces delicate wands of tiny flowers each with many lilac stamens and a sweet fragrance. As the flowering stems age and dry, they turn into 12-inch wands, the tops heavily studded with little pods. Start seeds early and space 6 to 8 inches apart.

Cockscomb

Globe amaranth

Florist's statice

Swan River everlastings

The unicorn flower (*Proboscidea louisianica*) is a sprawling plant that bears beautiful, orchid-like but strange-smelling flowers of white, yellow, and violet. The smell can be so intense on a hot day that plants should be placed away from the garden proper. Space them at 5 feet apart. The pods, upon ripening, split into two parts, the inspiration for a common name of ram's-horn. They are used to make unusual additions to dried arrangements and many craftsmen make miniature birds and animals out of the pods.

Paper moons (*Scabiosa stellata* **'Drumstick'**) are a new garden flower cultivar. When the plants are in bloom they look like a rather washed-out scabiosa (the pin-cushion flower), in an unattractive shade of blue. But they soon ripen into bronze-colored, round seed heads that look more like coral fossils than plants. Stems reach 40 inches in length. Space the plants 8 inches apart. They are hardy annuals.

Gomphocarpus (*Asclepias fruticosa*) is a member of the milkweed family. Its flowers are small, white, and intricate in design. But this plant is grown for the pods, which form yellow to greenish brown balls, each covered with soft, green spikes. They are large, spreading plants best started at least six weeks before the last spring frost in order to guarantee flowering. Space 12 inches apart. Although listed as tender annuals, plants will survive fall temperatures of −26°F.

There are two ornamental corns for this garden of seeds and pods. One, called strawberry corn, is grown for the small, almost round ears which are about 2 inches long and covered with deep crimson kernels (*Zea mays* var. *praecox*). Strawberry corn is an excellent popping corn, too. The other ornamental corn is shaped more like a typical ear of corn but the kernals are many colored (*Z. mays*). This is the popular Indian corn. Both these ornamentals are tender annuals and belong at the back of the garden as they can reach 6 feet in height.

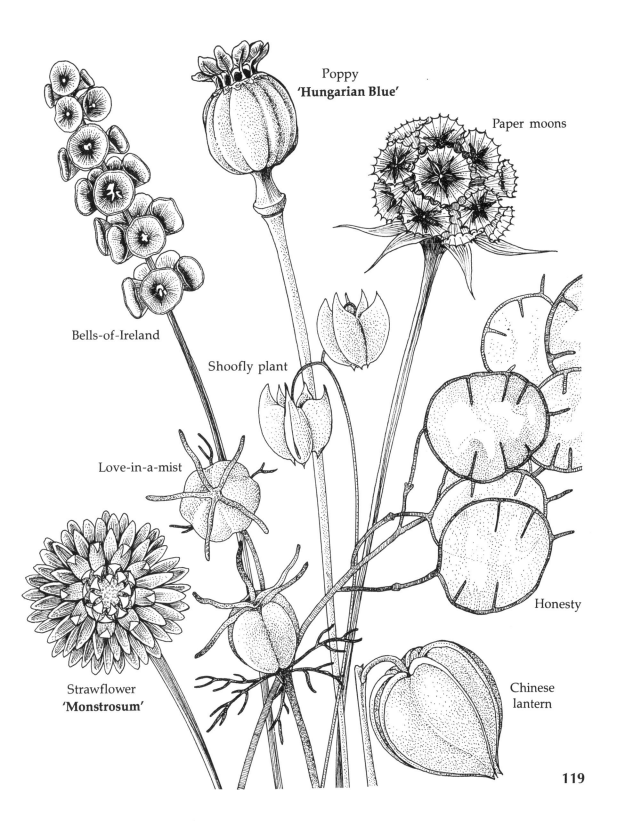

Poppy
'Hungarian Blue'

Paper moons

Bells-of-Ireland

Shoofly plant

Love-in-a-mist

Honesty

Strawflower
'Monstrosum'

Chinese
lantern

119

A GARDEN FOR SHADE

Jill-o'er-the-ground is purple blue,
Blue is the quaker maid,
The wild geranium holds its dew
Long in the boulder's shade.

William Vaughn Moody, *Gloucester Moors*

No white nor red was ever seen
So amorous as this lovely green.
Meanwhile the mind, from pleasure less,
Withdraws into its happiness; —
Annihilating all that's made
To a green thought in a green shade.

Andrew Marvel, *The Garden*

There is an apple tree on our land that deeply shades the ground beneath. It is not too old and sits just back from the edge of our pond forming a rough circle 30 feet wide that reaches a few feet over the water's edge and 40 feet into the air. The tree bears green apples every year. It is on a slight rise, surrounded by a field of sedges and grasses sparked here and there with wild raspberries. Fast by the water is a deer path that goes straight through the mud, and where it is not worn by hooves, some smaller grasses and buttercups trail along the edge. Farther up the rise a Virginia creeper grows. Its vines at one time reached a now dead blueberry bush and were able then to climb to the upper branches of the apple. Now the creeper winds throughout the tree doubling the shade below.

In the morning the sun filters through the sedges and forms dim shadows on the moss-covered trunk. Even on the hottest day when an August sun is high above, it's cool and green beneath that tree. Then the late afternoon sun strikes the pond and every whirlygig beetle sends rippled reflections back to sparkle on the bark.

In spring the foamflowers bloom in that shade; ground ivy (*Glecoma hederacea*) bears small blue-purple flowers and violets (*Viola* spp.) of every color from deepest purple to lightest blue, yellow, and

The plants on the opposite page are happy in the shade of a white pine. At the left is the sensitive fern and at the right, the foamflower.

121

the brightest of whites cover the ground. Emerging from the water the yellow iris blooms and later in July and August, back near the trunk, the common nightshade (*Solanum nigrum*) bears its purple flowers each with a yellow beak.

And since early May, a large green frog has lived in the middle of the deer path, to jump with a splash and a startled squeak whenever we—or, I assume, the deer—walk by. Andrew Marvel could have sat beneath this tree.

Definitions of Shade

Everyone knows what is meant by the term "sunny." A sunny day, as Gertrude Stein might say, is a sunny day is a sunny day. But mention shade and immediately there are as many interpretations as there are gardeners. So it would seem the best thing to do at this point is to give five definitions to cover the basic varieties of shade:

Light shade is open shade like that found beneath a tall and stately tree, where sun is available in the early morning and late afternoon but the area is protected from the intense light of midday.

Medium shade is found under a group of trees, where light is dappled as in the woods; you will see reflected sunlight but not the direct sun.

Full shade means it's getting darker. Closely grouped trees and thickets intertwine and effectively cut out direct sun and even bright indirect light.

Deep shade is truly dark. Either buildings, trees, natural or artificial barriers, or a combination of all four cut off most of the outdoor light.

Seasonal shade is the result of the leafing out of deciduous trees and shrubs. That means in late winter and early spring, the sun shines through.

Soil for the Shade Garden

The condition of soil has been mentioned before. In the shade garden it is even more important. In full sun, most plants must struggle if they are in dense and poorly drained, clay-packed clumps of soil. When moved to the shade, the combination of poor drainage and dense soil is deadly.

So when you garden in the shade, be sure and incorporate leaf litter, garden compost, or peat moss into the soil. In our garden, since the soil slated for the shade plants was a layer of hardpan topped by clay, I was forced to dig down 18 inches and place a 2-inch layer of pea gravel into the bottom of the excavation. Then, while replacing the clay, I mixed it with wet peat moss, compost, and some soil from our woods. If the woods had not been handy, I could have replaced some of the soil with bagged top soil from a local garden center. I sometimes buy a few bags in the fall when the sales are on and store it for future needs.

A Plan for the Shade Garden

The garden plan incorporates areas of all four of the defined kinds of shade. It shows the north wall of a garage next to a thick grove of rhododendrons producing deep shade; a 60-foot high white pine at the garden's southern edge, with a 30-foot spread and branches starting 10 feet up the trunk, giving light shade; the medium shade resulting from Japanese maples growing within the spread of the pine; and the full shade found beneath a weeping birch that in turn stands beneath a white ash with a 16-foot diameter.

Since the birch, maples, and white ash are deciduous trees, theirs is a seasonal shade and there is plenty of spring sunlight for flowering bulbs. Only the area under the rhododendron bushes is really dark most of the year.

The plan for a shade garden.

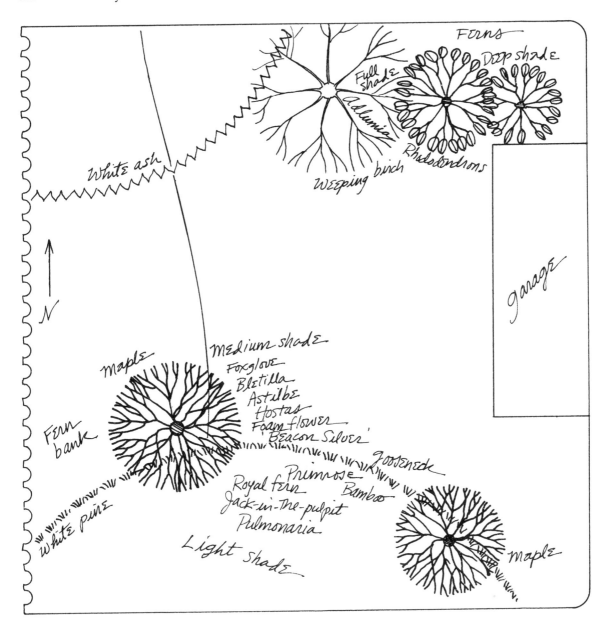

Ferns
Deep shade
Full shade
Adlumia
Rhododendrons
Weeping birch
White ash
garage
N
Medium shade
Foxglove
Bletilla
Astilbe
Hostas
Foam flower
'Beacon Silver'
Gooseneck
maple
Fern bank
Primrose
Royal fern
Bamboo
Jack-in-the-pulpit
Pulmonaria
White pine
Light shade
maple

Plants for Light Shade

In this part of the garden, dominated by the white pine, the soil is never allowed to completely dry out. If we don't get a weekly rain, I carefully water this area. The following flowers all grow well together. All are hardy in Zone 5.

The Jack-in-the-pulpit (*Arisaema triphyllum*) is a charming wildflower that loves a shady spot. In spring it produces what can best be termed an "entertaining" bloom that is followed in late summer by a cluster of red berries. The large leaves are lush and tropical looking.

For all-season color, the plant to grow is the Kamurozasa bamboo (*Arundinaria viridistriata*). In the grass garden (see page 68) this bamboo grows comfortably in a pot, but here it's allowed to run free, as our Zone 5 temperatures successfully keep it from being a rampant spreader. If you garden farther south, be sure and contain your planting with a metal or plastic collar. The leaves of this bamboo are a rich, velvety combination of gold and green.

Planted in and about the shade garden are forget-me-nots (*Myosotis sylvatica*), in shades of white, pink, and blue. These flowers freely self-seed and provide ample bloom every spring. If plants get a bit thick, they are easily pulled up.

The royal fern (*Osmunda regalis* var. *spectabilis*) grows well in this area of the garden but, since the soil is never really wet, the leaves stay about 4 feet tall. In late summer, the fertile leaflets at the top of the leaf are light brown. My original plant came from Terry Curtis in Callicoon, New York and its descendants are quite happy in Zone 5.

For vibrant spring color, primroses are the thing. Mixed together—and I try to keep them about 6 inches apart—are the Japanese primrose (*Primula japonica*) in a bright fuchsia; the polyanthus primrose (*P.* × *polyantha*) in colors of white, yellow, or orange; and to my mind the most charming of all, the **'Gold Lace'** polyanthus. This flower looks as though its edges were intricately embroidered with gold thread while sitting on the lap of Queen Victoria. Although they should be divided every second year at the end of August, these plants will continue to bloom a few years more, but then it must be done or flower production decreases. They are hardy in a protected area in Zone 5. They are easily raised from seed.

Next on the list for the light shade garden are the lungworts (*Pulmonaria officinalis*). They produce lovely flowers that open in early spring, starting out red but turning blue. Leaves are spotted

Jack-in-the-pulpit

with white. The plants adapt to most any soil, only needing moisture at the roots. They are called lungwort according to the Doctrine of Signatures, medieval medical practice wherein various plants were used to cure diseases indicated by the form and color of their leaves, roots, or flowers. The leaves of lungwort were thought to look like lung tissue. Mature plants are 1 foot high and have a 3-foot spread. To cover ground quickly, plant them 9 inches apart. *P. officinalis* var. *immaculata* has plain green leaves. The plants are hardy in Zone 4 and will also do well in medium shade.

You might not expect to find a rose listed for a shade garden but one particular variety of the French rose (*Rosa gallica* **'Versicolor'**) has brightened this corner of our garden for over ten years, sending forth its sweet-smelling white, pink, and red-petalled blossoms every June. Often called the Rosa Mundi, the dried petals of this rose were thought to have medicinal value and were used as a flavoring for other medicines in years gone by. Our bush remains small, never topping 3 feet in height, and is hardy here in Zone 5 but only in a protected spot.

Pulmonaria officinalis

Primula **'Gold Lace'**

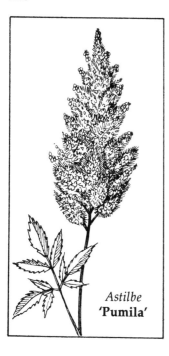

Astilbe
'Pumila'

Plants for Medium Shade

This area of the garden is shaded by a Japanese maple, a bank that rises behind and some residual shade from the white pine. At the other end of the garden, a white ash (*Fraxinus americana*) provides medium shade during the summer months.

The astilbes (*Astilbe* spp.) have long been favorites in the sunny border, but they are far better when granted a bit of shade during the hot summer months. In fact, I've found one particular plant, *A. chinensis* **'Pumila'**, that is a perfect groundcover for an area of medium shade. The late English gardener, Margery Fish, painted this foot-high flower as mauvish pink, while George Schenk, late of America and now living in New Zealand, terms the blossoms "shocking pink." I would strike a balance between the two and call it a medium pink with faint overtones of lavender. While not a spectacular blossom, with color easily washed out by the sun, it is in keeping with light tempered by shade. Plant these astilbes 9 inches apart.

There is a terrestrial orchid from China and Japan that is perfect for the shade garden. The books all say it isn't hardy north of Zone 8, but I've found that with a bit of shelter from the winter winds and either snow or pine boughs for cover, *Bletilla striata* will smile through a Zone 5 winter to bloom in the spring. The light purple flowers sit atop foot-high stems that rise from a crown of pleated leaves. There is also a white-flowered form, **'Alba'**, but it's very hard to find. In colder areas, lift the rhizomes in the fall and store them where temperatures are between 35° and −40°F. Space the plants 6 inches apart.

The common foxglove (*Digitalis purpurea*) is an annual (look for the cultivar **'Foxy'**), biennial, or under perfect conditions, a short-lived perennial. But it will easily reseed itself in your garden and provide you with years of 4-foot-tall shafts of flowers. There are many colors available but the white is especially fine in the shade. Plant 9 inches apart.

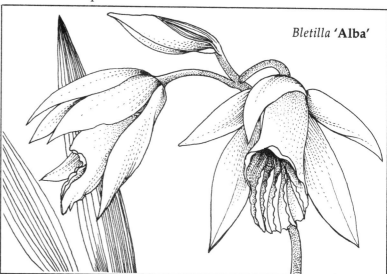

Bletilla **'Alba'**

Daylilies (*Hemerocallis* spp.) are among the most popular flowers in America. The American Hemerocallis Society publishes a quarterly bulletin that rivals *T.V. Guide* in format and number of pages. These plants are hardy almost to a fault, are generally disease resistant, tolerant of almost any soil around, and, according to type, bloom from early spring to late fall. There are now thousands of listed varieties in the United States with colors from the palest of yellow to dark mahogany. There are miniatures only 12 inches tall—**'Eenie-Weenie'** springs to mind (please overlook the name, many breeders are guilty of succumbing to the cute)—and other cultivars 3 feet tall. All daylilies will grow and bloom in medium shade. We have used them as a foundation planting on the north wall of our house. They only get sun for an hour in the morning, and then only before the leaves appear on the trees, yet they bloom every summer.

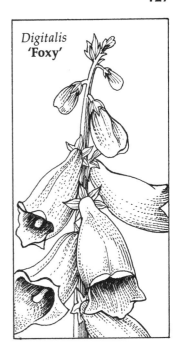

Digitalis **'Foxy'**

The hostas (*Hosta* spp.) are probably one of the most popular plants of today. Their willingness to thrive in the shade, coupled with the variety of available leaf shapes and colors, plus the benefit of blossoms, has catapulted hostas to the top of every gardener's want list. The blue-leaved types (**'Blue Angel'** and **'Blue Moon'**, for example) will do well in medium shade, but will even live in full shade. The greens (**'Green Fountain'** and **'Green Wedge'**) adapt from medium shade to full sun, and the variegated types (**'Resonance'** and **'Frances Williams'**) prefer shade. Space plants 12 to 24 inches apart, depending on their ultimate size and, if you don't wish to disturb them for years, just let them be. They will grow happily for decades.

Back in 1980, I ordered some *Lamium maculatum* **'Beacon Silver'** from the Hardy Plant Society Seed Exchange. This was the first mention that I had seen of this plant, a variety rated superb for the shaded border by English gardeners. I had a bumper crop in the spring of 1981, and the plant lived up to all expectations. Its bright silvery leaves lit up the shade like aluminum reflectors highlighting the faces of sun worshipers on the beach. By 1984, it seems that

Lamium **'Beacon Silver'**

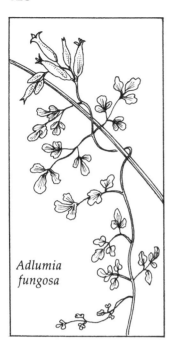

*Adlumia
fungosa*

every nursery in the United States had the plant in stock, and it's apparently another hit plant among gardeners. Don't let familiarity breed contempt. Try it. The stems reach about 6 inches high before they bend over to scramble along the ground, producing light purple snapdragon type flowers in the summer. With plenty of moisture, the plants will grow in light shade. Kept in dry soil, they do well in full shade. Space plants about a foot apart. They will quickly join up.

There is a native American flower that the rest of the gardening world loves. It's called the foamflower (*Tiarella cordifolia*) and it revels in a good woodsy soil in medium to full shade. Maple-like leaves grow close to the ground and produce clusters of tiny white flowers on foot-high stems in the spring. Foamflower makes an excellent groundcover, its light green leaves being most attractive, and they turn a fine bronzy hue in the fall. The little flowers are only 1/4 inch across, but each has ten long stamens so a blooming stem looks like foam. Plant *Tiarella* 9 inches apart.

The final plant for medium shade is the myrtle, or lesser periwinkle (*Vinca minor*). Do not think of the species name as being belittling, for this is a workhorse of a plant. It is often found in old cemeteries where it winds between shaded tombstones, bearing lovely 1-inch-wide violet-blue flowers in the spring and often again in the fall. Plant rooted stems 6 inches apart. It will take some years to make a large bed, but it's worth the wait.

Vinca minor

Plants for Full Shade

This part of the garden lies beneath the hanging branches of a weeping birch (*Betula pendula* **'Tristis'**) which is in turn shaded by the larger white ash. The choice of plants gets more limited in this environment. Shade-loving ferns, the ubiquitous Japanese pachysandra, some shade-loving wildflowers like trillium and the violets, and the plants listed below are the best choices.

The Allegheny vine or what I think is the better name, climbing fumitory (*Adlumia fungosa*), is a biennial vine that looks like a fern during the first year, then begins to climb and bloom with small white flowers the second. I plant it directly beneath the birch so the plant can journey up the pendant branches. I've also grown it beneath a multiflora rose where it does just as well. This plant needs to be protected both from sun and wind, so the perfect home is a thicket.

The bedding or wax begonia (*Begonia × semperflorens-cultorum*) is found in every garden center, its waxy leaves and white, pink, or red flowers blooming all summer long. If started out in pots for the spring and early summer, the wax begonias can later be moved to deeper shade, where it will continue to bloom far into the fall, when the frosts cut it to the ground.

I can only safely speak of one ivy, called Baltic (*Hedera Helix* **'Baltica'**), an extremely hardy cultivar originally from Latvia. With

Hedera **'Baltica'**

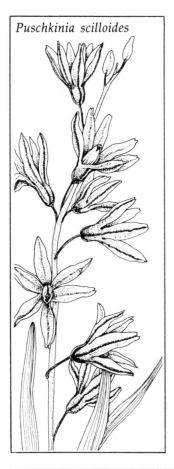

Puschkinia scilloides

some protection from harsh winter winds and hot summer sun, Baltic ivy makes a perfect groundcover. In my garden the plants gain some strength from the additional light of early spring and fall (after the birch loses its leaves) but also do well in the reduced light of summer. Plant rooted cuttings about 1 foot apart.

The jewelweed or impatiens (*Impatiens* spp.) have been grown for decades in the shade garden. Both *I. Balsamia* and *I. Wallerana* are found at garden centers in an amazing array of colors, chiefly white, purple, pink, red and salmon. *I. Wallerana* is the taller of the two, reaching 3 feet in a good spot. Start impatiens indoors, six weeks before the last spring frost, so you have plenty of plants for the garden. Nothing is more delightful than a number of the white-flowered plants winking out from the shade on a summer's day.

I don't mean to malign pachysandra, but it seems that every garden center's answer to shade gardening is to sell a flat of this enduring creeper. If it was rare, you might want it, but it isn't, so turn it aside. However there is a native American plant that is not only finer, but has prettier flowers. It's called Allegheny spurge (*Pachysandra procumbens*) and grows about 1 foot high. Its leaves are oval and gently toothed, with lighter areas of green marking the regular dark green surface of each leaf. The flowers have a purplish cast and consist mostly of stamens. Plant 9 inches apart.

For flowers in the spring, I use the striped squill (*Puschkinia scilloides*). The plant is named for Count Apollos Apollosovich Mussin-Puschkin (1760–1805), who left Russia in the year 1800 for the Caucasus in search of mineral wealth and never returned. This is a gem of a flower, resembling a small hyacinth but slim and refined with porcelain blue flowers, not gaudy in the least. Bulbs are planted at the base of the birch tree and get enough sun for the next year's bloom before the birch leafs out.

Allegheny spurge

Deep Shade Gardening

If you have a spot of deep shade, and wish to have a bit more growing than moss, charming as that can be, try moving a few of your jungle houseplants outdoors for the summer. A few of these plants will tolerate light down to 10 foot candles (20 foot candles is considered to be a good light for reading a newspaper). Most philo-dendrons, *Dracaena marginata* and *D. sanderiana*, *Ficus elastica* **'Dec-ora'**, and the parlor palm (*Chamaedorea elegans*) will go along for a few months, if you then give them better light to once again stimulate their growth.

THE HOSTA OR THE FUNKIA

Garden writers are a strange lot and once they get locked into something, even decades will not force them to give up a notion. Take the hosta as a case in point.

Hostas come from Japan and China. There they have been cultivated for centuries. The Japanese grow them in gardens, in pots, in deep shade and full sun, in rock gardens and in temple gardens, and they even use them cut up in stir-fry. (I assume the Chinese do something of the same but I can find no documentation for this statement.)

In 1894, William Robinson, the world-renowned English gardener, called these plants Funkia, or Niobe. They were named in honor of Heinrich Christian Funck (1771–1839), a German doctor. By the turn of the century the name had been changed to Hosta in honor of Nicolaus Host (1761–1834), another German doctor, this one in the service of the Emperor in Vienna.

After 1900 and to this day, every writer of any depth on the subject of these shade-loving perennials starts out by saying "Hostas or plantain lilies (after their resemblance to this other member of the lily family) or funkias . . ." So even today, some 85 years later, the name funkia persists. And I'd dearly love to know why Funck lost to Host. What dastardly deed did he do to lose his namesake and what noble thing did he do to hang on so long?

As to the plants themselves, they are the mainstay of a shady garden. One of the large cultivars, such as *Hosta* **'Big Daddy'** (I must apologize for many of these cultivar names that have a tendency to make the garden sound like a place for Barbie and Ken), has large puckered leaves of a deep blue. The plant will reach 30 inches in

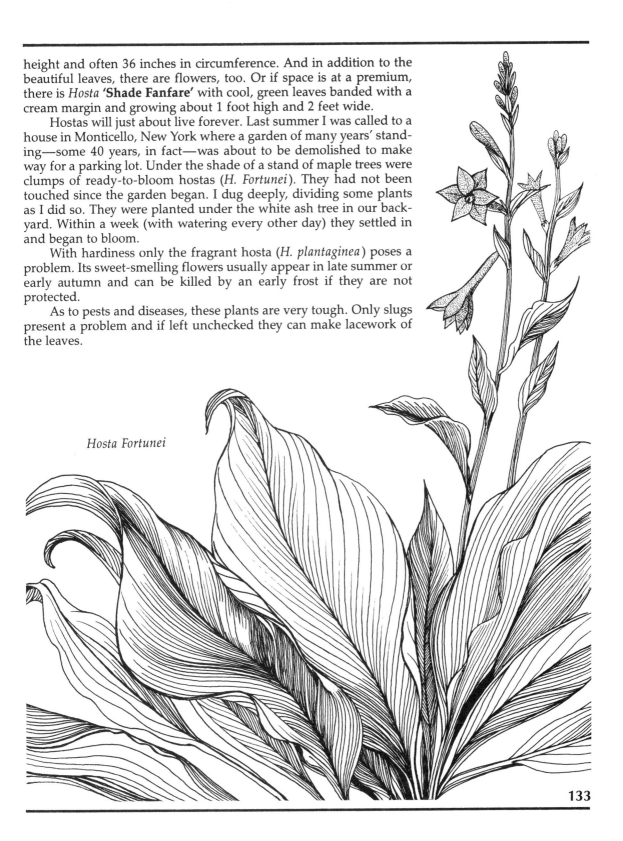

height and often 36 inches in circumference. And in addition to the beautiful leaves, there are flowers, too. Or if space is at a premium, there is *Hosta* **'Shade Fanfare'** with cool, green leaves banded with a cream margin and growing about 1 foot high and 2 feet wide.

Hostas will just about live forever. Last summer I was called to a house in Monticello, New York where a garden of many years' standing—some 40 years, in fact—was about to be demolished to make way for a parking lot. Under the shade of a stand of maple trees were clumps of ready-to-bloom hostas (*H. Fortunei*). They had not been touched since the garden began. I dug deeply, dividing some plants as I did so. They were planted under the white ash tree in our backyard. Within a week (with watering every other day) they settled in and began to bloom.

With hardiness only the fragrant hosta (*H. plantaginea*) poses a problem. Its sweet-smelling flowers usually appear in late summer or early autumn and can be killed by an early frost if they are not protected.

As to pests and diseases, these plants are very tough. Only slugs present a problem and if left unchecked they can make lacework of the leaves.

Hosta Fortunei

133

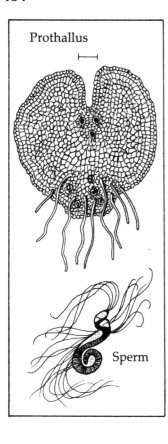

Prothallus

Sperm

A CIRCLE OF FERNS

For years whenever we have gone for a walk in the woods, any woods in the Northeast, I have kept my eye on the ground. Not from fear of stumbling, or losing my way, but simply because I don't want to miss a thing, either plant or animal. And one of the plants that I'm always looking for is the maidenhair fern. I consider it to be one of the most beautiful ferns in the forest, but it's not too common in our area of the Catskill Mountains. When I do spot a clump of these graceful fronds growing at the edge of a woods, I call everyone over with the cry, "I've found the elusive maidenhair!"

Once found, it's duly admired, and occasionally I might take a picture, but we never dig it up, for most large nurseries in the United States usually keep it in stock.

The maidenhair is but one of many beautiful members of the fern family, a group of plants that are among the oldest on the earth. When you look at a typical fern you are looking at a plant that stretches back some 350 million years to the Carboniferous Age, when the carbonized remains of these plants formed the vast coal beds that are mined today.

From spring when new, coiled fronds (called fiddleheads) emerge from the ground until early winter when the fronds are silhouetted against the virgin snow, ferns are delightful additions to the shady garden.

A Fern Garden

Ferns number some 10,000 species worldwide, far less than the 300,000 species of seed-bearing plants and yet with some 100 species available for cultivation in a fern bed, they become an interesting plant family for gardeners who wish to specialize. In a reasonably small area a number of species may be grown. And to approximate the terrain they are found in when growing naturally, the gardener should provide positions for deep shade, light shade, and an open, partly sunny spot.

Soil should be light and moist, either naturally or by changing the quality of the existing mix. Heavy soils can be adapted to fern culture by adding leaf mold or peat moss. Their roots are thin and wiry and except for a few species (one being the hay-scented fern, *Dennstaedtia punctilobula*, and another the common bracken, *Pteridium aquilinum*) resent the thickness of clay soil. Sandy soils must also contain humus in order to constantly provide the moisture—only a few species can tolerate standing water—that fern roots require. If water is needed it can easily be supplied by the gardener with a hose on a weekly schedule.

If possible, bring in a few rocks to help in varying the terrain if your backyard is unnaturally—for ferns—flat. In nature these plants ramble over gentle slopes or sprout from a tiny bit of leaf litter lodged between boulders.

The Fern's Life Cycle

Ferns do not bear flowers and seeds but begin their life cycle by producing spores encased in tiny cases called *sori*. These spore cases turn brown as they age and when mature, and weather conditions are fairly dry, their walls bend back to release millions of dustlike spores to the air. If it's raining the sori remain closed in order to protect the spores from destruction by heavy rain drops.

The spores drift to earth and with a proper combination of temperature and moisture, grow into a flat, heart-shaped structure called a *prothallus*, which at maturity is about the size of an aspirin tablet. Separate and distinct male and female organs grow on the underside of the prothalia, producing eggs and sperm. Using dew, fog, rain, or even melting snow, the sperm swim to the egg for fertilization and soon an embryo fern begins to develop.

Propagating the Spores

Absolutely sterile conditions are mandatory for home propagation. Not that you have to create Frankenstein's laboratory, but fern spores are easily invaded by mold, fungus, and a host of other undesirables. Ripe spores can be sown at any time of the year. Use 3- or 4-inch scrubbed and clean clay pots. Clay, not plastic, is necessary to ensure both the free circulation of air and the absorption of water. Place a piece of crockery over the drainage hole in each pot and fill to 1 inch of the rim with a sterilized soil mix of 1/3 potting soil, 1/3 peat moss, and 1/3 sand. The mix needs adequate drainage, so don't omit the sand. Lightly tamp the mix with a knife or spatula, making the surface smooth and level. If you are unsure about the sterility of the mix put the pot and soil into a 250°F. oven and bake for two hours.

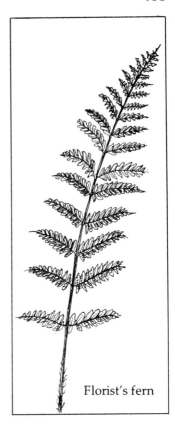

Florist's fern

Next soak the pots containing the mix until they are completely saturated; then drain off the excess water.

Using a piece of folded paper, cast the spores, one species to a pot. Label each pot with the date and species. Baby ferns all look alike so don't forget this step. Cover the pots with a sheet of glass, or rigid plastic, and put them in a warm spot at 65°-70°F. (18°-21°C.), with dim light. Since our house is old and chilly on many winter nights, I keep fern pots on a heating cable in the greenhouse below the level of the windows. At all times keep the pots away from the direct rays of the sun, as sunlight will impede germination. Check the medium for signs of drying out. If it starts, soak the pots again. Don't water from the top because the germinating spores should never be disturbed. If condensation on the glass becomes too heavy, remove the glass for a while. A thin beading of water is what we want, not huge drops of rain.

Many species will germinate within a few days, others will take a few weeks, so be patient. As the prothallia grow, a green cast will appear on the surface of the mix. In about three months they will reach their full size. If you get excellent germination, thin the prothallia to 1 inch apart. Falling condensation from the glass should provide enough water for the sperm to swim to the egg, but you might have to mist the soil surface, if it shows signs of drying.

The tiny fern plants will now begin to develop. When 3 or more fronds have appeared, transplant the small plants carefully to individual pots. It will take about two years for a mature plant.

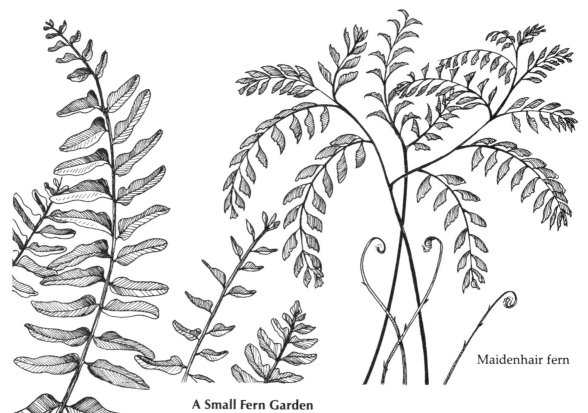

Maidenhair fern

Christmas fern

A Small Fern Garden

The fern garden is built against the western corner of the north side of my house. I used fieldstones to build a low wall to contain the royal fern and baltic ivy. The ground in front of the wall was mostly clay, so after removing the second-rate turf that makes up our lawn, I worked in a bale of partially moistened peat moss and a bushel of leaf litter from the woods.

A gutter is nearby and provides a great deal of moisture during and after rains, but this year we are having a drought—New York City is in imminent peril of being out of water in its Catskill reservoirs by December if we don't get more rain or snowfall at year's end—so I water with a hose when things get dry.

The light is bright on the bed most of the day but the only sun that falls on the ferns in front of the wall is in late afternoon and much of that is shaded by the lower branches of a weeping birch (*Betula pendula* **'Tristis'**).

The centerpiece of the garden is a cultivar of the royal fern (*Osmunda regalis* var. *spectabilis*). Roots of this fern when gathered in Florida have been used as a potting medium for orchids for generations. In their native haunts, royal ferns plants can reach 10 feet in height but this particular type settles for 6 feet in the garden. The parent of this cultivar is at home in northern woods and does need attention to watering; in nature it's often found growing next to streams or directly in bogs. If given adequate moisture it can tolerate some sun but it does better in light shade. The manner of growth is a crown rather than runners, so the plant spreads slowly. Leaflets turn a golden brown in autumn.

Around the royal fern I planted a flat of Baltic ivy (*Hedera Helix* **'Baltica'**), the only type in my experience that withstands Zone 4 and 5 winters. If temperatures fall much below 15°F. without snowcover, the plant's top leaves are killed back but the vines renew in the spring; if mulched with pine boughs or snow, this ivy is fine. It, too, does best in partial shade.

Christmas fern (*Polystichum acrostichoides*) is, as its name implies, green for Christmas and cut fronds make excellent Holiday decorations. It grows about 3 feet high and sterile leaves (those without sori) remain evergreen through the winter while the others wither, although leaflets are often burned with frost. This plant will also take some sun if kept in damp soil, but it prefers shade. Some authorities say the Christmas fern prefers limy soil but plants do quite well in an acid mix. Unlike many ferns, this one transplants well.

Maidenhair fern (*Adiantum pedatum*) is a great beauty. The fan-shaped, light green leaflets are set atop shiny, near-black stalks and the grace of the plant is evident to all. Fronds grow between 12 and 24 inches tall and spread slowly in partial shade. Every so often, a dwarf form listed as **'Nana'** is offered by a few nurseries.

Sensitive or bead ferns (*Onoclea sensibilis*) are grown for both their leaves, which are decidedly unfernlike, and their spore-bearing fertile spikes, which look like beaded feathers. These ferns were very popular in Victorian times for dried arrangements and shadow-box pictures. They are called sensitive because the leaves die quickly when touched by the first frost. The broad leaves are a good contrast to the typically ferny look of the other plants. This one must be watched as it can become invasive, but surplus plants are easily uprooted. They will grow in sun or shade.

Japanese painted fern (*Athyrium Goeringianum* **'Pictum'**) is another beauty. Its fronds are about 24 inches long and bend gracefully towards the ground. The color is gray-green lightly tinted with a brush dipped in maroon. The color is best displayed in partial shade. This fern needs water in hot summers or the leaflets turn brown. It seems too beautiful to be hardy, but like many plants from Japan, it is.

Lady fern (*Athyrium Filix-femina*) grows to 30 inches tall and likes a position in moist, partial shade though it will live—but not do well—in full sun. The name comes from the delicate structure of the leaflets, which are truly finely cut.

My final choice for the fern garden is the florist's fern (*Dryopteris spinulosa*), known also as spinulose woodfern. When approaching a grove of these plants in the woods you see a fern that typifies ferns. And when buying flowers from a florist, this fern usually supplies the leaves in the arrangement. The florist's fern needs light shade and must be well-watered to prevent burning of the fronds. Plants grow about 30 inches tall and form crowns.

Lady fern

Royal fern

THE WATER GARDEN

*Everywhere water is a thing of beauty, gleaming in
the dewdrop; singing in the summer rain; shining in the
ice-gems till the leaves all seem to turn to living
jewels; spreading a golden veil over the setting sun;
or a white gauze around the midnight moon.*

John Ballantine Gough, *A Glass of Water*

*Many owners of large ponds are anxious to have one
or more islands in them. Not infrequently a circular
wall is built in the middle, the space so enclosed is
filled with soil, and the island is finished! I
consider this method altogether wrong.*

F. W. Meyer, *Rock & Water Gardens*

Ever since I've become interested in gardening I've longed for water
in the backyard. My first dreams were of a large flagstone terrace
surrounded on three sides with ivy-covered stone walls: The one at
left supporting awnings for afternoon shade; the center featuring an
antique lavabo set off on either side by climbing roses; and the right
wall delineating an area for dining *alfresco*. The fourth side would be
open to the woods and hills beyond.

In the center of my imaginary terrace is the pool (40 feet square),
lined with blue tile, deep enough for a quick swim, and highlighted
by a fountain with lead fishes on stone waves, squirting water high in
the air. Scattered about would be tables and chairs designed by
Edwin Lutyens—Gertrude Jekyll's partner who created houses to
match her gardens—and a number of *large* terra cotta pots housing
rare tropical plants.

Needless to say the dream never happened.

But plastic did! By using the new PVC sheeting, a garden can
now include a pond of decent size for a very reasonable price. And if
the gardener does not have the time to properly install such a pool,
he or she need only excavate a small hole and set within it one of the
many free-form fiberglass jobs, or for a very small expenditure, fill a

**The magnificent lily on
the opposite page is the
lotus.**

wooden or plastic tub with water and grow a single exquisite water lily and a cattail.

Never underestimate the power of water in a garden. The sound of it, especially on a torrid day, is hypnotic. The look of it as lazy ripples widen where dazzling dragonflies have quickly trod, enchants the eye. And while most of us will miss the opportunity of worrying about F. W. Meyer's view of island construction, we need not miss water in our gardens.

Planning for a Water Garden

After many years of planning and then a summer of actual work, last year we finally put in a pond. A number of uses were to be served: Swimming, boating, a home for wildlife, stocking for fish, the aesthetic joy of water, and a home for a number of deep-water and shallow-water plants. By last June, we already had memories of great water sports, the new wildlife was wonderful, we were still debating over the type of fish to introduce (pond owners get as excited over favorite fish as gardeners do over tomatoes), and lost most of the water plants (except those in deep water) to our old friends the deer.

This meant we had to put in an ornamental pool in the garden as a home for these marvelous plants that I had been looking forward to growing during all the years of pond planning.

I looked around the yard and determined that the pool, whatever size, could not be concrete—both the climate and my continual garden changes ruled against such a permanent approach. A tub garden would be fine but too small. So I opted for a larger pool that I would excavate by hand and install a vinyl liner to hold the water. Believe me, I always distrust people who say something is an easy job, because it always turns out to be untrue. In this case, it isn't. Putting in a pool using this method is a weekend's work (unless you live and garden in a rock quarry).

Nymphaea odorata

Where To Put the Pool

I finally chose for my garden pool a level spot that would be in the sun from late morning on. It was also close to the terrace so we could comfortably sit and yet be able to watch the water and its reflections. An electrical outlet was also installed nearby in case I want to add lights sometime in the future.

Next I consulted the catalogs to see what size of vinyl liner was available. I found that a 10 by 10 foot liner of extra thick (20 mil.) plastic would make a pool just under 6 by 6 feet, about 18 inches deep. A simple rule of thumb for figuring how much liner to buy is: Add to your maximum width twice the depth, plus 2 feet, to allow a 1-foot overlap on each side. Do the same for the length. The color of the liner I chose is battleship gray, and does not make the brash statement in the garden that a turquoise or blue liner would.

To make your pool, first dig a hole 18 inches deep. If you plan on a large pool, use a garden hose to lay out the shape. Use a line and line-level to make sure your excavation is level; now is the time to be careful. Remove all the rocks, pebbles, or other debris. Next put a 1/2-inch layer of sand on the bottom and work sand up the sides to

The plan for a water garden.

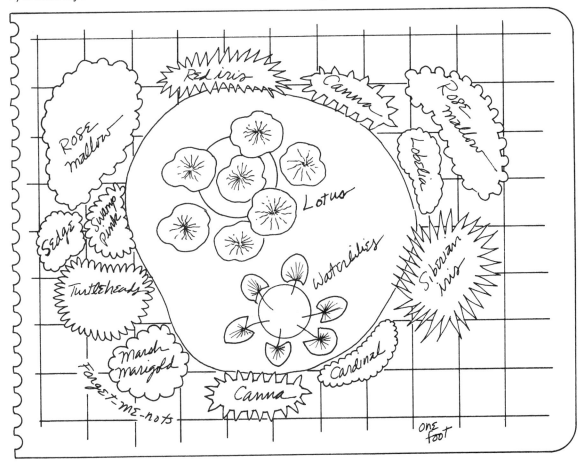

Iris fulva

Canna
hybrids

fill any holes left by removed stones. If you have especially rocky soil—like we do—lay a layer of .002-inch commercial building polyethylene over the sand, before you lay the liner.

Drape the liner into the hole, placing bricks or stones on the sides to hold it down. Now start filling it with tap water. As the pool fills, occasionally remove the stones to allow the liner to fit tightly into the hole. After the pool is full, trim the liner to a 6-inch overhang and cover that with a layer of fieldstone slabs. If you want a very formal look, you could lay stone paving on a bed of mortar. If you do intend to put fish in the pool, let the water settle for a week before they join the swim. Use a siphon to empty the pool. If you use cement try to keep it out of the pool—it's deadly where fish are concerned.

Planting the Water Garden

Instead of throwing soil directly into the pool, put both waterlilies and other aquatic plants into individual pots. A good soil mix for both is three parts of good topsoil—and in this case a heavy clay soil is fine—and one part of well-rotted cow manure. Cover the soil after planting with a 1-inch layer of clean gravel to prevent the soil from riling up the water. Then saturate the pot and earth before setting it into the pool.

Never plant the tropical lilies in water under 70°F. They will not snap out of dormancy.

Different plants require a different water depth but you can easily adjust this by placing the pots on bricks or stones.

Keep tight control over the number of plants! A pool will only hold so much and keep in a healthy state. A 6 by 6-foot pool has a surface area of 36 square feet and will hold three or four small to medium waterlilies and one or two other water plants, plus those that will grow about the outer edge of the pool.

In the North, you can treat tropical lilies as annuals and replace them every garden season or bring them into a greenhouse pool. In the South where winters are Zone 10, and temperatures rarely fall below 30°F., they can be left out all year.

The hardy lilies are stored over winter in a cool basement where temperatures hold between 40° to 50°F. In the fall before a hard freeze, lift the lily pots from the pool, drain well, and store them leaves and all by covering with damp peat moss so they will not dry out over the winter. In the spring, empty the rhizome from the pot, clean it off, remove any suckers—small, yellow leaves—and repot as you did the year before. Hardy lilies may only be left outside in a pond deep enough that the ice line is above the tuber and the pot.

Tropical water plants can be held over in the greenhouse or sunporch.

Plants for a Water Garden

The following plants are meant either for the pool itself or for around the edge where the ground should be damp at all times. The plants mentioned in the tub garden section (see page 148) may also be used. Unless otherwise mentioned, the terrestrial plants are hardy in Zone 5.

The marsh marigold or cowslip (*Caltha palustris*) blooms in early spring with bright yellow flowers on 1- to 2-foot stems with heart-shaped leaves. They like a boggy condition with plenty of humus and should never dry out. They go dormant in midsummer and can be overplanted with a crop of annual summer forget-me-not (*Anchusa capensis*) or, if the garden is permanent, biennial forget-me-nots (*Myosotis sylvatica*). Propagate from seed or division in spring.

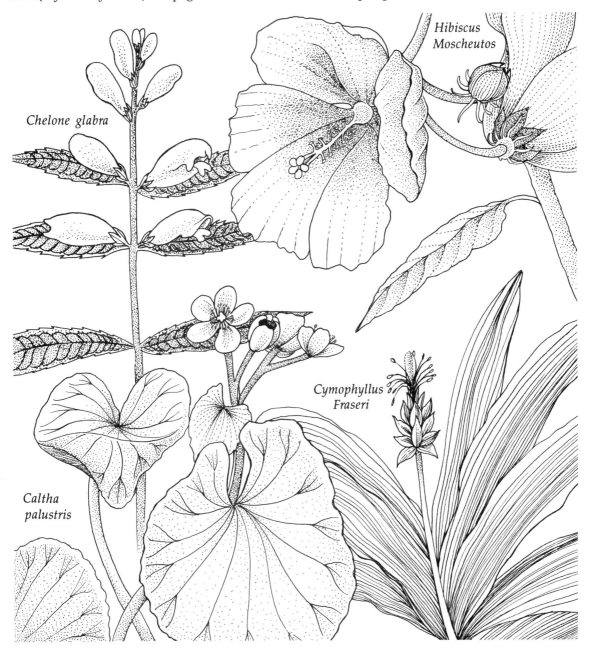

Hibiscus Moscheutos

Chelone glabra

Cymophyllus Fraseri

Caltha palustris

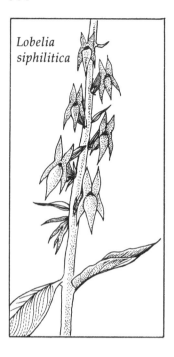

Lobelia siphilitica

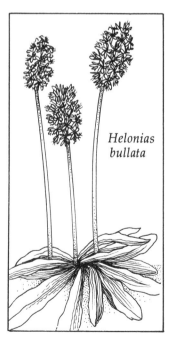

Helonias bullata

The water cannas (*Canna* hybrids) are tropical hybrids of the typical bedding canna and are meant for planting in water up to 6 inches deep. They are 4 feet high and blossom either in red or yellow with orange spots. They can also grow around the pond margin.

Fraser's Sedge (*Cymophyllus Fraseri*) is a family of one plant often called *Carex Fraseri* in old catalogs. It needs damp soil with a good deal of humus and a spot with filtered shade, either from an overhead tree or larger plants in the vicinity. The evergreen, strap-like leaves are usually 12 inches long with white flower spikes on 20-inch stems in early spring. While hardy in Zone 6, it will survive in Zone 5 if given a good winter mulch. Propagate by division in spring but only with mature plants.

The white turtlehead (*Chelone glabra*) is aptly named, for the flower when viewed from the side looks just like a turtle. Blossoms are on 2- to 3-foot stalks and appear in late summer to early fall. Plants like wet feet so they will do well on the edge of the pond or pool (deer relish them). Propagate with seed or division in spring.

Swamp pink (*Helonias bullata*) is a very rare American flower of great beauty, usually only available from seed. It is another family of one. Its tufted leaves grow 1 foot long and are evergreen. In spring a 2-foot branch will appear, topped with a very dense raceme of fragrant pink flowers. It prefers a swamp or bog and likes wet feet. Propagate from seed or division in spring.

Rose mallows (*Hibiscus Moscheutos* subsp. *palustris*) are graced with summer-long 4-inch-wide blossoms of pink or white, each like a tropical hibiscus. Plants like a wet place in full sun and will reach 7 feet in a good spot. They will eventually fill a good area, so allow for a 2- to 3-foot spread. Propagate by seed or division after the shoots emerge in spring.

Red iris (*Iris fulva*) grow to 2 feet in wet soil to a water depth of 6 inches. The flowering period is short, in mid-spring, but the leaves are very attractive all summer long. They are hardy in Zone 5 with a winter mulch. Divide in late summer.

The Siberian iris (*Iris siberica*) forms huge clumps in damp soil or in water up to a depth of 4 inches. Purple flowers on 3-foot stems stand above sharply pointed leaves that would be grown in gardens even without flowers. Propagate by dividing the clumps in early fall.

Cardinal flowers (*Lobelia Cardinalis*) are among the most beautiful of American flowers. Brilliant red blossoms march up 3-foot stems in late summer. In nature they often grow along the bank of a stream with some shade in midday from overhanging branches, a winter mulch of leaves, and plenty of water at the roots. If your climate is colder than Zone 6, be sure you give a winter mulch and don't let plants go into a winter in dry soil. Propagate from seed.

The great blue lobelia (*Lobelia siphilitica*) resembles the cardinal flower except that the flowers are not quite as graceful and of a light blue color. These plants are a bit hardier and seed more freely in the garden. The species name refers to the alleged efficacy of blue lobelia in curing syphilis.

The lotus (*Nelumbo nucifera*) is a grandiose flower. Its blossoms exude a rich fragrance and stand with the leaves above the water on stout stems. When blooming is over, the seed pods remain. Colors are white, rose, pink, yellow, and red. The American lotus (*Nelumbo lutea*) has yellow petals and is only slightly less impressive than its tropical kin. Treat it as a hardy lily. Leaves are often 2 feet across and quite unusual in that they shed water as if they were the back of a duck.

You must have space for both of these plants. Tubers are placed in a tub 20 inches in diameter or larger and kept with 6 to 12 inches of water above the soil. They must have six hours of sun a day.

The fragrant, day-blooming waterlily (*Nymphaea odorata*) has white or pink petals and is hardy. Leaves are up to 10 inches across. This tuber may be placed in a 6-inch pot for a small pond. Propagate by separating roots in spring when they become crowded.

The hardy water lilies (*Nymphaea* spp.) come in varying sizes which spread from less than 6 square feet to over 12. Colors are white, pink, yellow, and red, in a bewildering number of cultivars. A few varieties will bloom in partial shade, but all need at least three hours of direct sun every day. The flowers open during the day and close at night. Propagation is by dividing the tubers.

The Victoria water lily (*Victoria amazonica*) was discovered in 1837 in British Guiana. Seeds packed in wet clay and flowers preserved in alcohol were brought back to England in 1846. The first flower appeared in 1849 and was presented to Queen Victoria. She must have loved it. Blossoms are 16 inches across and have a pleasant smell of sweet pineapple. Petals appear as white on the first day, turning to rose early on the second morning, then rapidly change to red, finally dying some 48 hours later as crimson. Each flower is surrounded in the water by leaves 5 to 6 feet in diameter, with edges turned up and so buoyant from air-filled veins beneath, they will usually support a child's weight—and have been known to float 200 pounds.

This water lily is not for the small pond. It can cover an area up to 30 feet across. The species usually grown is *V. Cruziana*, which can take a lower water temperature than the queen's. Roots must be started in water of 70°F, and you must make sure all of the water is warm. If any part of the plant hits colder water, it goes into dormancy. I tried it in our pond and never got more than two leaves because of cold springs along the bottom. Plants cost around $40 but if you have the place for it, the Victoria is a great entertainment value.

Victoria waterlily

DRAGONFLIES AND CATTAIL LEAVES

When water is added to a garden in the form of a pond, a small pool, or even a plastic tub that either sits upon or is sunk into the ground, certain very small visitors will arrive. If the gardener lives in the suburbs or the country (or anywhere except in the center of a large city) frogs inevitably find their way, ready for bathing on a hot day; small butterflies, called skippers, will delight in treading on the damp ground at the pool's edge, and if the pool is large enough, water birds will fly down looking for the frogs, tadpoles, small fish (either your own imports or nature's additions), and water insects that will quickly accumulate as spring advances into summer.

To me the most interesting to watch and delightful to have around are the dragonflies and the damselflies. They are very similar except when resting. Then the dragons hold their wings outstretched and the damsels fold them neatly over their bodies.

Fossils of these insects date back some 300 million years and the originals had wingspans of over a foot. Today they are much smaller. The green Heroic Darner (*Epiaeschna heros*) that lives from Mexico to Quebec, has a wingspan of 5 1/8 inches and is 3 5/8 inches long. The dragonflies' slender "darning needle" bodies end, it seems, with only two gigantic, swiveling eyes that sparkle in the sun and obscure most of the head. Helicopters owe their original design to these creatures.

Sharp jaws are used to cut up insect prey and four powerful wings move independently of each other. In fact dragonflies fly quite differently from other insects. Recent studies have shown that the wings twist on the downstroke to create whirlpools of air over the top surface, providing a lift of up to ten times the insect's body weight.

Dragonflies and damselflies mate in flight and lay their eggs in the water. These eggs hatch into underwater youngsters called *naiads*, Latin for a water nymph. Nymphlike they are not. These predators will capture tadpoles, all manner of insects, even small fish using a lower lip armed with jaws that are amazingly fast. The term "water tigers" is a more fitting appellation.

When the naiad matures, it crawls out of the water onto a handy leaf—usually belonging to a cattail or another type of aquatic plant—and, holding tight with crossed legs, splits its skin down the back, allowing the adult insect to emerge. Soon the wings unfold and dry in the morning sun. Then some 30 minutes later, the insect flies off in search of food.

There are about 450 species in North America but the usual visitors to your garden will be the Heroic Darner, the Green Darner, the White Tail, the Twelve-spot Skimmer, the Short-stalked Damselfly, the Circumpolar Bluet, and the Elisa Skimmer.

Every morning from mid-July on, when we walk around the edge of our new pond, we see the empty cases of naiads that have recently escaped the bonds of adolescence. Each case is so perfect that even the individual facets of the compound eyes are visible under a hand lens.

A dragonfly naiad climbs out on a leaf.

These insects are voracious and consume many times their body weight in pests, including mosquitoes. But on sunny afternoons when the air is warm and ripples sparkle on the pond, they dart and skim the water, hovering first in one place and then another, obviously enjoying the gift of flight and the joy of life.

Four-leaf
water clover

WATER IN A TUB

Early last spring while walking through a large garden center in upstate New York, I spotted a pile of used wine barrels that had been cut in half. The barrels measured 24 inches across and 17 inches high. They were on sale for $12.00 apiece and I immediately thought what great little water gardens these barrels would make. I knew that keeping the water pure in these casks might be a problem but I had no intentions of adding fish and they seemed clean enough. They could also be lined with heavy plastic, carefully stapling the plastic's edge to the inside top of the cask. Or a readily available plastic tub of 19-inch diameter and 9-inch depth could be set inside the barrel after using some concrete blocks to line up the edges.

Some years ago I remembered reading an article in *Flower and Garden* (April, 1979) which reported that Joseph Dayton had successfully planted water lilies in two 12-gallon sauerkraut crocks (18 inches wide by 24 inches deep). The lilies were planted in 8-inch clay pots, and they bloomed, each plant bearing 4 to 6 flowers. I decided to try it for myself.

I bought a tub, washed it out carefully, and let it sit in the sun for a few days.

Next I ordered one white pygmy water lily, one spike rush, and one dwarf papyrus, from a water garden nursery for spring delivery. I kept the number of plants low, realizing that with a tub this size it is best to underplant.

Upon arrival in mid-May, the water lily went into an 8-inch plastic pot, the type with many openings on the bottom. The other two plants went into 6-inch clay pots. Either plastic or clay pots can be used. I used 3/4 heavy garden soil and 1/4 composted manure. The soil was topped with a layer of pea gravel to prevent escaping dirt from muddying the water. Each pot was then plunged into a pail of water to completely soak the soil.

After being put in its final place on the terrace, the tub was filled to within 4 inches of the top with water from the hose, and was left to sit for a day. The next morning I placed the water lily on the tub bottom. The spike rush and the papyrus were then placed on bricks so the water level was about 5 inches above their dirt when the tub was full. I topped off the water.

The tub sat on the terrace where it received sun most of the day. You have to add water to a tub garden every week or so to replace any that evaporates.

The little water garden was a success. The lilies bloomed, the spike rush grew into a healthy fountain of green tipped with brown non-flowering buds, and the dwarf cyperus shot up 2 1/2 foot stems topped with a fan of leaves.

Once autumn arrives and temperatures start to fall, the water garden should be emptied until the following spring. Hardy water lilies will survive outside if the water above them never freezes solid. But in a tub exposed to the weather this will be the natural order of things.

If you wish, the lilies can be kept over the winter in a cool basement (45 to 50°F.). The roots should be stored in moist sand and need not be kept in water. The papyrus can be a happy houseplant if kept warm (62 to 80°F.), in maxium light, and moist soil. As to the spike rush, I do not know, but I suspect it, too, will keep indoors if given plenty of light and at least six weeks of temperatures averaging about 42°F.

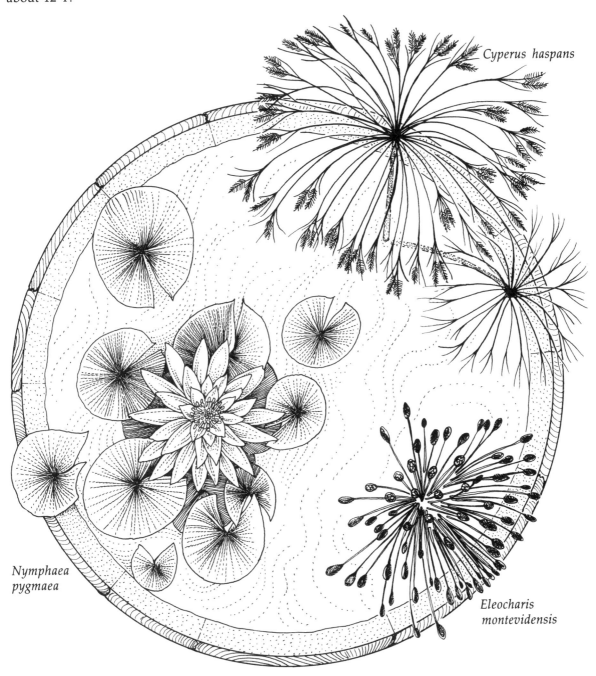

Cyperus haspans

Nymphaea pygmaea

Eleocharis montevidensis

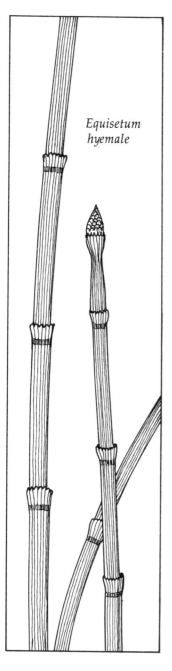

Equisetum hyemale

PLANTS FOR THE TUB GARDEN

There are a number of pygmy water lilies on the market today. They are all cultivars of *Nymphaea pygmaea* so I will just list some of the cultivar names. **'Yellow Pygmy'**, **'White Pygmy'**, and **'Joanne Pring'** (with 2-inch, dark pink flowers) need full sun. **'Helvola'** has flowers the size of a 50-cent piece and needs at least five hours of sun to bloom.

Nymphaea colorata has blossoms colored a wisteria blue and needs three to five hours of sun to bloom.

Nelumbo nucifera **'Momo Botan'** is a rose-colored lotus that will live and bloom in a tub with six hours of sun.

All the pygmy water lilies should have 4 to 6 inches of water above the top of the pot. Use an 8-inch pot for each plant.

The following water and bog plants will all do well in 6-inch pots, using the same soil mix as with the water lilies.

The water arum (*Calla palustris*) has small white flowers over dark green, spear-like leaves. It needs 6 inches of water and at least six hours of sun.

Dwarf papyrus (*Cyperus haspans*) sends up 2 1/2-foot stems when grown in 6 inches of water. They need full sun.

The water poppy (*Hydrocleys nymphoides*) bears 2-inch, three-petaled yellow flowers just above the water's surface. Its leaves are 3 inches wide. Water poppies need three hours of sun to bloom and 4 to 12 inches of water.

Nymphoides cristatum

The spike rush (*Eleocharis montevidensis*) bears 2-foot quill-like leaves and needs three hours of sun to succeed.

Water snowflake (*Nymphoides cristatum*) has 3/4-inch white flowers and heart-shaped leaves and needs three hours of full sun to bloom. It requires 4 to 10 inches of water.

Four-leaf water clover (*Marsilea malica*) grows 3-inch leaves like perfect clovers floating on the water. It needs three hours of sun and 4 to 10 inches of water.

Sweet flag (*Acorus calamus*) likes full sun and needs 6 inches of water to succeed. The leaves have a sweet smell when crushed and are the source of the drug, calamus.

Horsetail (*Equisetum hyemale*) is a primitive plant and looks it. The jointed stems will grow up to 3 feet tall, and the plant is happy in full to partial sun in up to 6 inches of water. This plant has a striking, architectural beauty all its own.

Gardener's garters (*Phalaris arundinacea* var. *picta*) has been grown as an ornamental grass for centuries. But few gardeners know that it will also do well in water. Leave 3 inches between the gravel topping the pot and the water's surface.

The blue flag (*Iris versicolor*) will grow to 24 inches high and bear its lovely flowers in early summer. It needs full to partial sun and up to 6 inches of water.

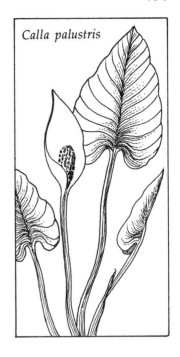

Calla palustris

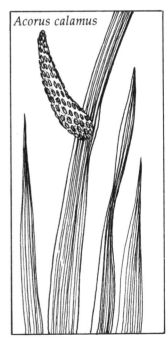

Acorus calamus

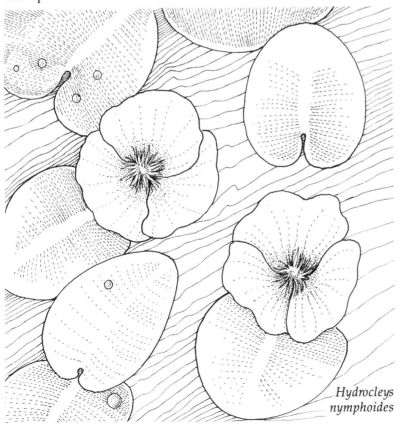

Hydrocleys nymphoides

THE WILD GARDEN

Actually the word wildflower *is a paradox to start with. Many species tulips are wildflowers in Turkey or Greece but treasured as garden delights in the rest of the world. . . .*
Obviously what is a wildflower depends on where your garden is. In my own garden . . . are regal lilies from the mountains of China, snowdrops from the Caucasus, caladiums from South America, and calla lilies from Africa—all of them wildflowers in their place of origin.

Bebe Miles, *Wildflower Perennials for Your Garden*

Our garden began on a piece of land that was cleared for farming some 110 years ago and then neglected for years. By the time we purchased the property, the wild trees and shrubs had walked back like Birnam Wood from the nearby thickets. Since then, we've had a great deal of experience with wild plants.

Because there was only one large nursery in our area (specializing in trees for road works) when we moved in 16 years ago, and all our available funds had to go into renovating our old farmhouse, work in the garden meant transplanting wild ferns and flowers from the woods or fields and selectively cutting some of the available trees. Since many of these plants have a natural beauty and fit perfectly within our country surroundings, much of our landscaping continues to deal with wild plants.

Today we have a wonderful white ash in the backyard that appeared as a sapling 14 years ago (and is now 30 feet tall) and a bank of hay-scented ferns that have developed and spread naturally over many springs; a colorful group of staghorn sumac that I'm pruning and shaping into a grove (after seeing it done in the Wave Hill Gardens up in the Bronx, New York), and banks of daylilies (many over 60 years old according to neighbors) and sensitive ferns along the driveway.

On the opposite page, a butterfly with a wonderful name—the little wood satyr—flies in a counterclockwise direction to visit a goldenrod, bottlebrush grass, sundrops, and the purple coneflower.

153

Allium tricoccum

*Aquilegia
canadensis*

Over the seasons we've planted seven different fern species, some wild orchids (to save them from the destruction of a bulldozer), trailing arbutus (also rescued from highway department, this time when they scraped the roadside to improve drainage), white and red trilliums, violets galore, wild grasses of many species, wild columbines, Jack-in-the-pulpit, wild rushes, and a host of others.

The beauties of a wild garden that develops over many years are the memories associated with gathering the plants. Each one tugs at the mind until you suddenly recall the spring day that you collected that violet in the back of your own woods or the walking fern from a friend's collection of rarities. I should also point out that permission should be asked if you are on other folks' land, and you should never disturb any endangered or protected plants unless they stand in the path of a developer's machinery.

Because so many gardeners in recent years have discovered for themselves the beauty inherent in our native plants, a number of specialized nurseries have started around the country.

A Place for the Wild Garden

The plan for the wild garden is smaller than the others in this book. Wildflowers are never quite as grandiose as the plants used in a typical garden or herbaceous border. They need a more intimate setting.

This plot is designed for a corner of a property and asks that a deciduous tree—here a Japanese maple—be included for open shade during the hot summer. A birdbath is provided since birds and wildflowers go together. Stepping stones should be in the plan so you can walk directly into the garden to see the flowers close-up. Bloom will begin in early spring and continue into the fall.

The soil should be well-laced with humus or leaf litter to a depth of at least 6 inches. If you are in a dry area of the country, remember to water this garden well at least once a week. The plants I've chosen do not like to wallow in water but do need moisture at all times. A mulch (see page xxix) is helpful and if your garden is in Zone 5, the entire bed should be protected by evergreen branches or a carpet of leaves if snow is lacking.

The following are American natives (with one exception) and have been chosen either for their charming flowers or attractive leaves, and a few provide interesting seeds and pods.

Plants for the Wild Garden

The wood leek or ramp (*Allium tricoccum*) is a member of the lily family. Its cluster of small, white, star-shaped flowers appears on a 12-inch stem early in summer after the leaves of the leek have burgeoned and disappeared. You know it's a member of the onion clan if you bruise a leaf or mistakenly cut into a bulb. Since all trace of the plant is gone by midsummer, I've placed it next to the bloodroot which shares the same habit; overplant this area with some white alyssum (*Lobularia maritima*) to provide continuing bloom. These plants are gathered for food by people of the Appalachians. Propagation is both by seeds and offset bulbs.

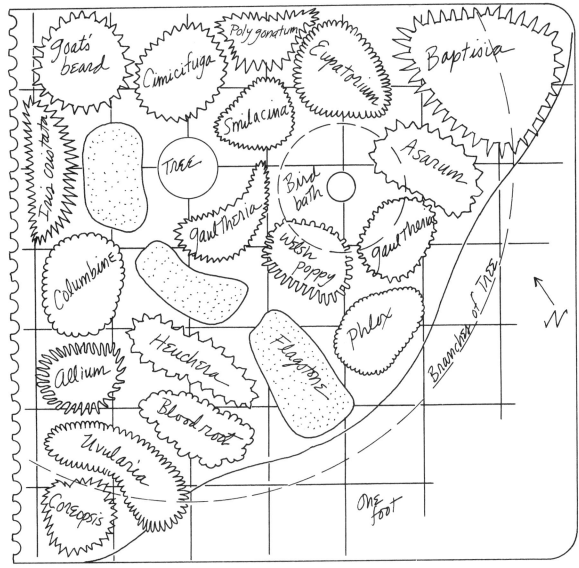

The plan for a wild garden.

American columbines (*Aquilegia canadensis*) are easy to grow compared to many other wildflowers. Given good drainage—the roots revel in rock laden soil—they adapt to most situations. In this garden they are planted towards the outside so they get some afternoon sun. The flowers have spurred petals of red, lined with yellow, and are usually on 1-foot stems. Since the blossoms hang upside down, the garden bees become quite acrobatic in their approach, an entertaining thing to watch. Hummingbirds, too, love this flower. The compound leaves are attractive in their own right and from Zone 6 south, are often evergreen. If the leaves get tracings on their surface, like unintelligible handwriting, it is the work of leaf miners, tiny insects chewing away inside the leaf. Just overlook them.

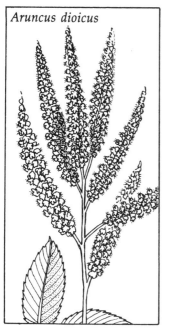

Aruncus dioicus

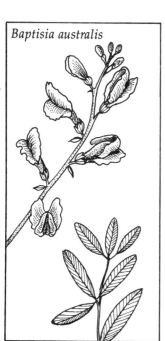

Baptisia australis

The common name is said to be derived from the Latin word *columbinus* or dove, referring either to the bird-like claws or the beak-like spurs of the blossom. Mrs. William Starr Dana in her classic wildflower book, *How to Know the Wildflowers*, writes that one Dr. Prior maintains the name refers to the "resemblance of its nectaries to the heads of pigeons in a ring around a dish, a favorite device of ancient artists." The generic name is believed to be derived from *aquila*, an eagle, referring once again to claw or beak. Frankly, the flower is a gem, as is Columbia. The plants self-seed with ease.

Goat's-beard or wild spirea (*Aruncus dioicus*) will form a large clump of attractive, compound leaves that frame frothy sprays of tiny white flowers on stems that can reach to a height of 6 feet, blooming in summer. Plants are set at the rear of this garden because of ultimate size and a liking for a bit of afternoon sun. The flowers, when dried, are very attractive in winter arrangements. Watch out for Japanese beetles, they love this plant as it belongs to the rose family. Pick them off when they show up or use one of the new scent traps. Propagate by division in spring.

Wild ginger (*Asarum Shuttleworthii*) is a southern plant growing only a few inches high, that produces big, heart-shaped, evergreen leaves with a high surface gloss. It's hardy to Zone 6. If your garden is Zone 5 then buy the European relative, *A. europaeum*. This plant is also an evergreen and grows to about 6 inches. They both make splendid groundcovers. Even in Zone 4, there is a ginger for you. Try *A. canadense*, also called Canada snakeroot. The leaves are taller, to 12 inches, often 6 inches wide, but unfortunately the leaves disappear in winter. Propagate by division in spring.

All three gingers have a strange flower. It resembles a little brown jug—almost like the tiny wax bottles full of sweet syrup we remember from childhood days—that rests on the ground in spring, hidden under the leaves. Why, you ask? What bee would travel there? In spring there are many little bugs, flies, and other tiny insects that live in the litter of the forest floor. They approach the blossom and wander in for shelter, carrying pollen from plant to plant.

Blue false indigo (*Baptisia australis*) was once to be a commercial treasure of early America, providing the blue dye, indigo. Unfortunately, the dye was not as reliable as that derived from the Asian species and the market for it collapsed. As a plant, the light green, oval leaves form a fine seasonal bush with a bonus of blue, pea-like flowers and big, black seed pods that rattle when they shake. Foliage dies down to the ground in late fall but turns black while doing so. It belongs on the outer edge of the wild garden with just a bit of filtered shade. It will take a few years to become established but once it does, one plant will cover several feet. It self-seeds with ease.

The black cohosh or snakeroot (*Cimicifuga racemosa*) blooms in early summer and sends forth 6- to 7-foot tall stems with tiny, star-like flowers. The Latin generic name means bugbane and refers to the somewhat rank odor of the flowers. Flies love them but other bugs shy away. A southern relative, the fairy candle (*C. americana*) bears flowers on 3- to 4-foot stalks, is odorless, but only hardy to the southern part of Zone 5. Both plants are fine perennials in the wild garden and if the summer has plenty of rain, snakeroot will often bloom again. The seed pods are very attractive and persist into late autumn. Propagate by division in spring.

The whorled coreopsis (*Coreopsis verticillata*) likes a bit of sun so it's placed on the outer edge of the garden. The yellow daisies are on 2-foot stems and if you remove spent blossoms, the plant will bloom from summer into fall. Soil need not be as good as for the other wildflowers: This plant will do well in a hot, dry spot. Propagate by seed.

Coreopsis verticillata

White snakeroot (*Eupatorium rugosum*) dwells on the border between woods and field. The clusters of mist-like white flowers appear on the top of 3-foot stalks. The blossoms are a sure sign that autumn is near; they bloom in our area about mid-September. It is the most attractive of the thoroughworts (the *Eupatorium* Tribe). Boneset (*E. perfoliatum*) is almost too clunky in appearance, even for a wild garden—the name refers to the leaf: It completely wraps the stem and in the Doctrine of Signatures would be used to heal a broken bone. Propagate by division in spring.

Creeping wintergreen, checkerberry, partridge-berry, mountain tea, ground tea, and deer, box, or spice berry are all common names for *Gaultheria procumbens*. White, often solitary, bell-shaped flowers nod from 4-inch stems. They turn to bright red berries—not true berries but merely the flower's calyx that turns color and guards 5 seeds within—for the fall. If the birds leave them be, they will persist throughout the winter, brilliant against the snow. The leaves are green and shiny, evergreen, and smell of wintergreen when crushed. They provided both the oil and a tea in days gone by. Wintergreen makes an elegant groundcover and spreads by underground runners. Propagate from seed or by rooting runners.

You will have to grow the next flower from seed; I've never seen it offered as a plant at a dealer, but the various rock garden seed exchanges usually carry it. Any finding is worth the effort. *Heuchera cylindrica* has no common name and is native to southwestern Canada and south to Wyoming. It resembles the common garden coralbells (*H. sanguinea*) but the flowers are tiny, green bells that rank along a 30-inch stem. The leaves are rounded, with smoothly toothed edges and make an excellent ground cover. While they do well in sun, these plants prefer partial shade.

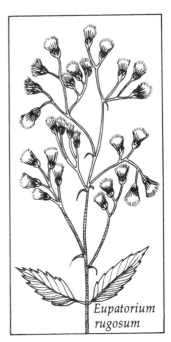

Eupatorium rugosum

The dwarf crested iris (*Iris cristata*) grows naturally from Maryland south to Georgia, and a prettier native it's hard to imagine. The leaves are 6 inches high and the flowers nestle within with lilac-purple petals (called *falls*) topped with gold. Unlike other irises, these plants slowly spread in partial shade and a good woodsy soil. **'Alba'** bears white flowers and is especially pretty in the wild garden. Propagate by division in midsummer.

In the midst of all these American plants I've included one from foreign shores, the Welsh poppy (*Meconopsis cambrica*). It's mentioned in the alpine garden as a relative of the fabled Himalayan poppy (see page 8) but is in truth a common wildflower of England. The four-petaled flowers of June and July are golden yellow and

Sanguinaria canadensis **'Multiplex'**

Uvularia grandiflora

nestle in the shadow of our garden birdbath, glowing in the shade. These plants like cool summers, hence their success in a wildflower glen. But if your summers bring lots of temperatures in the 90s pass this plant by. Propagation is from seed.

The dwarf phlox (*Phlox subulata*) is called ground pink, moss pink, or in our area, mountain pink. In partial shade the plants form mats of evergreen foliage only a few inches high. Then in spring, they are covered with flat, five-petaled flowers of white, pink, rose, or lavender. There are so many blatantly colored cultivars now on the market that it's hard to remember that this plant is an American native. When planting out phlox, try not to mix too many colors together. Instead stick with the white and the pink, for these look best when mixed with other wildflowers. Dwarf phlox need some sun, so are placed at the edge of the garden. Propagate by seeds or division in spring.

The great Solomon's-seal (*Polygonatum commutatum*) is a member of the lily family with a thick rootstock with many joints. Each spring one long stem arises from this root and shoots toward the sky, often 6 feet high. When it dies back in the fall, a round scar is left. An early imaginative naturalist likened this to the seal of King Solomon. While the flower and the red berries are not spectacular, their wand-like appearance is most attractive. Propagate by seeds or division in early spring.

For a white water lily on dry land try the double bloodroot *Sanguinaria canadensis* **'Multiplex'** (and that cultivar name must be one of the worst ever coined, especially for such a beautiful flower). The single bloodroot has large white flowers often 2 inches across, with prominent yellow stamens all on 8-inch stems. The double-flowered form bears 16 petals, lacks stamens, and is stunning. Both bloom in early spring. The leaves last until summer then disappear. Hence an overplanting of an annual is advised. The rootstocks, which bleed red sap if cut, slowly expand to make a colony of plants. Propagate by division of the rootstock after the leaves die back. Allow the cut to air-dry for a day before replanting.

I first met Solomon's-plumes (*Smilacina racemosa*) growing along the stone wall surrounding an old local cemetery. Alternate, strong-looking leaves climb a 30-inch stem, topped with a terminal cluster of tiny white flowers. Sometimes called false Solomon's-seal, this plant is a cousin but the roots bear no scars. Mrs. William Starr Dana notes a singular lack of imagination in naming this plant. "[It] has enough originality to deserve an individual title," she wrote. In the fall, bright red berries appear. It really needs extra water in dry summers. Propagate by seeds or division in spring.

Great merrybells sounds like an expletive from the old radio character, Gildersleeve. *Uvularia grandiflora* is the botanical name and is derived (according to Taylor's *Encyclopedia of Gardening*, second edition) from the Latin for palate, in reference to the hanging flowers. The Royal Horticultural Society maintains that the name is from *uva*, a bunch of grapes, referring to the form of the fruit. One never knows in the world of botany. The flowers are bright yellow and nod at the end of stalks up to 2 feet in height. The leaves are attractive throughout the summer. Merrybells like a neutral soil so in areas of heavy acidity, scratch in a few teaspoons of lime around the plant when you think of it, or mulch it with some marble chips. Propagate by seeds or division in spring or fall.

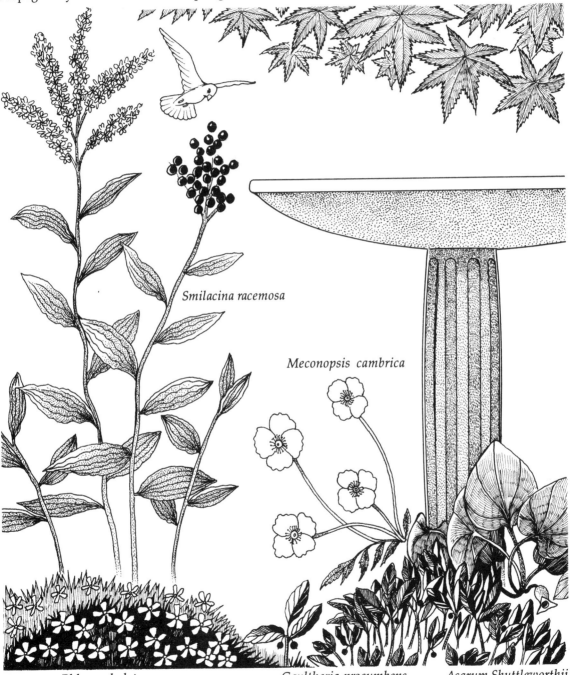

Smilacina racemosa

Meconopsis cambrica

Phlox subulata   *Gaultheria procumbens*   *Asarum Shuttleworthii*

THE MEADOW GARDEN

There are vogues in gardening as with anything else; fashion is not limited to food and clothes, although gardeners like to think they are beyond such short-lived fads. For years the vast majority of people cared not a whit about flower gardens or wildflowers except those few classified as conservationists. Then during the 70s conservation became popular and country weekenders up from the cities discovered both the beauties and physical rewards of gardening. Finally in the 80s, gardening has become a trendy avocation with many people vying with each other over unusual garden styles.

The English meadow garden (itself first discussed in the late 1800s by William Robinson who suggested planting hardy bulbs in meadow grass and naturalizing wildflowers under trees on great lawns) is one such garden fashion. The idea has hit the "arts and leisure" sections of the major newspapers. At the same time "meadows-in-a-can" and "Monet's garden" have been featured by camping and hiking equipment companies, in upscale mail order catalogs. Their colorful ads suggest to readers that vast sweeps of garden color can be theirs with a minimum of work over a short period of time.

Well it's a lot harder to establish such gardens than just opening up a can and sprinkling seeds about as you will discover by reading the small print on the labels. But the effort is worth the work involved when you see how beautiful a well-established meadow garden can be.

And what does a meadow garden look like? You get somewhat of an idea if in early summer under a clear blue sky you drive along a two-lane country road lined on either side with fields, in a county whose highway department does not use defoliants to rid the shoulder of what they love to call weeds. A meadow garden is tall, green grasses swaying in the wind and dotted everywhere with daisies and buttercups, it's bright pink mallows and pastel yellow cinquefoil, and it's butterflies—almost like in a Disney film—flying from flower to flower while shining yellow goldfinches dart from purple thistle to purple thistle.

The meadow was a common sight in rural England until the farmers learned how to get the most out of what was once termed unproductive land, and scarred and plowed the meadows, finally turning over to developers what they didn't destroy. And it's no different in the United States, where the desire to build has spread out from every city and flattened everything in its path, coupling with the mania of state highway departments for removing every roadside weed and flower.

Obviously a meadow garden is not for everyone. It does not belong in a single front yard in a suburban housing development where it will be surrounded by dozens of clipped and perfectly kept lawns. There the meadow would be viewed as a thorn among an acre of roses. But for a vacation home, a secluded backyard, or most any rural setting, such a garden is a joy to have.

Iris cristata

Glechoma hederacea

A Weekend Meadow Garden

We have friends who have a weekend home with a front yard some 30 feet wide and 40 deep. It is bordered on three sides by woods that are mostly made up of conifers mixed with beech and maple trees. When our friend's home was completed 12 years ago they were faced with the following choices: Plant grass on the now-barren ground and then cut lawn every weekend, establish a garden, or let everything alone. Neither of them wanted to get involved with cutting lawns. Since a garden in the wild has no protection from deer and rabbits, and our friends did not want to be surrounded with fencing; they struck a happy medium between the last two suggestions and decided to plant wildflowers. So, although the dirt around the newly built home was raked and leveled, no improvements were made to the soil, because wildflowers as a rule do better on poor soil.

Within the first year the "seeds of a troubled earth" appeared. These are the weeds like burdock (*Arctium minus*), ragweed (*Ambrosia artemisiifolia*), and crabgrass. But Janet and Tom patiently removed them and at the same time left in place the more attractive pasture grasses that blew in from nearby fields, and the ferns and annual wildflowers that moved in from the woods. The only major work they did was to put in a fieldstone path that led from the driveway to the front deck.

Violets of all kinds bloomed the second year, accompanied by daffodils and early iris (*Iris cristata*) that were put in as bulbs the fall before. Visitors included black-eyed Susans (*Rudbeckia hirta*), Queen Anne's lace (*Daucus Carota* var. *Carota*), and Gill-over-the-ground (*Glechoma hederacea*). They shared the yard with clumps of daylilies (*Hemerocallis* spp.), with the common orange daylily coming from an abandoned farm and a few more colorful cultivars purchased from mail-order catalogs. Some wild blue flags (*Iris versicolor*) and Joe Pye weed (*Eupatorium purpureum*) from a nearby streamside went into a shady spot along one border.

As year followed year, more flowers were added to the land along with many wild grasses. A large rock to the right of the path as one approached the house was left in place and became a home to all sorts of wild mosses and lichens (see Janet's Rock on page 166). Today our friends' yard is totally charming and upkeep is confined to cutting the tallest grasses every fall, either with a borrowed sicklebar or a machete.

Planting Wildflower Mixes

If your problem is not starting out from scratch but dealing with an existing field, you must spend some time in preparation. As I mentioned before, you cannot just throw seeds into the grass and expect them to germinate, much less survive. These native grasses can overpower the more delicate wildflowers.

If the grasses are worth saving, but you wish to add more flowers, first cut and rake the field in the fall of the year. In milder climates the seed—of either annuals or perennials—can be sown at

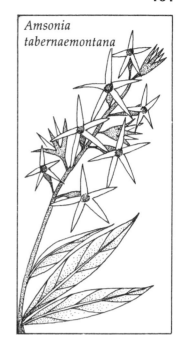

Amsonia tabernaemontana

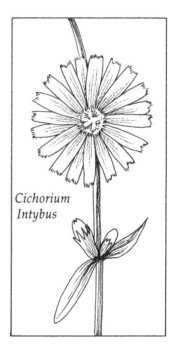

Cichorium Intybus

California poppy

Gentiana Andrewsii

that time. In the colder parts of the country, sow the seed in early spring.

If your intended meadow garden is mostly a motley collection of weeds, then you must plow and harrow, or at least use a professional rototiller. Then the earth must be raked and settled. Most desirable seed will not germinate if left on hard ground.

There are different seed assortments available for different needs: annual wildflowers, perennial wildflowers, desert mixes where sand is the norm, dry land mixes for areas where water is scarce, and mixes specifically for different climates and areas of the country.

When seed is purchased from reliable firms, the packages will tell you how much to use for the area chosen. The Clyde Robin Seed Company, one of the first to offer wildflower seeds, suggests: 5 pounds of seed per acre if the land already has some trees and shrubs; 8 pounds per acre on cleared land; and for truly lush growth, 15 pounds per acre on flat land and up to 20 pounds on steep slopes. They also suggest that an average city lot of 50 by 150 feet needs about 1 1/2 pounds of seed. Remember to mix the seed with sand or finely screened soil in order to spread it more evenly.

You might have to mow your meadow two or three times from spring to late summer during the first year in order to give the wild-flowers a chance against any weedy types that show up. Once established, cutting should be either in midsummer and late fall, or just late fall alone.

Cloud-Cutting

If you are lucky enough to have meadows surrounding your home but tired of mowing the whole works every fall, try the concept of cloud-cutting. It requires thinking in grandiose terms, but it saves a great deal of effort in the long run. Between the front of your meadow and your existing lawn cut the last swath of grass with graceful curves like the edges of clouds. In the fall of the first year cut only the front third of the meadow. The second year cut two-thirds of the meadow. Finally every third year cut the entire meadow.

The result is that the third of the meadow closest to the house changes the most. But the other parts, when allowed to mature, are open to all sorts of different field flowers and grasses from seeds brought by birds or blown in from land nearby. You're never sure just what you might find. And leaving a part of the meadow undisturbed is an invitation to birds and insects that choose to spend the summer near your home. This method of cutting looks especially fine when the meadow is on a gentle hill.

A List of Plants

The following is a very subjective list of wildflowers, shrubs, and grasses that do well in meadow gardens:

Achillea Millefolium, yarrow, 1-3 feet tall, white flowers

Amsonia tabernaemontana, star flower, 1-3 feet, a beautiful sky blue

Anaphalis margaritacea, pearly everlasting, 1-3 feet, everlasting white flowers

Asclepias syriaca, milkweed, 3-5 feet, home to the monarch butterfly

Aster novae-angliae, New England aster, 3-5 feet, many variations in the colors among plants

Baptisia australis, false indigo, 3-5 feet, seedpods called Indian rattles

Briza maxima, quaking grass, an annual, 2-4 feet

Chrysanthemum leucanthemum, oxeye daisy, 1-3 feet, the familiar field daisy

Cichorium Intybus, Chicory, 2-4 feet, flowers light blue, sometimes pink, even white

Daucus Carota var. *Carota*, Queen Anne's lace, 2-4 feet, biennial, white lacy flowers

Dianthus deltoides, Deptford pink, up to 16 inches

Echinacea purpurea, purple coneflower, 2-3 feet

Elymus villosus, wild rye, 3-4 feet

Eschscholzia californica, California poppy, an annual, 10-14 inches, glorious gold color

Eupatorium purpureum, Joe Pye weed, 3-6 feet, light purple, will take damp soil

Fragaria virginiana, wild strawberry, 3-6 inches

Galium boreale, northern bedstraw, white, to 30 inches

Gentiana Andrewsii, bottle gentian, 1-2 feet

Heliopsis helianthoides, oxeye sunflower, 3-5 feet

Helenium autumnale, sneezeweed, 3-5 feet

Hemerocallis fulva, common daylily, 3-5 feet

Hemerocallis cultivars, over 1,000 varieties

Hesperis matronalis, sweet rocket, 1-3 feet

Houstonia caerulea, Quaker ladies, tiny blue flowers, 2-3 inches

Hystrix patula, bottlebrush grass, 4-6 feet

Kalmia angustifolia, sheep laurel, becomes a shrub

Lathyarus latifolius, perennial sweet pea, large rose and white flowers, a vine

Liatris spicata, blazing star, pink flowers, 1-5 feet

Lobelia Cardinalis, cardinal flower, beautiful red, 2-4 feet, likes wet places

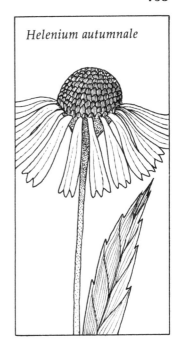

Helenium autumnale

Lobelia Cardinalis

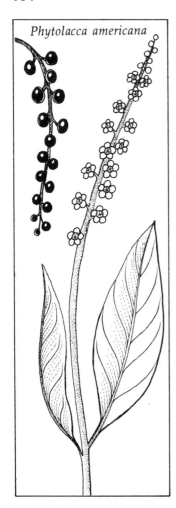

Phytolacca americana

Lobelia siphilitica, blue lobelia, light blue, 1-3 feet, likes wet places

Lotus corniculatus, birdsfoot trefoil, 6-8 inches, usually prostrate

Malva moschata, musk mallow, 1-2 feet

Melilotus albus, sweetclover, biennial, 2-4 feet

Nemophila menziesii, baby blue eyes and a charming annual, 6-12 inches

Oenothera biennis, evening primrose, 1-5 feet

Oenothera fruticosa, sundrops, 1-3 feet

Physostegia virginiana, obedient plant, so called because where flowers are pushed, they stay, 1-4 feet

Phytolacca americana, pokeweed, large with colorful, but poisonous berries, up to 10 feet

Potentilla canadensis, cinquefoil, yellow, creeper

Rosa virginiana, pasture rose, 1-3 feet

Rudbeckia hirta, black-eyed Susan, 1-3 feet

R. hirta **'Gloriosa Daisy'**, and all cultivars

Sambucus canadensis, elderberry, shrub to 8 feet

Sisyrinchium bellum, blue-eyed grass, 10-12 inches

Solidago spp., goldenrods, many species, up to 6 feet

Spiraea tomentosa, hardhack, pink spire, 2-4 feet

Vaccinium corymbosum, highbush blueberry, bush, to 12 feet

Verbascum Blattaria, moth mullein, yellow, 3-6 feet

Vicia americana, purple vetch, 2-3 feet, climbs up grasses

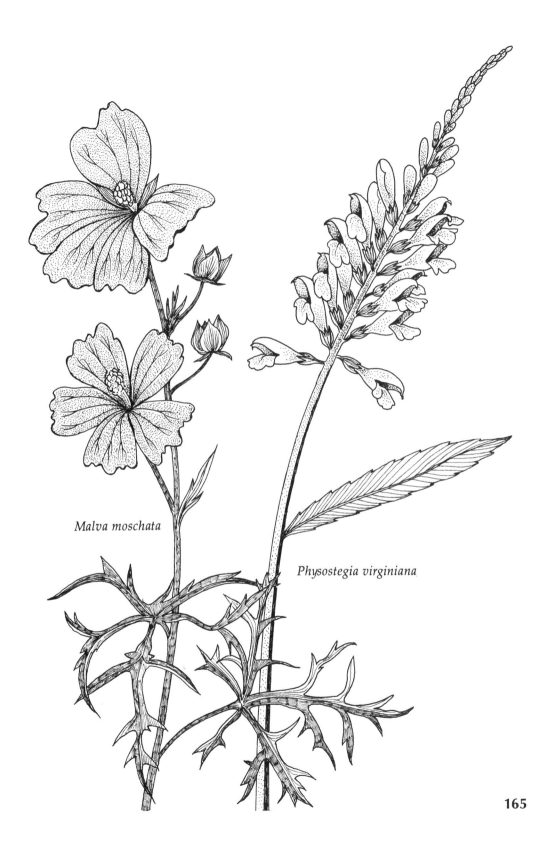

Malva moschata

Physostegia virginiana

Bartramia pomiformis

JANET'S ROCK

There is a rock in Janet's meadow garden that was brought there by the last glacier as it retreated through the Catskill Mountains 10,000 years ago. The rock is 8 feet long, close to 8 feet wide on the right side (facing west) and tapers to a 2-foot width on the left side. The top of the rock is 2 feet above the level of the yard. This rock is like an iceberg: Judging from the slope, only 10 percent is above ground. When Janet and Tom built their vacation home, the man who ran the earth-moving equipment said if they could live with the rock, they should; only blasting would make an impact on it and that was uncertain.

They decided to live with the rock and turn it into a moss, lichen, and whatever-else-happened-to-show-up garden. Last weekend on an August afternoon under a misty sky with a light, drizzling rain—the first rain we've had in weeks—Janet and I took inventory of the rock. Except for a few choice clumps of lichens and mosses brought back from nature walks to other parts of the property, everything growing on the rock has started on its own.

The rock is shaded from the direct morning sun by the house. By noon it is in the open shade of a very old beech tree that grows beside a fieldstone wall at the edge of the yard, and in late afternoon, sunlight is filtered through tall pine trees growing on the other side of the driveway. Until the trees leaf out in late spring and again in midsummer when the sun is high, the rock gets some direct sun.

The rock itself is surrounded by old daffodils (descendant bulbs of 50-year-old plants that came from Janet's home in Indiana), some wild iris (*Iris versicolor*), white crocus (also old and brought from Indiana), a large clump of lady fern (*Athyrium Filix-femina*), a trailing variety of the bouncing Betty (*Saponaria ocymoides*), and various wild grasses of short stature.

Almost at the rock's center and highest point, a 6-year-old white pine seedling (*Pinus strobus*) stretches 10 inches in the air. The roots are lost in a large clump of reindeer moss for there is as yet no soil on the rock. The little white pine has dwarfed naturally, each year's candles (new shoots) not any larger than an inch.

But the largest number of plants upon the rock are the mosses, small green plants that usually prefer shade, and lichens, strange plants that are a combination of green algae and colorless fungi.

Houstonia caerulea

Mosses and Lichens

Mosses need shade because they have poorly developed water distribution systems and the hot sun can dry them out before water can reach thirsty cells. Hair-cap moss will grow in open fields, but there grass provides some protection, and the dews of morning furnish needed water. Because mosses are subject to rapid loss of moisture, they "fold-up" their leaves when dry, markedly changing their appearance. But when water once again reaches the plant, individual cells quickly swell and the mosses revert to normal size. Mosses reproduce by releasing eggs and sperm that form seedlike spores.

Lichens are really algae and fungi living together in a partnership called *symbiosis:* The fungi provides a house for the algae which, in turn, provides food like any other green plant, with its ability to make nutrients from sun and air. Lichens provide food for small insects and large mammals. In the Arctic, reindeer moss (really a lichen) is the principal diet of caribou during harsh winters; in our own Northeast, deer often survive by feeding on tree lichens when no other food is available. Interestingly, lichens will not exist where the air is not pure. They are intolerant of sulfur dioxide and other impurities of city air. A few are found in the suburbs but most lichens prefer the rural life.

Lichens generally reproduce by asexual means, simply forming new plants from broken pieces of the old. They also produce fruiting bodies in many colors on top of their tiny branches, that in turn produce spores. But no one has ever successfully grown new lichens by germinating these spores. The action of sexual reproduction for lichens is complicated because botanists know that the fungal spore must find a compatible alga to join it before a lichen is formed, but have no idea how this is achieved in nature.

Both lichens and mosses can exist on bare rock. By chemical means they produce food. By mechanical means they can remove tiny pieces of hard rock, threading their *rhizoids,* or tiny roots into microscopic pores in the rock's surface, gaining trace elements for nutrition and slowly, over eons, making soil. Even airborne dust from mountain roads and shoulders is trapped by the tiny projections of the lichens and the leaves of the mosses, eventually to combine with old crumpled and dehydrated plants to form new accumulations of dirt. Given enough time, the little white pine will someday find soil on the top of Janet's rock.

An Inventory of the Rock

Upon the rock itself and in its crevices and crannies are nine different species of moss and eleven species of lichen; one sedge (unidentified, as it's never flowered); a bit of ground ivy (*Glecoma hederacea*); some partridge berry (*Mitchella repens*); two tiny meadow puffballs (*Lycoperdon pratense*); five tiny mushrooms, known as the little wheel Marasmius (*Marasmius rotula*), each having 1 1/2- inch wide caps on thin 2-inch stems; and three baby crickets, a few ants, one small, brown toad, and two efts (the immature, land-locked form of the common salamander).

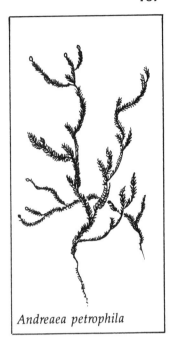

Andreaea petrophila

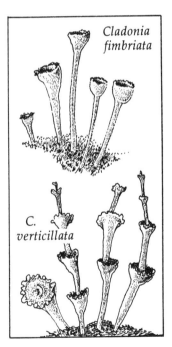

Cladonia fimbriata

C. verticillata

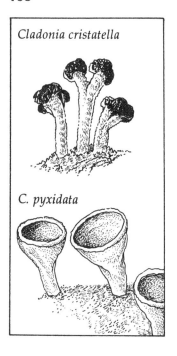

Cladonia cristatella

C. pyxidata

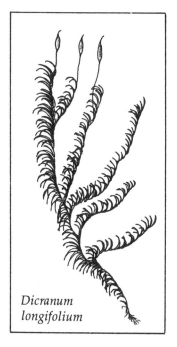

Dicranum longifolium

Using a few snippets of the mosses, previous knowledge of the lichens, plus three nature field guides, we identified the following mosses and lichens growing on Janet's rock.

The ostrich-plume feather moss (*Hypnum Crista-castrensis*) looks like a miniature example of its namesake. The term *hypnum* is Greek and supposes that these mosses were once helpful in bringing sleep.

The tiny cedar moss (*Thuidium delicatulum*) received its common name because of its close resemblance to a cedar tree in miniature. The cedar moss was well known to Linnaeus, the great Swedish botanist who worked out the Latin system of naming plants, who called it *delicatulum* in recognition of its dainty aspects.

Apple moss (*Bartramia pomiformis*) gets its name because the plant's tiny spore cases are found like apples. These cases resemble miniature salt shakers and release seedlike spores to the wind. Usually found growing in rock clefts, it was named after John Bartram (1699–1777), an early American botanist from Pennsylvania.

The fork moss (*Dicranum longifolium*) is named after the unusual formation of the teeth on its spore case and is among 65 species of *Dicranum* in North America. Male Indians called the fork moss "woman's heads" because when trampled underfoot they spring right up again, a not-so-subtle reference to the indomitable spirit of woman.

Pincushion moss (*Leucobryum longifolium*) look like pincushions. *Leucobryum* is Greek for white moss, referring to their usual pallid green color when compared to the other mosses.

The stone-loving andreaea (*Andreaea petrophila*) has a habit of growing on rocks in damp places. The plant is named for the German botanist, G. R. Andreae.

Hair-cap moss (*Polytrichum commune*) have been known and watched since ancient Greece. Pliny called them "golden maiden-hair" because of the golden gloss they exhibit when dry. They were once dedicated to Venus and then to the Virgin Mary and were the first plants to be recognized by early botanists as not having true flowers.

The glittering feather moss (*Hypnum* [*Pleurozium*] *splendens*) is a beautiful combination of gold, and green leaves on red stems.

And the last moss on Janet's rock has the most romantic common name of all: the triangular wood-reveller (*Hylocomnium triquetrum*). This particular moss grows only on wood with a luxuriant delight that led to the term, reveller. It was collected in a nearby wood and placed on the rock in a crevice that holds its wooden base. Triangular refers to the shape of the stems.

Lichens are not as soft and comfortable looking as the mosses, but make up for it in fanciful shapes and subtle colors.

British soldiers (*Cladonia cristatella*) are named after the redcoats of the Revolutionary War. After a rain, their red tips (really another type of spore case) glow in the sunlight and, though only an inch tall, can be seen for yards. *Cladonia* refers to the branchlike pattern of growth that this genus shows.

The goblet lichens (*C. pyxidata*) look like tiny cups made to hold beer or wine for elves.

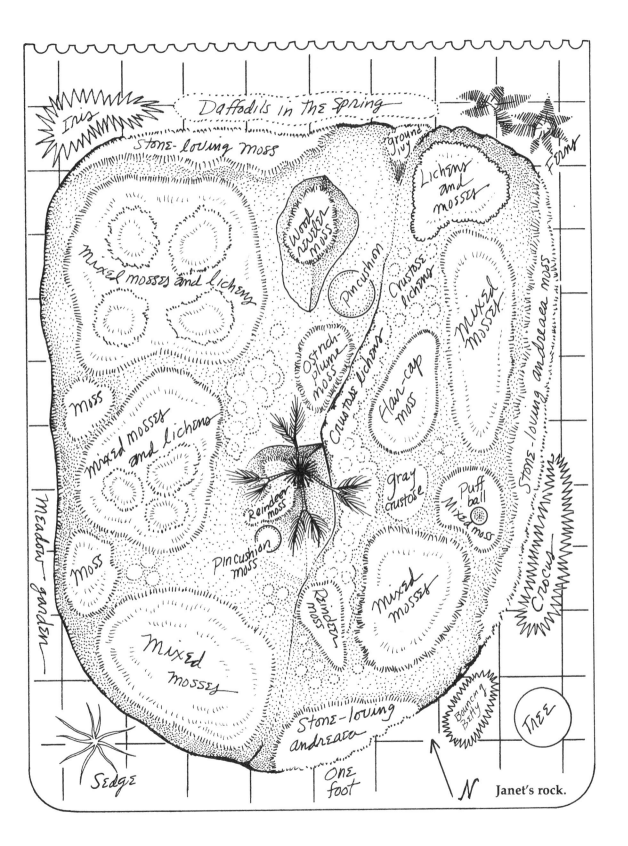

Janet's rock.

The reindeer mosses (*C. rangiferina*) grow into a tangle of inter-locking threads. There are two kinds on Janet's rock, the second of which is smaller and more tightly packed, and known as *C. rangiferina* var. *alpestris*.

Fringed cladonia (*C. fimbriata*) grows into tiny structures tipped with fringe.

And *C. verticillata*, has no common name, but the species name refers to little branches on the top of the plant that are arranged like spokes on a wheel.

Pink earth lichens (*Baeomyces roseus*) sport spore cases of a soft orange-pink.

Finally the rock is home to four so-called crustose lichens. Since

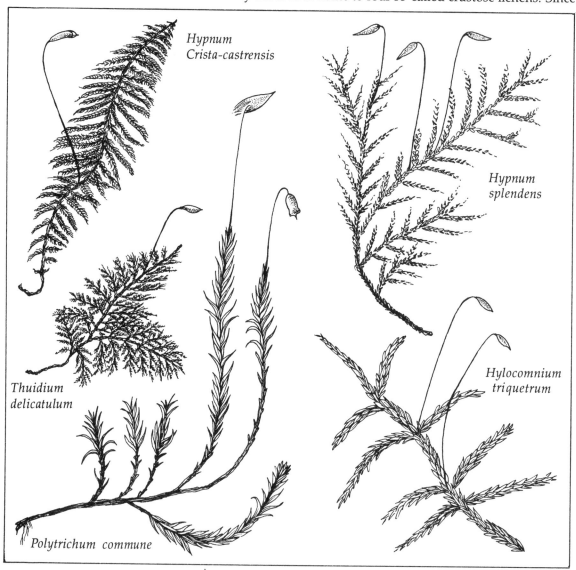

Hypnum Crista-castrensis

Hypnum splendens

Thuidium delicatulum

Hylocomnium triquetrum

Polytrichum commune

they are so flat and stick so closely to the rock's surface, they seem to be actually parts of the rock itself.

Physicia stellaris forms light gray rosettes dotted with tiny black spore cases.

Rhizocarpon concentricum consists of flat concentric circles of small bumps.

Lecidea speirea also grows in circles, and *Parmelia caperata* makes small round shields.

Janet's rock is not for everyone. It necessitates a delight in the small, a shunning of bravado, not to mention a rural location. But it fits the definition of a true wild garden and all that that term can mean.

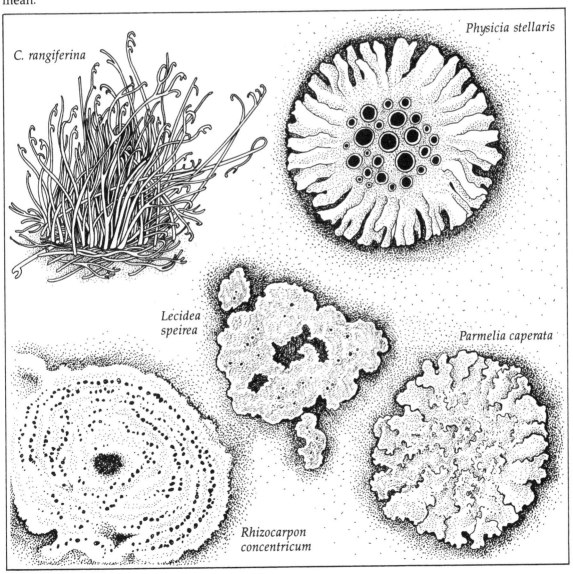

THE WINTER GARDEN

Oh, every year hath its winter,
And every year hath its rain —
But a day is always coming
When the birds go north again.

Ella Higginson, *When the Birds Go North Again*

One night last January the wind whipped through here at about 30 miles per hour, accompanied by a temperature of −25°F.—that's below 0° and so cold that windchill factors become lilygilding— under one of those clear skies that look like dimensional backgrounds for a space movie like "Star Wars." About 3:30 in the morning I got up to check the greenhouse heater and add a few logs to the woodburning stove in the living room. Even in our well-insulated house I felt the cold air scuttling along the floor and saw frost forming along the edges of the insulated glass in the kitchen windows: The house mice were not abroad this night.

The next morning saw a brilliant sun reflected in every icicle and by midday the thermometer on the shady side of the house registered 38°F.—and the groundhog wasn't due to emerge for another two weeks. Such is the weather in the Northeast.

After lunch we decided to take a walk around the pond, fill all the birdfeeders, and gather some kindling in back of the vegetable garden (where the compost heaps showed evidence of much wildlife dining). On the way we passed through the back garden and perennial border.

There, the birdbath was dolloped with whipped snow and stood next to the well-wrapped wisteria tree (without such a winter coat it would never survive, much less flower) the two of them looking like World's Fair trademarks from 1939. The seedheads of a small astilbe (*Astilbe chinensis*) were line etchings on superwhite paper, and the clumps of ornamental grasses were tangled masses of bronzed leaves complementing the severity of the red-twigged dogwood nearby. But the most complex pattern of all was formed by the Harry Lauder walking stick (*Corylus Avellana* '**Contorta**'), as each of its branches

On the opposite page, a nuthatch (the only bird that truly walks upside down), clings to the vines of the bittersweet bush while a yucca stands green against the snow.

173

Bergenias

ended in a curlicue of tan, tiny slinkies tipped with seedpods from the fall before.

Farther down the snowy garden path a clump of sedums were pincushions of mahogany and each of the dwarf conifers that edge the bank above showed myriad shades of green, subtly pastelled by their coat of snow. The fountain cotoneaster that flows from between a step of flagstones still bore a crop of scarlet berries and to the right, the weeping birch was an umbrella of countless ribs with two friendly chickadees precariously perched on the farthest side picking at the hanging seedpods.

On the way to the pond we walked through the copse behind the vegetable garden and saw the green, leathery blades of the Christmas fern poking up through the cover of snow. Though some individual leaflets were somewhat tattered and torn, they were still green.

Finally, just before the frozen edge of the pond and behind the lichen-covered fieldstone wall that divides that area from the swamp behind, we saw the thicket of winterberry, each of the many branches covered with hundreds of brilliant orange-red berries.

The pond was truly frozen, its snowcover stitched with the hoofprints of the local deer who come every day to an area just above its right margin for a ration of grain. Since fences never seem to work and deer repellents are useless, we've found the best way to protect the garden proper from their endless foraging is to provide them with food.

By midafternoon the temperature began to fall and the sky quickly darkened. An ominous orange stripe of weakened light appeared just above the horizon in the west and snow began to fall, big flakes first then small. "Little snow, big snow" is the saying here in the Catskills and by early evening we knew it to be true.

Had we world enough and time I could actually see planting a garden especially for winter. As things stand now it's an impractical suggestion. Yet with a bit of planning any projected or existing garden can include a number of plants that are especially beautiful when looked at with a winter's eye. And if you are lucky enough to reside south of Zone 6 or if you have a small area that is well-protected farther north, even a few winter flowers are within your grasp.

Plants for the Winter Garden

On the wall over my desk is a map of the United States published by the U.S. Department of Agriculture. The map shows in living color the ten climate zones that ribbon across our country. Zone 5 (where minimum winter temperatures average −20° to −10°F.) is colored green and extends from Newfoundland, through most of New England and New York, splits Pennsylvania, Ohio, Illinois, takes a third of Missouri, half of Kansas and New Mexico, one quarter of Arizona, then blots out most of Nevada, a smidgen of California, half of Oregon and a third of Washington, before shooting back up to Canada. North of Zone 5 (except for a few areas around large bodies of water) is a gigantic area that includes four more colder zones. Only 14 states on the continent are without that tint of green—even Texas has a telltale dot of that color in the upper northwest corner.

The majority of plants usually suggested for the winter garden are happy only when temperatures stay above 0°F. I have chosen hardier plants so my plan for a winter garden is for the majority of readers. Like the autumn garden, it is not a specific spot of ground. Rather it consists of small trees, shrubs, and a few plants to be spread about the garden, bringing welcome color to the snow and ice.

Bergenias (*Bergenia cordifolia*) are plants from Siberia and Mongolia. As such they are perfectly happy in temperatures of −30°F, but when exposed to winds at this point, leaves will turn brown and burn at the edges. Plants are evergreen above 0°F. and turn a reddish bronze when colder. They prefer partial shade in the summer and a soil that is well-drained but moist with humus or leaf mold. In such a spot it is an excellent groundcover. Space plants 12 inches apart. As a bonus, they flower with rose-pink, waxy blossoms in spring.

The weeping birch (*Betula pendula* **'Tristis'**) has been in our backyard garden for about six years. The white-barked trunk is 6 feet high then splays out with branches that now cover a circle with a 12-foot diameter. In the summer it is a cool, green haven on a hot day; in fall a shower of golden leaves; but in winter when the branches sparkle after an ice storm or are lightly frosted with snow, it is a sight beautiful to see.

Heathers (*Calluna vulgaris*) are hardy in our garden when planted out of the worst of the winter winds and given a well-drained but acid soil. I've dotted the bank that faces southeast and rises above the scree bed with a number of these small shrubs from England and Europe. There they form 1-foot-high mounds of evergreen needle-like foliage with different colors according to their cultivar. *C. vulgaris* **'Blazeaway'** is a golden-yellow mound about 18 inches high, turning to orange in winter, while **'Golden-Carpet'** changes to reddish orange in winter. They usually blossom in the fall but *C. vulgaris* **'H.E. Beale'** produces pink flowers in November.

The heaths (*Erica carnea*) require the same general conditions as the heathers do and if so rewarded will actually flower on the milder days of winter and on into early spring. Their leaves are more needle-like than heathers. *E. carnea* **'King George'** grows about 12 inches high and blooms from January to May with crimson flowers. **'Pink Spangles'** is about 10 inches high and produces pink flowers from mid-February to April. **'Winter Beauty'** is perhaps the best; it will begin to produce pink flowers, covering an 8-inch mound of leaves, in late December and intermittently on to early April. Naturally, if covered with many feet of snow, these plants will not perform on schedule but will make up for lost time later in the season.

The Siberian dogwood (*Cornus alba* **'Sibirica'**) is a shrub hardy in Zone 3 and especially valuable for the 6- to 7-foot brilliant red stems. Plants like a moist soil in sun or partial shade. The 4-inch-long oval leaves are dark green above, paler beneath with clusters of tiny white flowers in the spring. To walk out to the garden on a winter's day and see the colored stems against the snow is a treat for cabin-

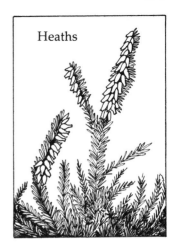
Heaths

Heathers

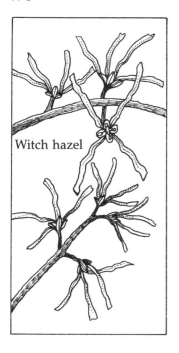

Witch hazel

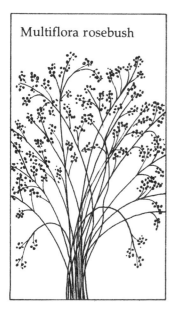

Multiflora rosebush

fevered eyes. There is a yellow-branched form, *C. sericea* **'Flaviramea'**, but it is difficult, if not impossible to find in the United States.

Harry Lauder's walking stick (*Corylus avellana* **'Contorta'**) is named for the Scottish baritone who sang *Roamin' in the Gloamin'* and brandished the contorted namesake of the bush. This is a cultivar of the European filbert and an absolute must as a highlight to the winter garden. The 'stick' will eventually grow up to 8 feet high, and every stem and branch is twisted like a corkscrew. Hardy in Zone 4, even the early spring flowers or catkins are off-center. Plants like full sun but will grow in partial shade as well. The leaves are large, up to 4 inches across and relished by Japanese beetles.

The compact form of this euonymus, the burning bush, is popular in the autumn garden, but the winged euonymus (*Eunonymus alata*) holds its scarlet leaves for later in the season. Then, as leaves fall to the ground, bright orange berries show up against the unusual bark, a bark that looks as though someone came through the garden and pasted rectangular sections of cork along the round green stems of the bush. When dusted with snow it becomes especially attractive. The bush is hardy in Zone 3 and will grow to a height of 8 or 9 feet in any good soil with full sun or partial shade.

Blue fescue (*Festuca ovina* var. *glauca*) is a useful ornamental that forms 10-inch-high mounds of steely blue rounded blades of grass. Not particular as to soil, this fescue gives the best color when that soil is poor. Like most ornamental grasses, it grows in individual clumps and is not invasive. Full sun is best, but partial shade is accepted. The plant is hardy in Zone 3.

There are vast thickets of witch hazel (*Hamamelis virginiana*) in the woods of our Catskill Mountains. Local journeymen would boil the astringent bark and leaves to distill a tonic used either medicinally or as skin toner. In late autumn and early winter, 4-petaled yellow flowers appear along the branches.

Luckily there are other more graceful types available. *H. × intermedia* is a hybrid between the Japanese and Chinese witch hazel, forming a tree up to 25 feet tall. It has produced two cultivars: **'Diana'**, with flowers of copper-red opening on mild days in February in the South and later on in March up North; and **'Arnold Promise'**, with yellow flowers opening in February around New York City and a bit later farther upstate. *H. vernalis* is smaller, reaching only to 6 feet. It blossoms with warm weather in late January or in early to mid-February. All three like moist soil in full sun or partial shade.

Winterberries (*Ilex verticillata*) are small trees or shrubs between 5 and 10 feet tall. They have smooth, dull gray bark and are fond of damp or swampy sites. Most of the year they go unnoticed. The flowers are very small and hidden by the leaves. Then in late autumn, when all the leaves are gone, the beautiful, brilliant orange-red berries are seen. They dot the winter landscape until the local bird population starts collecting. They are hardy to Zone 3 and will do well in any type of acid soil. If you are cutting branches for a winter bouquet, be sure and keep them in water or the berries will shrivel and fall off.

Weeping birch

Harry Lauder's
walking stick

Siberian
dogwood

177

The Bar Harbor juniper (*Juniper horizontalis* **'Bar Harbor'**) and the gray owl juniper (*J. virginiana* **'Grey Owl'**) will grow in partial shade but do best in full sun and like dry, well-drained soil that is slightly alkaline. Both can be pruned in either spring or fall if they are spreading out of control. They make excellent groundcovers.

'Bar Harbor' forms a low-growing mat up to 10 feet wide and is at its best when pouring over the edge of a stone wall. The yearly growth is 15 inches. The branches are gray-green during the growing season but turn a beautiful mauve-purple in the winter.

'Grey Owl' grows about 3 feet high and spreads to 8 feet. The branches are light and airy and maintain a beautiful shade of gray-green.

Russian cypress (*Microbiota decussata*) is native to the Valley of the Suchan, near Vladivostock in eastern Siberia, and that's not a bad pedigree for a plant to survive in the northern United States and in Canada. Russian cypress is hardy to −50°F. The branches are flat-topped and hug the ground. Leaves turn a reddish bronze in winter. This plant resents hot and humid summers.

The white willow is hardy to Zone 2 but is usually not thought to be a fit subject of a reasonably sized winter garden. Although the twigs are used for wicker in furniture and basketry and could keep idle hands busy during long winter nights, it is the variety *vitellina* that is especially decorative. Willows start the garden year at the end of winter, and this type colors the young branches a bright yellow-

Bar Harbor juniper

orange. To keep the tree in scale and force it to produce new branches with the best coloring, it should be coppiced by cutting all the main growth to within a few inches of the base, then mulching the plant well. By fall the shoots will lose their leaves and give you the colored stems throughout the winter. Then in spring, prune it again. If you have the room, you could pollard the tree by allowing a single stem to grow to the required height, say 5 feet, then prune back the stems the same way as before.

Looking out of my studio window I see barren ash trees; the leafless Manchurian apricot; the Persian lilac, all brown branches and twigs. Then beyond, the tan and lifeless fields. Yet there is one spot of true color: fans of sharply pointed leaves, dark green and strong, bringing the look of the Arizona desert to the Catskills. These plants are the yuccas (*Yucca filamentosa*), the hardiest of the species and able to endure even the cold of Zone 4.

In the middle of the summer a strong flower stem appears (see the Night Garden, page 91) but it is the stern quality of the leaves that make the plants so welcome in winter.

Yuccas like well-drained, sandy soil in addition to a lot of sun. They are, after all, plants of the desert. Once in the ground they should be left alone as they form a taproot that digs deep into the earth. Plants reach about 3 feet in height, forming a clump. The variegated yucca *Y. filamentosa* **'Bright Edge'** is especially beautiful in the winter garden.

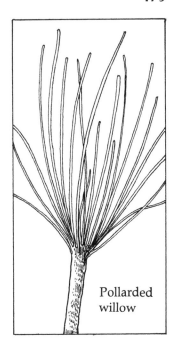

Pollarded willow

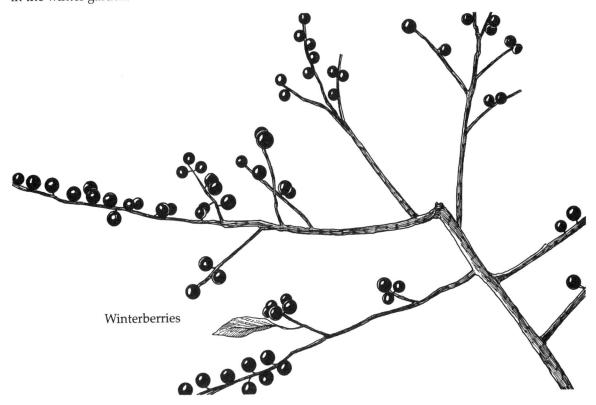

Winterberries

BIRDS IN THE WINTER GARDEN

We have a prefabricated English arbor in our front yard. It straddles the concrete landing before the steps that descend to the driveway at the bottom of a 6-foot bank. The bank is covered with old-fashioned daylilies. The steps were installed 55 years ago when the former owners attempted to establish a degree of gentility in the wilds of the Catskills. The arbor was added by us last year.

To the right and the left of the arbor are American bittersweet (*Celastrus scandens*), and I've trained some of their branches to wind about the plastic and metal hoops. They have, in fact, wound so much and so tightly, that if the arbor breaks up in pieces, its shape will remain in the branches. Bittersweet is classified as a weed by many gardeners and there is good reason: They send out curling tentacles in all directions and if given half an opportunity, they would probably engulf the house. But I simply cut them back and continue to wind a few strays about the arbor top. The resulting growth is now 18 feet long and 4 to 8 feet wide: In summer a marvelous hummock of leaves, rising slowly to engulf the arbor, in winter an abstract jumble of dark brown lines.

To the right of the bittersweet is a Persian lilac. The original base of the trunk is still there, very old and gnarled, but the great bulk of this large bush is made of maturing suckers that themselves are now 15 years old.

We don't spend much time in this area during the summer because the back gardens, the pond, and the nearby woods take all our attention.

Except for the robins who claim the front and backyard as home territory, the cat birds who meow in the garden proper most of the day, the hummingbirds who claim the flowers (and they do rest after a meal, quietly sitting on the tip of a daylily leaf to survey the scene), and the house wrens who claim everything, most of the summer birdlife is in the fields and meadows that stretch to the woods. Part of this decline in birds closeby is the result of the garden cat's wanderings as she guards against rabbits. But the above-mentioned birds are not bothered by her attentions and continue to go about their garden business. They appear to be too catwise for serious worry.

As twilight falls a veery will give its tin-whistle call from the trees that edge the meadow and the swallows give way to the brown bats who sail through the night eating midges. Yet often we take no notice of the birds for they must share our attention with animals, insects, plants, vegetables, trees, people, and the weather.

But when winter arrives and cold concentrates the mind, we hang three bird feeders in the lilac and spend the snowy months happily watching the birds from our library window. All three feeders contain sunflowers—our small mountain birds will eat nothing else but that and suet.

And the birds in winter are legion. We have blue jays, cardinals, chickadees, evening grosbeaks, mourning doves, nuthatches, purple finches, slate-colored juncos, fox sparrows, and titmice. An occa-

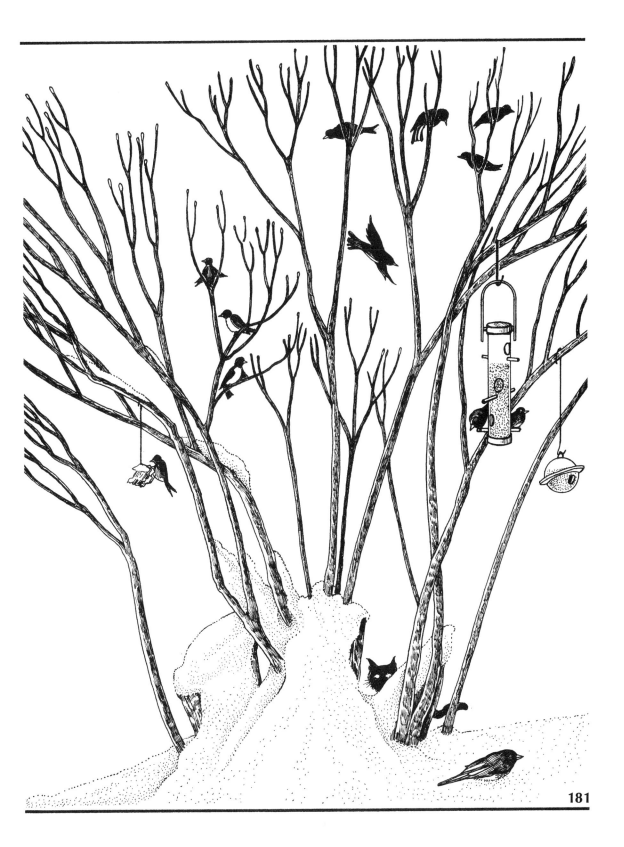

sional interloper might appear on the way south, but these birds make up the bulk of the neighborhood.

The small birds have discovered the tortured and twisted bittersweet vines. Here under the protection of a viny screen, they are safe and secure. Although the garden cat is still about, in winter she is much too visible against the snow and that coupled with warning cries and the security of the tightly meshed bittersweet branches, allows all the birds to fly in to the bittersweet with a beak full of sunflower seed and settle down for breakfast. Chickadees sit along the topmost branches like notes on a music staff, lacking only a notation of time before a tune could be played. The juncos and fox sparrows do a Michael Jackson shuffle on the snow beneath, picking up fallen seeds while the nuthatches walk upside down using the vine as a spiraling road to nowhere.

At night when temperatures fall and a chill wind blows, the bittersweet vines become an even more important shelter. Many a bird has spent the night beneath those twisted boughs.

The vines bear their orange and yellow-bright berries in the fall, their warm colors echoed in the flaming red hips of a huge multiflora rosebush 10 feet distant.

Chickadees spend some time in the back garden searching the umbrella birch for leftover seeds and the juncos will strut about for a while, but the majority of the birds now identify with that bittersweet.

Below the rosebush, the bittersweet, and the daylily bank that slopes to the old driveway, fields begin. In addition to feeding the birds, we give the local deer cracked corn after the snow and ice storms freeze up their browse. This is necessary because they would completely ravage the garden of all visible plants including dwarf conifers. State conservation departments say deer should not be fed or they will become spoiled and never return to the wild. This, of course, is bureaucratic nonsense spun by people who never leave a desk to take a walk in the woods. When our fields green up in spring, the deer change their dining habits and proceed to eat grass, leaves, and tender branches (local vegetable gardens too, if allowed) until the next winter starts.

After the deer—usually we see about 12 of them—finish eating a light breakfast on a winter morning, the mourning doves fly down for a kernel or two, only to be followed by the vociferous blue jays who make beelines for the corn, ruling the roost so to speak until the crows arrive from the nearby woods.

Such a hustle and a bustle there is around our place in the winter! It does not do away with the discomforts of snow and ice but it goes a long way towards making the whole process more palatable.

A WINTER GARDEN OF GRASSES

Part of our garden sits upon a ledge of rock with about 6 inches of topsoil. The rock runs down two miles towards the Delaware River, descends 800 feet, then rises again to merge with the strata that form the Pocono Mountains. And starting about the end of July, gardeners in this region begin to feel the first hints of the coming cold air of winter: Early in the evening the chill slowly flows down from the mountain tops to settle eventually at the bottom of the hill.

If you live all year 'round in such a climate, it's not too long before the thought of the garden in winter rises to the top of your gardener's consciousness. You quickly become aware of your limitations. Soon comes the knowledge that your climate will not support Christmas roses (*Helleborus niger*) blooming in January, winter-flowering camellias (*Camellia japonica*), or clumps of winter daphne (*Daphne odora*) scenting the frigid January air.

In addition to the temperature problems of a Zone 4 to 5 climate (−30 to −20°F.), even the protection afforded by snowcover cannot be counted upon. In our area we never get a guaranteed snow fall: In one out of five years, the snow accumulations total less than 1 inch. Instead we get endless coverings of sleet and downpours of rain. In these years, what the wandering and hungry deer do not polish off, winter burn from the harsh and drying winds does.

Luckily there is a group of plants that offers hope for all seasons: the ornamental grasses. These plants are unlike the grasses used for lawns or cattle fodder, which spread roots in all directions. Instead, the ornamental grasses grow in self-contained clumps. Their leaves and some of their flowering spikes persist well into winter and often 'till early spring—unless literally beat into the ground by a blizzard equal to the famous storm of '88, when snow buried New York City.

In winter the colors of these grasses are never blatant or bold. Tone here is mellow: Shades of brown or buff mingle with warm,

Fountain grass

M. sinensis
'Zebrinus'

burnished yellow ochers highlighted with the worn silver white of the seed plumes that wave above, welcome and beautiful against the snows, glowing when held within a sheath of ice.

The various cultivars of the eulalia grasses (*Miscanthus* spp.) grow over 7 feet in one summer season, on the average, and usually show their plumes as fall approaches. When the days grow shorter and colder, growth stops. Then with the first killing frost the leaves turn a rich golden yellow or light brown.

The dying leaf blades are borne on sturdy stems: Maiden grass (*M. sinensis* **'Gracillimus'**) arches in a graceful manner; striped eulalia (*M. sinensis* **'Variegatus'**) and zebra grass (*M. sinensis* **'Zebrinus'**) are straighter in silhouette; and eulalia stands like a sentinel against the winter skyline. Even after the seed plumes begin to shatter, there is still enough structure to hold visual interest.

The clumps slowly increase in size over the years and usually look their best at the back of a border or in specimen plantings in an open lawn. Old stems are cut back in the early spring so there is room for the new growth. If it looks like the grass is becoming too large in scale for the area, I break up the clump with an ax, and give the surplus sections to other gardeners.

Fountain grass (*Pennisetum alopecuroides*) and purple moor grass (*Molina caerulea* **'Variegata'**) both bring to mind the lilting waters of a garden sprinkler, the first being of a browner shade, the other truly golden. They are best planted in groups and are striking when the leaves are covered with a light sprinkling of snow. They, too, grow slowly and should not be divided until they have gotten completely out of hand.

Feather reed grass (*Calamagrostis acutiflora* var. *stricta*) has thinner leaf blades than the other grasses. They stand straight into the air rather than curving and when broken by the wind or rain, the stems come to rest in odd angles against the remaining clump. Then the

Poverty grass

falling snows settle along their length making sculptural shapes that could grace a Madison Avenue Gallery.

We have a rather steep bank that rises up behind our garden. I've mentioned before that it is of poor soil, with a large percentage of small rocks and red shale. We've tried many things over the years to at least give it the flavor of belonging to civilization. We finally solved the problem by planting staggered rows of little bluestem grass (*Schizachyrium scoparium*). This grass also grows in a fountain-like fashion, though smaller in scale, and in late summer its small, white, seed plumes rise on reddish stems. Most of the year it's just there, but when the winter winds blow, the leaves turn a rich reddish brown, and literally glow when seen against a drift of falling snow.

At the base of the bank the lichens and mosses grow, for winter has no effect on them, and curling about the grays, greens, and browns is a colony of poverty grass (*Danthonia spicata*). By summer the 6-inch leaves of poverty grass are nondescript but by November, the leaves curl even tighter than usual, looking more like wood shavings left by a tiny carpenter than any grass. Heavy snows may come and bury these plants, but with every thaw their elfin beauty returns.

Back in the perennial border we planted a group of sedums (*Sedum Telephium* **'Autumn Joy'**) in front of a clump of cord grass (*Spartina pectinata* **'Aureo-Marginata'**). In winter the sedums turn a rich mahogany brown, each bunch of blossoms becoming a glowing pincushion set off by the curving golden tan leaves of the grass.

Next to the birdbath, sits a clump of northern sea oats (*Chasmanthium latifolium*) that turns golden brown in the winter's sun, and

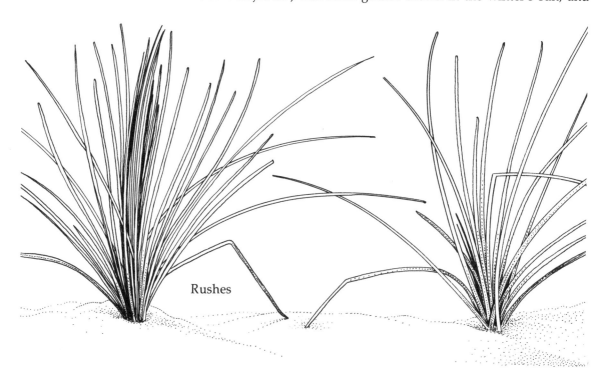

Rushes

sports its oat-like seed heads, that by December will each have a frosting of ice. In front sits one Japanese sedge grass (*Carex Morrowii* var. *expallida*)—truly a sedge, not a grass. Unless the winter is truly bad, the sedge grass will remain evergreen until new leaves arise the next spring. It's only 12 inches tall, with graceful arching stems of a dark, shiny green edged with creamy white.

Finally, a group of three common rushes (*Juncus effusus*) stand guard next to a row of Bar Harbor junipers (*Juniperus horizontalis* **'Bar Harbor'**). The rushes are truly primitive and their leaves are really pith-filled stems, round and tapering, each 16 to 20 inches long and curving in all directions from a common center. I dug them up from a cow field nearby and as they become accustomed to a better kind of soil, they are growing larger every year. In winter, their color changes from light green to a lustrous brown and are strong enough to make lacework of falling snow.

Cultural demands are few. Average garden soil will suit the grasses, just place them in a sunny location. Sedges and rushes will do better if given a little shade part of the day and prefer a soil that is slightly damp.

We have many dwarf conifers in the garden, their steely blue and green foliage bright against the snow. A weeping birch that becomes an abstract pattern of waving lines in the winter shares attentions with the mahogany colored sedums. But every year when winter truly descends from leaden skies above, it's the ornamental grasses that bring warmth and beauty to the garden until it's time for spring to return to the mountains.

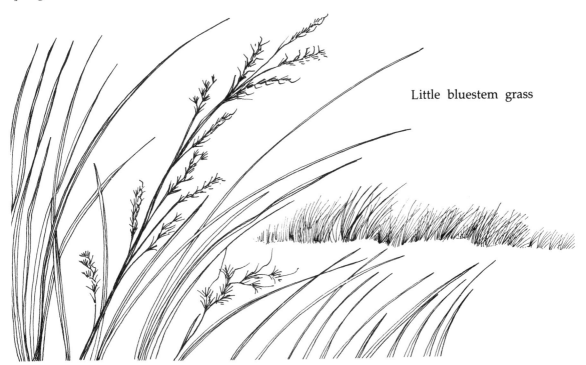

Little bluestem grass

A GARDEN FOR THE HANDICAPPED

Before we moved into our country house in mid-1969, we spent a year of weekends driving up from Manhattan every Friday night and returning either late Sunday night or very early Monday morning. There was more work than play involved in those country weekends, for most of the time was spent in an effort to turn back years of neglect to the house and surrounding yard.

The house was originally built in 1875, enlarged in 1912 when it became a summer boarding establishment, and misused from 1939 until 1951 when it was turned into a weekend summer colony that the owners left closed and unheated every winter until we finally bought the property in late 1967.

My wife's mother, Ruth, was living with us then. She had a severe stroke in 1950, and through years of effort and plain hard work she could talk (though slowly), walk (once again slowly), and she had a mind as sharp as well-edged steel.

Ruth loved to garden. She had her own set of small but strong garden tools (marketed at that time as gardening tools for children) each with a forged rubber handle. But as to other items to make her gardening life easier, for the most part they did not exist. She could not stand for long periods of time, but every Saturday morning if the weather was at all clement she would take a small wooden basket, and aided by a strong brown walking stick, aim for the nearest clump of weeds in the front yard. There after carefully sitting herself down (and she was fiercely independent; there would be no broaching the subject of aid), she would begin to pull up field goldenrod, dandelions, dock, spent daisies, and a host of other weeds.

When we finally dug up a small plot of ground for a vegetable garden, Ruth was delighted. The wooden fence we built from scrap

On the opposite page, a gardener with a bad back welcomes the comfort of a garden scoot, especially when weeding between the rows.

lumber gave her support as she walked about the garden's edge; and weeding between the slight rows of radishes and tomatoes gave her needed exercise.

At that time, about the only product on the open market listed as an aid to the handicapped was an aluminum walker with rubber-tipped feet. Outdoors this was a hopeless item, especially on slopes and in soft earth. Ruth would be surprised today by the number of

A plan for a garden for the handicapped.

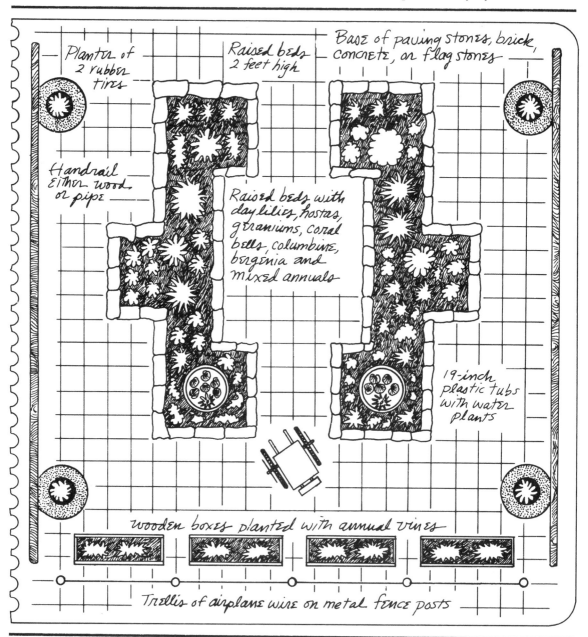

tools especially designed for people who by dint of age, illness, or disability, have found it difficult to get about the garden.

Most of these garden aids were developed in England, a country long involved with the problems of an aging population fanatically disposed to gardening, and people injured during the bombings of the Second World War.

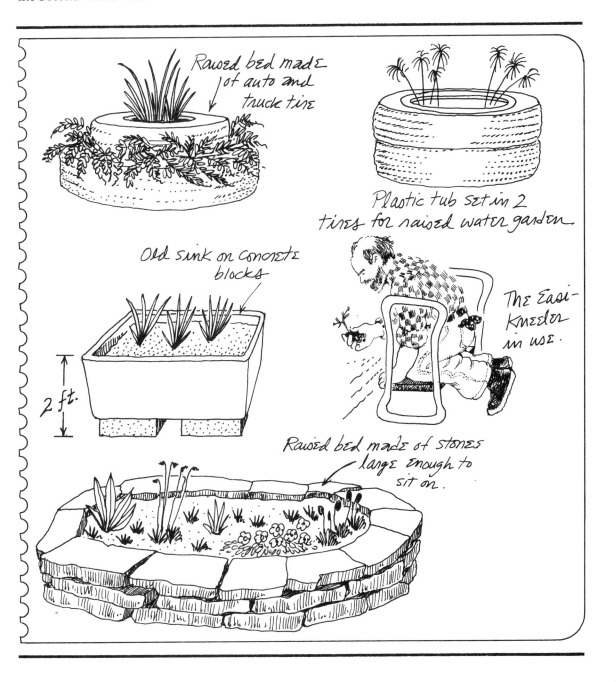

Raised bed made of auto and truck tire

Plastic tub set in 2 tires for raised water garden.

Old sink on concrete blocks

2 ft.

The Easi-Kneeler in use.

Raised bed made of stones large enough to sit on.

Tools for the Handicapped

The following are just some of the tools available. See the Appendixes for sources of supply and the Bibliography for details on a few books devoted to this subject. Mary Chaplin's book, *Gardening for the Physically Handicapped and Elderly* is published in England and covers everything you'll ever need to know including a list of plants that are especially easy to divide when they outgrow their bounds. *Tools and Techniques for Easier Gardening,* published by The National Association for Gardening, includes a list of resources for horticultural therapists and institutional garden program leaders and a further bibliography of resource books for the disabled.

The first two items to be covered are not limited to the handicapped: kneepads and croakies. When the human knee was designed, it seems little if any thought was given to kneeling; or if it was, the assumption was to make kneeling as uncomfortable as possible. The other problem I've found with human anatomy is the ear as it is used to hold up glasses that will slip down the nose the harder one works.

Kneepads can help with the first problem. They are available in either leather padded with felt or formed on a mold with foam rubber. When either type is buckled about the knee, pants stay drier, and the pain of little pebbles digging into the sparse flesh covering the patella, is absolved.

Croakies are bonded and rubberized elastic bands that fit around the side pieces of a pair of glasses and hold them tightly on the bridge of the nose. Their use keeps lenses free from scratching with dirt and prevents a buildup of soil around the edge of the ear after repeated attempts to adjust the falling frames.

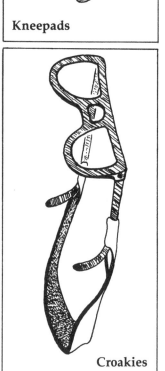

Kneepads

Croakies

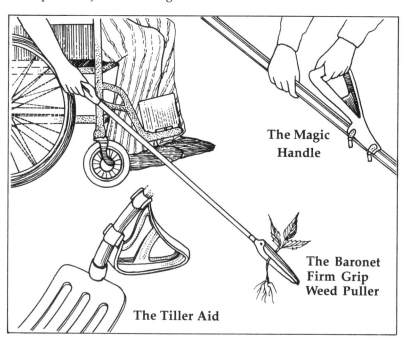

The Magic Handle

The Baronet Firm Grip Weed Puller

The Tiller Aid

The Merrifield Tool Tree is placed in the center of the garden. There in full view you can hang your tools, gloves, hats, and twine. In fact, there is space for most everything and the tool tree saves endless trips on tired legs back and forth to the garage or tool shed.

The Garden Scoot is really a swiveling tractor seat on wheels. You can actually sit down on the job without bending, stooping, or squatting. The wide rubber tires roll through garden dirt. The two-wheeled model is for the more agile, the three-wheeler is perfectly balanced for the person who needs additional stability.

With the **Corrie Easi Kneeler** you can kneel in comfort on a padded cushion that covers a finished wood platform, and you can use the tubular steel frame as support in rising to your feet. Turning over, the kneeler turns into a comfortable seat for a short rest from gardening chores. This equipment is very well made and will stand up to a great deal of punishment.

The Easy Grabber weighs 2 pounds and resembles a large, scissor-type salad server with bent handles. It just about eliminates stooping to pick up leaves and piles of garden debris. If you are taller than 5 1/2 feet you will bend a little, but in turn the grabber can be used by wheelchair gardeners.

The Magic Handle is a hand grip that is strapped to the wooden shaft of a shovel. This small item makes it much easier to hold any such tool and cuts down on arm and back strain.

The Tiller Aid is clamped to a fork, spade, or shovel just above the spot where the handle meets the tool. By acting as a fulcrum it saves much of the energy needed to "dig up" a load of soil.

The Long Handled Trowel is just that. The handle helps in getting leverage and is especially useful for wheelchair gardeners.

The Baronet Cut and Hold Flower Gatherer

The Long Handled Trowel

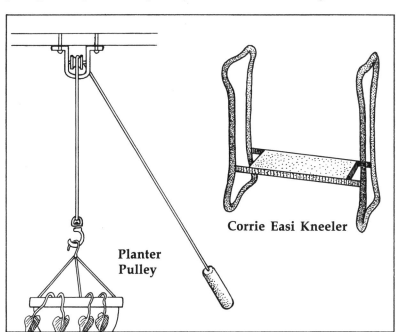

Planter Pulley

Corrie Easi Kneeler

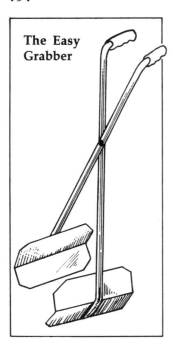

The Easy Grabber

The German Hand Tool Set enables the gardener to fit seven different tools to one 30-inch lightweight handle. All the tools are steel with polished zinc finish, and dimple-grip orange plastic handles. They easily twist on and off the handle. The tools include: a trowel, a combination furrow and hoe, a combination rake and weeder, a 15-inch long brush rake, a weeder knife, a steel dibber for making holes for planting seeds, and a combination grubber and claw-hoe.

The Baronet Cut and Hold Flower Gatherer makes cutting and holding a flower a one-hand operation. It's 31 inches long and perfect for pruning soft wood, gathering fresh flowers, and removing dead ones. Use it on vines and climbing roses.

The Baronet Firm Grip Weed Puller is designed to grip and pull out the most obstinate weed from cultivated land using one hand. At 34 inches it's invaluable for such work.

The Clean Up Caddy has a free standing, self-supporting heavy metal frame that holds the bag open. You can rake and sweep garden debris directly into the bag. It's permanent and reusable and holds more than 8 bushels. Just grab the handle to move the caddy about. It folds flat for easy storage.

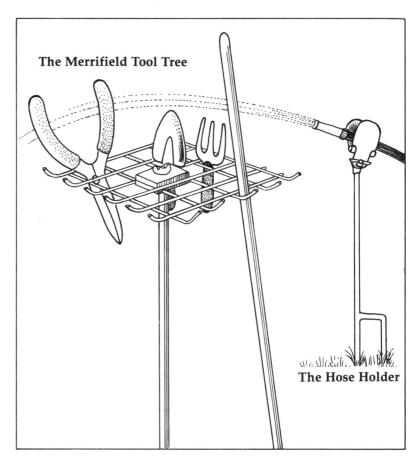

The Merrifield Tool Tree

The Hose Holder

The Hose Holder clamps onto the hose (not the nozzle) so any hose attachment or style of nozzle can be held in place by a spring-loaded clamp and aimed in any direction. Tough steel spikes are pushed into the ground by foot and the holder stands 30 inches high. No stooping is necessary, and it holds the hose as long as you need it.

Finally for ease of care with houseplants there is the **Planter Pulley.** This self-locking pulley is designed to raise and lower hanging plants for watering and tending. A stout nylon cord will support up to 20 pounds. It's also handy for bird cages.

There are many things that I learned from living with a handicapped person over the years. The most important to me was patience, not only in my daily routines but in dealing with other handicapped people. I also learned how important gardening can be, not only as a vocation but as the finest of avocations, an activity that blends beauty, nature, and philosophy into one greening package.

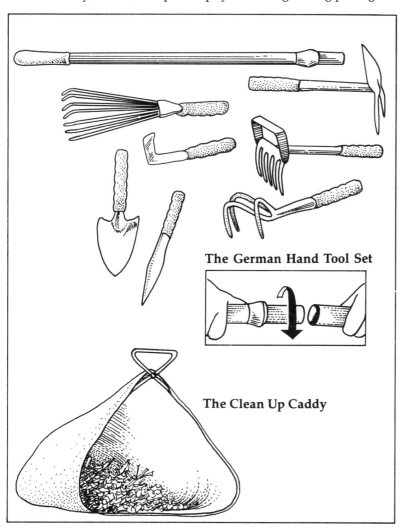

The German Hand Tool Set

The Clean Up Caddy

APPENDIXES

APPENDIX 1:
Magazines and Newsletters

The following publications are all available by subscription in the United States and Canada, including three published in England.

American Horticulturist publishes six magazines and six newsletters per year at a cost of $20 and is part of the membership in the American Horticultural Society. The magazine is one of the best for all serious gardeners, with an emphasis on flowering plants. Production and illustrations are excellent. (Also listed in Appendix 2.)
—American Horticultural Society, Mount Vernon, Virginia 22121.

The Avant Gardener is a monthly newsletter costing $15 per year and dealing with all aspects of horticulture. It's for the serious amateur and professional, covering news items and developments in horticulture and related subjects.
—Box 489, New York, New York 10028.

Flower and Garden is a bimonthly magazine that's been a friend to gardeners for years. It covers both flowers and vegetables in a newsy, how-to manner. Price: $6.00 per year.
—4251 Pennsylvania Avenue, Kansas City, Missouri 64111.

Flower Arranging Quarterly appeared on the scene in early 1985. It is a small but elegant quarterly magazine devoted to the art of flower arranging in America. Membership is $14 per year.
—Floramerica, P.O. Box 263, Westwood, Massachusetts 02090.

Garden is a bimonthly magazine published by the New York Botanical Garden for $10 a year. It is scientific in approach and free with membership at the garden.
—New York Botanical Garden, Bronx, New York 10458.

The Garden comes from London and is the monthly magazine published by the Royal Horticultural Society of England. From garden design to the newest in both indoor and outdoor plants, it has something to offer for everyone. The cost is $20 per year, but exchange rates vary (see Appendix 2).
—Vincent Square, London SW1P 2PE, England.

Garden Design appears four times a year and is the showcase magazine for the American Society of Landscape Architects. It presents fine photos and plans of large gardens both here and abroad and costs $20 a year.
—1733 Connecticut Avenue, N.W., Washington, D.C. 20009.

Green Scene is published by the Pennsylvania Horticultural Society and appears on a bi-monthly schedule with fine articles on gardening, indoors and out. One wishes for more when reading it. While dealing with the Delaware Valley in Pennsylvania, most of the information is good throughout the country. Price is $8.50 per year.
—325 Walnut Street, Philadelphia, Pennsylvania 19106.

The Herb Quarterly is a well-produced and interesting quarterly devoted entirely to herbs and their cultivation for $15 per year.
—Newfane, Vermont 05345.

Horticulture is a monthly covering all aspects of gardening and has been one of the more accomplished publications on the market for many, many years. A subscription of 12 issues is $18 per year.
—755 Boylston Street, Boston, Massachusetts 02116.

HortIdeas is a monthly newsletter that reports on the latest research, methods, tools, plants, books, etc., for vegetable, fruit, and flower growers, all gathered from hundreds of popular sources. A yearly subscription is $10.00.
—Route 1, Box 302, Gravel Switch, Kentucky 40328.

The Maine Organic Farmer and Gardener is a bi-monthly newspaper with headquarters in Augusta, Maine. It writes of life on the farm in the rural Northeast, covers vegetables but often has articles about flowers, too. Subscriptions are $5 per year.
—P.O. Box 2176, 283 Water Street, Augusta, Maine 04330.

The Minnesota Horticulturist has been in business since 1866 and deals extensively with the northern garden in a highly professional manner. It is published nine times a year for $12 single membership and $18 family membership.
—Minnesota State Horticultural Society, 1970 Folwell Avenue, St. Paul, Minnesota 55108.

National Gardening was originally *Gardens for All* but recently changed its name. A monthly newsmagazine, it deals with both flowers and vegetables. A subscription is $15 per year.
—180 Flynn Avenue, Burlington, Vermont 05401.

Pacific Horticulture is a quarterly out of California but always with something of interest to all gardeners in the country. Illustrations and articles are excellent. Price: $12 per year.
—P.O. Box 485, Berkeley, California 94701.

Plants and Gardens is a quarterly published by the Brooklyn Botanical Garden and covers a different garden theme with each issue. The backlist has many excellent issues available. Price: $15 per year.
—1000 Washington Avenue, Brooklyn, New York 11225.

Practical Gardening is Britain's number 1 garden monthly and absolutely fun to have. Much of the information is as useful here as in England, and is a bit more realistic than that found in the expensive English garden books now flooding the market. The cost is about $18 a year but changes slightly with the exchange rates.
—Competition House, Farndon Road, Market Harborough, Leics LE1 9NR, England.

The Plantsman is a quarterly from Kew Gardens in England and, while very scientific in its outlook, it has much information of value to the serious gardener. The price is $18 per year, but the exchange rates will vary.
—Artists House, 14–15 Manette Street, London W1V 5LB, England.

Rodale's Organic Gardening is no longer just for the backyard vegetable gardener. Today's issues deal with all the sophisticated aspects of horticulture but still remain true to their original commitment of working with chemical-free soils. The cost is $12.97 per year.
—33 East Minor Street, Emmaus, Pennsylvania 18049.

The Texas Gardener was bound to happen in a state the size of Texas. Flower and vegetable gardening is covered with an emphasis on native state plants. A yearly subscription is $15.
—P.O. Box 9005, Waco, Texas 76714.

In addition to the above, there are many decorating magazines on the market. Most, like *House & Garden,* have garden features and columns; a few, such as *Architectural Digest,* feature well-known gardens both here and abroad.

APPENDIX 2:

Organizations that Publish Bulletins and/or Sponsor Seed Exchanges

The following organizations all have publications and/or seed exchanges of great diversity. Many are overseas, but do not let that stop you from joining: The mails go through, albeit slowly.

Alpine Garden Society is mainly concerned with alpine and rock garden plants. Its quarterly bulletin is stocked with valuable information and photos of rare plants. The seed exchange is annual and lists well over 4,000 species. Both are available to members for $15 per year but varies with the exchange rates.
—Lye End Link, St. Johns, Woking, Surrey GU21 1SW, England.

American Horticultural Society sponsors a seed exchange for members that is included in the membership fee. See Appendix 1.

American Rock Garden Society publishes an interesting quarterly bulletin and sponsors the biggest seed exchange in the United States and Canada. Over 3,500 different species are offered as part of membership. Cost is $15 per year.
—15 Fairmead Road, Darien, Connecticut 06820.

Hardy Plant Society is a fine old English organization that publishes various news bulletins, one annual bulletin, and sponsors a fine and select seed exchange dealing with perennials. Cost is $8 and varies with the exchange rates.
—10 St. Barnabas Road, Emmer Green, Cabersham, Reading RG4 8RA, England.

Japanese Rock Garden Society recently opened its doors to world-wide membership. The yearly journal is in both Japanese and English; the seed exchange is fascinating. Cost is $15 per year and requires an International Money Order.
—Noriyoshi Masuda, 943–123 Nibuno, Himeji, Japan.

Royal Horticultural Society is one of the all-time greats. In addition to *The Garden,* the monthly magazine, a membership includes a free pass to the Chelsea Flower Show, and the seed exchange that covers the world with 1,200 entries.
—Vincent Square, London SW1P 2PE, England.

Scottish Rock Garden Society publishes two fine bulletins per year and sponsors a seed exchange of surprising diversity with 3,200 entries. Membership is $12 per year.
—21 Merchiston Park, Edinburgh EH10 4PW, Scotland.

The following seed exchange does not easily fall into any other category so I list it here.

Major Howell's International Seed Collection stocks hundreds of varieties of seed from all types of botanical collections throughout the world. Membership and lists are $10 per year, including the first six seed choices.
—Fire Thorn, 6 Oxshott Way, Cobham, Surrey, KT11 2RT, England.

APPENDIX 3:
Plant Societies

The following plant societies are dedicated to the pursuit of special interests as their names imply. Memberships usually include special publications, seed exchanges, and invitations to regional meetings. Many groups publish bulletins that are among the most professional in the plant world. *The Daylily Journal,* for example, averages 100 pages per issue and includes dozens of photos and intricate articles on breeding procedures and unusual cultivars, while *The Bulletin* of the American Orchid Society is as large as *T.V. Guide.* Find one that interests you and expand your garden horizons.

Actinidia Enthusiasts Newsletter, P.O. Box 1064, Tonasket, WA 98855

African Violet Society, Box 3609, Beaumont, TX 77704

African Violet Society of Canada, 8 Smith St., Moncton, NB E1C 8G2, Canada

American Bamboo Society, 1101 San Leon, Solana Beach, 16505

American Bonsai Society, Box 385, Keene, New Hampshire 03431

American Begonia Society, Box 1129, Encinitas, CA 92024

American Boxwood Society, Box 85, Boyce, VA 22620

American Bryological and Lichenological Society, Missouri Botanical Garden, 2345 Tower Grove Ave., St. Louis, MO 63110

American Camellia Society, Box 1217, Fort Valley, GA 31030

American Conifer Society, 1825 North 72 St., Philadelphia, PA 19151

American Daffodil Society, 2302 Byhalia Rd., Hernando, MS 38632

American Dahlia Society, 159 Pine Street, New Hyde Park, NY 11041

American Fern Society, Botany Dept., University of Tennessee, Knoxville, TN 37916

American Fuchsia Society, Hall of Flowers, Golden Gate Park, 9th Ave. and Lincoln Way, San Francisco, CA 94122

American Ginger Society, P.O. Box 600, Archer, FL 32618

American Gloxinia Society, Box 493, Beverly Farms, MA 01915

American Gourd Society, Box 274, Mount Gilead, OH 43338

American Hemerocallis Society, Route 5, Box 874, Palatka, FL 32077

American Hibiscus Society, Drawer 5430, Pompano Beach, FL 33064

American Hosta Society, 9448 Mayfield Road, Chesterland, OH 44026

American Iris Society, Box 10003, Huntsville, AL 35801

American Ivy Society, Box 520, West Carrollton, OH 45449

American Magnolia Society, Box 129, Nanuet, NY 10954

American Orchid Society, 6000 South Olive Ave., West Palm Beach, FL 33405

American Penstemon Society, Box 33, Plymouth, VT 05056

American Peony Society, 250 Interlachen Rd., Hopkins, MN 55343

American Plant Life Society, Box 150, La Jolla, CA 92038 (Amaryllis Society)

American Poinsettia Society, Box 706, Mission, TX 78572

American Pomological Society, 103 Tyson Bldg., University Park, PA 16802

American Primrose Society, 6730 West Mercer Way, Mercer Island, WA 98040

American Rhododendron Society, 14635 S.W. Bull Mountain Rd., Tigard, OR 97223

American Rose Society, Box 30,000, Shreveport, LA 71130

Aril Society International, 5500 Constitution, N.E., Albuquerque, NM 87110

Azalea Society of America, Box 6244, Silver Spring, MD 20906

Bamboo Society of America, 1101 San Leon Court, Solan Beach, CA 92075

Bonsai Canada, 12 Beardmore Crescent, Toronto, ON M2K 2P5, Canada

Bonsai Clubs International, Box 2098, Sunnyvale, CA 94087

British Columbia Fuchsia and Begonia Society, 2175 West 16th Ave., Vancouver, BC V6K 3B1, Canada

Bromeliad Society, P.O. Box 41261, Los Angeles, CA 90041

Cactus and Succulent Society of America, 2631 Fairgreen Ave., Arcadia, CA 91006

California Rare Fruit Growers, Fullerton Arboretum, CSU, Fullerton, CA 92634

Canadian Chrysanthemum and Dahlia Society, 83 Aramaman Dr., Agincourt, ON M1T 2P7, Canada

Canadian Geranium Pelargonium Society, 254 West Kings Rd., North Vancouver, BC V7N 2L9

Canadian Gladiolus Society, 1274–129A Street, Surrey, BC V4A 3Y4, Canada

Canadian Iris Society, 199 Florence Avenue, Willowdale, ON M2N IG5, Canada

Canadian Rose Society, 18–12 Castlegrove Boulevard, Don Mills, ON M3A 1K8, Canada

Carniverous Plant Society, The Fullerton Arboretum, California State University, Fullerton, CA 92634

Cycad Society, 1191 4th Avenue West, Seattle, WA 98119

Cymbidium Society of America, 469 W. Norman Ave., Arcadia, CA 91006

Delphinium Society, 1630 Midwest Plaza Bldg., Minneapolis, MN 55402

Desert Plant Society of Vancouver, 2941 Parker St., Vancouver, BC V5K 2T9, Canada

Dwarf Conifer Notes, Theophrastus, P.O. Box 458, Little Compton, RI 02837

Dwarf Fruit Tree Association, 303 Horticulture, MSU, East Lansing, MI 48823

Epiphyllum Society of America, Box 1395, Monrovia, CA 91016

Friends of the Fig, 840 Ralph Road, Conyers, GA 30208

Garden Club of America, 598 Madison Avenue, New York, NY 10022

Gardenia Society of America, Box 879, Atwater CA 95301

Heliconia Society International, 6450 S.W. 81 Street, Miami, FL 33143

Herb Society of America, 300 Massachusetts Ave., Boston MA 02115

Holly Society of America, 304 Northwind , Baltimore, MD 21204

Home Orchid Society, 2511 S.W. Miles St., Portland, OR 97219

Hoya International, Box 54271, Atlanta, GA 30308

Indoor Citrus and Rare Fruit Society, 176 Coronado Avenue, Los Altos, CA 94022

Indoor Gardening Society of America, 128 West 58th Street, New York, NY 10019

Indoor Light Gardening Society of America, RD 5, Box 76, East Stroudsburg, PA 18301

International Aroid Society, P.O. Box 43–1853, Miami, FL 33143

International Asclepiad Society, 10 Moorside Terrace, Drighlington, BD11 1HX, England

International Cactus and Succulent Society, P.O. Box 253, Odessa, TX 79760

International Clematis Society, Burford House, Tenbury Wells, Worcester, WR15 8HQ, England

International Geranium Society, 5861 Walnut Dr., Eureka, CA 95501

International Lilac Society, Box 315, Rumford, ME 04276

International Palm Society, Box 27, Forestville, CA 95436

International Protea Association, P.O. Box 269, Kula, HI 96790

International Tropical Fern Society, 8720 S.W. 34th St., Miami, FL 33165

Los Angeles International Fern Society, 14895 Gardenhill Dr., La Miranda, CA 90638

Marigold Society of America, Box 112, New Britian, PA 18901

Men's Garden Clubs of America, 5560 Merle Hay Road, Des Moines, IA 50323

National Chrysanthemum Society, 2612 Beverly Rd., Roanoke, VA 24015

National Fuchsia Society, 2892 Crown View Drive, Rancho Palos Verdes, CA 90274

National Oleander Society, Box 3431, Galveston Island, TX 77552

Nerine Society, Brookend House, Welland, Worcestershire, England

North American Fruit Explorers, 10 S. 055 Madison, Hinsdale, IL 60521

North American Gladiolus Council, 8524 Vollmert Ave., Baltimore, MD 21236

North American Heather Society, 62 Elma-Monte Rd., Elma, WA 98541

North American Lily Society, Box 476, Waukee, IA 50263

Northern Nut Growers Association, Broken Arrow Rd., Hamden, CT 06518

Palm Society, Box 368, Lawrence, KS 66044

Peperomia Society, 100 Neil Ave., New Orleans, LA 70114

Perennial Plant Association, 217 Howlett Hall, 2001 Fyffe Court, Columbus, OH 43210

Plumeria Society of America, 1014 Riverglyn, Houston, TX 77063

Rare Fruit Council International, 13609 Old Cutler Road, Miami, FL 33158

Rhododendron Society of Canada, 4271 Lakeshore Road, Burlington, ON L7L 1A7, Canada

Saintpaulia International/Gesneriad Society International, Box 549, Knoxville, TN 37901

Sempervivum Fanciers Association, 37 Ox Bow Lane, Randolph, MA 02368

Society for Louisiana Irises, Box 40175 USL, Lafayette, LA 70504

Soil Conservation Society of America, 7515 Ankeny Road, Ankeny, IA 50021

Solana Newsletter, 3370 Princeton Ct., Santa Clara, CA 95051

Terrarium Association, 57 Wolfpit Ave., Norwalk, CT 06851

Toronto Gesneriad Society, 70 Enfield Rd., Etobicoke, ON M8W 1T9, Canada

Vancouver Island Rock and Alpine Society, 575 Towner Road, RR 1, Sidney, BC V82 3R9, Canada

Waterlily Society of America, Box 104, Lilypons, MD 21717

APPENDIX 4:
Commercial Seed Companies

The following list consists of catalogs issued by seed companies mostly involved with flowers, although a few also stock vegetables. Because of fluctuating costs, I've not included any charges incurred with receiving these publications, so write first.

Remember, too, that each seed company is—at least up to now—unique in one way. Each carries a few species or cultivars that are theirs and theirs alone. Many items will be repeated from house to house, but every catalog will have a few surprises. Over the years, I've dealt with all the businesses listed below. They will all, I think, deliver satisfaction.

This list is in no way a complete count of seed companies in business today. Every year there are more.

Abundant Life Seed Foundation, P.O. Box 772, Port Townsend, Washington 98368. Dedicated to keeping species from disappearing from the garden scene.

Applewood Seed Company, 5380 Vivian Street, Arvada, Colorado 80002. Wildflower seeds.

The Banana Tree, 715 Northampton Street, Easton, Pennsylvania 18042. Exotic seeds: bananas, trees, flowers.

BioQuest International, P.O. Box 5752, Santa Barbara, California 93150. Many interesting South African seeds and bulbs.

Burpee Seeds, Warminster, Pennsylvania 18974. One of the oldest companies around today.

John Chambers, 15 Westleigh Road, Barton Seagrave, Kettering, Northants NN15 5AJ. A large collection of wildflower and grass seeds.

Chiltern Seeds, Bortree Stile, Ulverston, Cumbria LA12 7PB, England. One of the largest collections of annual and perennial garden seeds.

The Cook's Garden, Box 65, Londonderry, Vermont 05148. Unusual gourmet vegetable seeds.

The Country Garden, Route 2, Box 455A, Crivitz, Wisconsin 54114. A very large collection of annuals and perennials both for cutting and the border.

William Dam Seeds, P.O. Box 8400, Dundas, Ontario, Canada L9H 6M1. An old and established firm.

DeGiorgi Company, Inc., Council Bluffs, Iowa 51502. Another old American company in business for 80 years. Good selection of ornamental grasses.

J. A. Demonchaux Company, 827 N. Kansas, Topeka, Kansas 66608. Very fancy seeds from France.

Jack Drake, Aviemore, Inverness-shire, Scotland PH22 1QS. Rare flower seeds from around the world.

Epicure Seeds, Box 23568, Rochester, New York 14692. Very fancy vegetable seeds for the gourmet table.

Far North Garden, 16785 Harrison, Livonia, Michigan 48154. A wonderful collection of seeds, many rare.

The Fragrant Path, Box 328, Fort Calhoun, Nebraska 68023. A wonderful collection of fragrant plants and a few night bloomers.

Gleckler's Seedsmen, Metamora, Ohio 43540. Giant marigolds, a specialty.

L.S.A. Goodwin & Sons, Goodwins Road, Bagdad, Sth 7407 Tasmania. Yes, specialized seeds from Tasmania and well worth writing for.

Gurney's Seed & Nursery Co., Yankton, South Dakota 57079. An old-fashioned catalog with old-fashioned pictures and many interesting varieties.

Horticultural Enterprises, P.O. Box 340082, Dallas, Texas 75234. Wild plants and the world's most complete selection of hot peppers.

C. W. Hosking, Exotic Importer, P.O. Box 500, Hayle, Cornwall, England. Large collection of tropical seeds and many night bloomers.

J. L. Hudson, Seedsman, P.O. Box 1058, Redwood City, California 94064. A giant selection of interesting seeds from all over.

International Seed Supplies, P.O. Box 538, Nowra, N.S.W., Australia 2541. Many rare seeds from all over the world.

Johnny's Selected Seeds, Albion, Maine 04910. Mostly vegetables but a few good flowers and many herbs.

Jung Quality Seeds, Randolph, Wisconsin 53956. Another fine American seed house with many flowers.

LaFayette Home Nursery, Inc., Lafayette, Illinois 61449. Seeds of prairie plants and native grasses.

LeMarch Seeds International, P.O. Box 566, Dixon, California 95620. Many unusual gourmet seeds.

Earl May Seed & Nursery, Shenandoah, Iowa 51603. One more famous American nursery with a large selection of seeds.

Maver Rare Perennials, P.O. Box 18754, Seattle, Washington 98118. Hundreds of rare and interesting flower seeds.

Nichol's Herb and Rare Seeds, 1190 N. Pacific Highway, Albany, Oregon 97321. A large collection of special seeds: herbs, flowers, and bulbs.

Olds Seed Company, P.O. Box 7790, 2901 Packers Avenue, Madison, Wisconsin 53707. Annuals, perennials, and vegetables.

Geo. W. Park Seed Company, Greenwood, South Carolina 29647. One of the most famous in America, with many unusual seeds.

Plants of the Southwest, 1570 Pacheco Street, Santa Fe, New Mexico 87501. An interesting catalog with many wildflowers and grasses.

Clyde Robin Seed Company, P.O. Box 2855, Castro Valley, California 94546. One of the major dealers in wildflower seeds.

Rocky Mountain Seed Service, Box 215, Golden, British Columbia, Canada V0A 1HO. Native Canadian seeds.

R. H. Shumway, Rockfor, Illinois 61101. Another American institution where seeds are concerned.

Southern Seeds, The Vicarage, Sheffield, Canterbury, New Zealand. Rare alpine seeds from the New Zealand wilds.

Stokes Seed Company, Box 548, Buffalo, New York 14240. An attractive catalog with many flower offerings.

Thompson & Morgan, P.O. Box 100, Farmingdale, New Jersey. One of England's oldest seed houses, with a vast selection of seeds and now with offices in America.

Otis Twilley Seed Company, P.O. Box 65, Trevose, Pennsylvania 19047. Select flower and vegetable seeds.

APPENDIX 5:
Live Plants by Mail

The following suppliers grow and sell live plants to be shipped either by mail or United Parcel. Over the years I've ordered hundreds of such plants and most everything has arrived in fine shape. The firms listed below have learned through experience how to wrap plants for rough handling and they are eminently fair people, ready to hear from you, the buyer, if you have a problem.

Like seed suppliers, no two nurseries are alike. Each firm will have a few unusual things to offer.

I have not listed catalog fees because they continue to change so drop the supplier a note asking for the catalog and fee.

Alpenglow, 13328 King George Highway, Surrey, B.C., Canada V3T 2T6. A large variety of alpines, perennials, and shrubs for the garden.

B & D Lilies, 330 "P" Street, Port Townsend, Washington 98368. A tremendous selection of garden lilies.

Kurt Bluemel, Inc., 2543 Hess Road, Fallston, Maryland 21047. The largest collection of ornamental grasses in this country and includes many sedges, rushes, and unusual flowering perennials.

The Bovees Nursery, 1737 S.W. Coronado, Portland, Oregon 97219. A large collection of rhododendrons, azaleas, and companion plants.

Coenosium Gardens, 425 N. Fifth Street, Lehighton, Pennsylvania 18235. A fascinating and complete selection of dwarf conifers.

C.A. Cruickshank, Ltd., 1015 Mount Pleasant Road, Toronto, Ontario M4P 2M1, Canada. Many garden bulbs, perennials, and gladiolus.

The Cummins Garden, 22 Robertsville Road, Marlboro, New Jersey 07746. A fine selection of dwarf and small evergreens along with companion plants.

Endangered Species, 12571 Red Hill Avenue, Tustin, California 92680. A big selection of bamboos and many unusual in- and outdoor plants.

Far North Gardens, 16785 Harrison, Livonia, Michigan 48154. They are listed here because of the fine collection of primroses and wild plants, though they mainly deal in seeds.

Fjellgarden, P.O. Box 1111, Lakeside, Arizona 85929. A fine selection of unusual alpine plants.

Garden Place, 6780 Heisley Road, P.O. Box 83, Mentor, Ohio 44060. A good all-around selection of hardy garden perennials from *Achillea* to *Yucca*.

Gardens of the Blue Ridge, P.O. Box 10, Pineola, North Carolina 28662. A number of wildflower perennials along with shrubs, ferns, and vines.

Girard Nurseries, P.O. Box 428, Geneva, Ohio 44041. A fine selection of small evergreens and hollies.

Russell Graham, 4030 Eagle Crest Road, N.W., Salem, Oregon 97304. Many unusual alpine plants plus a large number of bulbs.

Greenlife Gardens Greenhouses, 101 County Line Road, Griffin, Georgia 30223. The largest selection of hybrid epiphyllums plus many other succulents.

Greer Gardens, 1280 Goodpasture Road, Eugene, Oregon 97401. A bewildering selection of rhododendrons, azaleas, and many maple cultivars.

Hatfield Gardens, 22799 Ringgold Southern Road, Stroutsville, Ohio 43154. A staggering number of daylilies and hostas.

High Country Rosarium, 1717 Downing Street, Denver, Colorado 80218. Many unusual hardy roses.

Holbrook Farm, Rte. 2, Box 223B, Fletcher, North Carolina 28732. An interesting collection of native American wildflowers and bulbs.

International Growers Exchange, P.O. Box 52248, Livonia, Michigan 48152. A clearinghouse of many perennials, herbs, and exotic bulbs and flowers.

Kester's, P.O. Box V, Omro, Wisconsin 54963. A complete stock of water plants for larger ponds and foods for wildlife.

Klehm Nursery, 2 East Algonquin Road, Arlington Heights, Illinois 60005. Many peonies, daylilies, hostas, and iris.

Lamb Nurseries, E. 101 Sharp Avenue, Spokane, Washington 99202. Many hardy perennials, alpines, and garden mums.

Las Pilitas Nursery, Star Rte., Box 23x, Santa Margarita, California 93453. They feature native plants of California, many hardy to − 20°F.

Lilypons Water Gardens, 6800 Lilypons Road, Lilypons, Maryland 21717. A complete selection of plants for the pool or pond, including the Amazon lily.

Logee's Greenhouses, Danielson, Connecticut 06239. A vast collection of indoor and outdoor plants including many herbs.

Lowe's Own Root Roses, 6 Sheffield Road, Nashua, New Hampshire 03062. New and rare hybrid perpetual roses.

John D. Lyon, Inc., 143 Alewife Brook Parkway, Cambridge, Massachusetts 02140. Send a SASE for the list of many unusual bulbs for naturalizing.

McClure & Zimmerman, Bulb Brokers, 1422 West Thorndale, Chicago, Illinois 60660. Outstanding selection of bulbs, corms, and tubers including the Devil's tongue.

Mellinger's, Inc., 2310 W. South Range Road, North Lima, Ohio 44452. Many unusual plants and seeds plus much garden equipment.

Milaeger's Gardens, 4838 Douglas Avenue, Racine, Wisconsin 53402. A fine list of hardy garden perennials.

Oliver Nurseries, Inc., 1159 Bronson Road, Fairfield, Connecticut 06430. Oliver's does not ship but the nursery includes such a perfect collection of fine pines and rock garden evergreens that they are included here for those of you who live close enough to visit.

Paradise Gardens, 14 May Street, Whitman, Massachusetts 02382. Another large collection of plants and fish for the water garden.

Powell's Gardens, Rte. 2, Highway 70, Princeton, North Carolina 27569. Many daylilies and hostas.

Rocknoll Nursery, 9210 U.S. 50, Hillsboro, Ohio 45133. A very personal collection of rock garden plants and hardy perennials; many coralbells.

Roses of Yesterday and Today, Brown's Valley Road, Watsonville, California 95076. A must for the rose lover.

Sandy Mush Herbs, Rte. 2, Surrett Cove Road, Leicester, North Carolina 28748. A diverse selection of herbs and garden perennials, especially thymes.

Shady Oaks Nursery, 700 19th Avenue N.E., Waseca, Minnesota 66093. Specialists with plants for shady places.

David B. Sindt, Irises, 1331 W. Cornelia, Chicago, Illinois 60657. The most complete selection of irises in the United States.

Siskiyou Rare Plant Nursery, 2825 Cummings Road, Medford, Oregon 97501. The best in alpines, including ferns.

Louis Smirnow, 85 Linden Lane, Glen Head, Brookville, New York 11545. Tree peonies and herbaceous peonies.

Slocum Water Gardens, 1101 Cypress Gardens Road, Winter Haven, Florida 33880. Plants and lilies for the water garden.

William Tricker, Inc., 74 Allendale Avenue, P.O. Box 398, Saddle River, New Jersey 07458. Plants and fish for the water garden.

Van Ness Water Gardens, 2460 N. Euclid Avenue, Upland, California 91786. Another major supplier of water garden items.

Andre Viette Farm & Nursery, Rte. 1, Box 16, Fishersville, Virginia 22939. Many daylilies, hostas, ornamental grasses, and garden irises.

Wayside Gardens, Hodges, South Carolina 29695. A tremendous number of plants, shrubs, and small trees.

We-Du Nurseries, Rte. 5, Box 724, Marion, North Carolina 28752. A very large collection of both native and foreign wildflowers.

White Flower Farm, Litchfield, Connecticut 06759. The catalogs are $5 per year and price includes spring and fall editions, with a large number of perennials described.

Woodlanders, 1128 Colleton Avenue, Aiken, South Carolina 29801. Many fine wildflowers and native shrubs and trees.

APPENDIX 6:
Garden and Greenhouse Equipment Sources

The following firms stock tools, garden gadgets, garden lighting, and many greenhouse items.

American Sundials, Inc., 300 Main Street. Point Arena, California 95468. All types of sundials for the garden.

Charley's Greenhouse Supplies, P.O. Box 2110, LaConner, Washington 98257. A major supplier of greenhouse-related items, including the new bubble insulation.

Clapper's, 1125 Washington Street, West Newton, Massachusetts 02165. Tools, garden furniture, and garden lighting.

Faire Harbour Ltd., 44 Captain Peirce Road, Scituate, Massachusetts 02066. Kerosene heaters and replacement parts.

Gardener's Eden, P.O. Box 7307, San Francisco, California 94120. A large selection of garden items, many of which make good gifts.

Gardener's Supply Co., 133 Elm Street, Winooski, Vermont 05404. Many interesting and well-made garden tools including the best long-handled trowel and Reemay cloth, perfect for protecting plants against frost.

Green River Tools, 5 Cotton Mill Hill, P.O. Box 1919, Brattleboro, Vermont 05301. Unusual garden tools including many stout items imported from Europe. They also carry the bat box and believe it or not, an earwig house.

Gro-tek Supplies, South Berwick, Maine 03908. Greenhouse supplies and sun shades for greenhouse glass.

Hanover Lantern, 470 High Street, Hanover, Pennsylvania 17331. A distributor of garden lighting. Write for local retail outlets.

Kim Lighting, Inc., 16555 E. Gale Avenue, P.O. Box 1275, Industry, California 91749. Modern garden lighting fixtures. Write for local retail outlets.

A. M. Leonard, Inc., 6665 Spiker Road, Piqua, Ohio 45356. A major horticultural tool and supply catalog.

Loran, Inc., 1705 East Colton Avenue, Redlands, California 92373. Distributors of *Nightscaping* outdoor lighting systems. Write for local retail outlets.

Mellinger's, 2310 W. South Range Road, North Lima, Ohio 44452. Although they are listed under plants, they do stock a large amount of pots, tools, and a variety of supplies.

Walt Nicke, Box 667L, Hudson, New York 12534. The original garden supplier with a catalog that's like a supermarket for all kinds of garden equipment. There are many items from Great Britain including the Scottish plant supports and items of great help to handicapped gardeners.

Smith & Hawken Tool Company, Inc., 25 Corte Madera, Mill Valley, California 94941. Quality garden tools and watering devices.

Wood Classics, Inc., RD #1, Box 455E, High Falls, New York 12440. Makers of classic Adirondack furniture and 2 new lines of English-style garden furniture, both in kit form.

APPENDIX 7:

Garden Book Dealers

No gardener should be without books to mull over during long winter nights while dreaming of the garden next spring. The following bookstores deal in gardening books by mail, both new and used, and include a goodly number of American books in their collections. Many dealers started as hobbyists but in time found more enjoyment in selling books than anything else—except gardening.

The American Botanist, P.O. Box 143, Brookfield, Illinois 60513.

Anchor & Dolphin Books, 20 Franklin Street, P.O. Box 823, Newport, Rhode Island 02840.

George A. Bibby, 1225 Sardine Creek Road, Gold Hill, Oregon 97525.

Warren F. Broderick, 695 4th Avenue, P.O. Box 124, Lansingburgh, New York 12182.

Editions, Boiceville, New York 12412.

Hortulus Books, 101 Scollard Street, Toronto, Canada M5R 1G4.

Hurley Books, Westmoreland, New Hampshire 03467.

Ian Jackson, P.O. Box 9075, Berkeley, California 94709.

Lion's Head Books, Academy Street, Salisbury, Connecticut 06068.

Timothy Mawson, 134 West 92nd Street, New York, New York 10025.

Pomona Book Exchange, Highway 52, Rockton, Ontario L0R 1X0, Canada.

Savoy Books, Box 271, Bailey Road, Lanesborough, Massachusetts 01237.

Second Life Books, P.O. Box 242, Quarry Road, Lanesborough, Massachusetts 01237.

Edward F. Smiley, RFD 5, 43 Liberty Hill Road, Bedford, New Hampshire 03102.

Jane Sutley, 1105 W. Cherry Street, Centralia, Washington 98531.

Sweetgrass & Company, P.O. Box 711, Alhambra, California 91802.

Gray Wayner, Bookseller, Rte. 3, Box 18, Fort Payne, Alabama 35967.

Robin Wilkerson Books, 24 Groveland Street, Auburndale, Massachusetts 02166.

Elisabeth Woodburn, Booknoll Farm, Hopewell, New Jersey 08525.

APPENDIX 8:
Measuring Foot Candles with an
In-A-Camera Reflected Light Meter

Set film speed to ASA 200 and
shutter speed at 1/500 second

F22	5000 FC	F 6.3	550 FC
F16	2500 FC	F 6.3	300 FC
F11	1200 FC	F 4.5	150 FC

APPENDIX 9:

**Measuring Foot Candles with a
Weston-Type Meter**

Reading	Foot Candles	Reading	Foot Candles
2	.4	10	100.
3	.8	11	200.
4	1.6	12	400.
5	3.2	13	800.
6	6.4	14	1600.
7	12.8	15	3200.
8	26.	16	6400
9	52.		

APPENDIX 10:

A Metric Conversion System

When you know:	You can find:	If you multiply by:
Inches	Millimeters	25.
Inches	Centimeters	2.5
Feet	Centimeters	30.
Centimeters	Inches	0.4
Millimeters	Inches	0.04
Degrees Celsius	Degrees Fahrenheit	1.8 and then add 32
Degrees Fahrenheit	Degrees Celsius	0.56 after subtracting 32

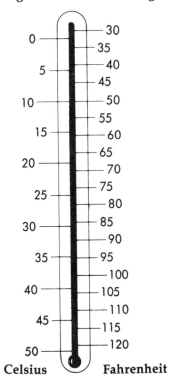

Celsius   Fahrenheit

BIBLIOGRAPHY

The following books are in my garden library. They are there because they are used. The English books herein have been chosen because they can be used by American gardeners (not so with many on the market today).

Allen, Oliver E. *Winter Gardens.* Alexandria, Virginia: Time-Life Books, 1979.
An excellent volume on gardens in the winter written by a fine gardener.

Bailey, L. H. *The Garden of Gourds.* New York: The Macmillan Company, 1937.
The only book on gourds from the gardener's point of view, written by a master American gardener.

Blanchan, Neltje. *Nature's Garden.* New York: Doubleday, Page & Co., 1904.
Full of wonders about wildflowers, how they grow and survive, and the bees who flit from blossom to blossom.

Britton, Nathaniel Lord, and Addison Brown. *An Illustrated Flora of the Northern United States and Canada.* 3 vols. 1913. Reprint. New York: Dover, 1970.
Covers just about all the wild plants growing in the United States. Some names have changed but still an excellent reference book.

Brown, Lauren. *Weeds in Winter.* Boston: Houghton Mifflin Company, 1977.
A charming book on the beauty of dried weeds in winter.

Brown, Vinson. *Reading the Outdoors at Night.* Harrisburg, Pennsylvania: Stackpole Books, 1972.
A perfect companion to the night garden telling you all you ever wanted to know about the animals that wander the land when evening falls.

Brookes, John. *Room Outside: A Plan for the Garden.* New York: Viking, 1970.
Covers everything you need to know about landscape design for a small plot of land.

Chaplin, Mary. *Gardening for the Physically Handicapped & Elderly.* London: B. T. Batsford, Ltd., 1978.
A thorough book that covers all aspects of gardening for the physically handicapped. It lists many plants suitable for such gardens and clear instructions on making raised beds.

Cobb, Boughton. *A Field Guide to the Ferns.* Boston: Houghton Mifflin Company, 1956.
The best field guide for ferns of northeastern and central North America.

Dana, Mrs. William Starr. *How to Know the Wild Flowers.* New York: Charles Scribner's Sons, 1895.
A wonderful book written in terms of days gone by. Look for a recent Dover reprint.

Dictionary of Gardening. The Royal Horticultural Society. 4 vols. and supplement. Oxford: Clarendon, 1965.
Next to *Hortus Third*, these volumes are the most used in my library. Fascinating not only for advice in plants and planting, but for the history of plants.

Earle, Alice Morse. *Old Time Gardens.* New York: The Macmillan Company, 1901.
All about American gardens and gardening from plants to ornament written in a delightful manner.

Embertson, Jane. *Pods.* New York: Charles Scribner's Sons, 1979.
Photos and descriptions of wildflowers and weeds. A fine book.

Encyclopedia of Organic Gardening. The staff of Organic Gardening Magazine. Emmaus, Pennsylvania: Rodale Press, 1978.
For all the information needed to grow a fine garden of flowers without resorting to artificial chemicals, this is the reference book to use.

Fink, Bruce. *The Lichen Flora of the United States.* Ann Arbor: The University of Michigan Press, 1935.
Covers most of the lichens found in the northern woods and fields.

Fish, Margery. *Gardening in the Shade.* London: Faber and Faber, 1983.
Well-written and full of usable information on shade gardening.

Frederick, William H., Jr. *100 Great Garden Plants.* New York: Alfred A. Knopf, 1975.
Good color pictures and a personal selection of plants that is very American in outlook.

Gault, S. Millar, and George Kalmbacher. *The Color Dictionary of Shrubs.* New York: Crown, 1976.
This, too, is an English book, but adapted to the American climate.

Genders, Roy: Bulbs: *A Complete Handbook.* Indianapolis/New York: Bobbs-Merrill, 1973.
Full cultural instructions for most bulbs, corms, and tubers being grown today.

Graf, Alfred Byrd. *Exotic Plant Manual.* East Rutherford, New Jersey: Roehrs, 1970.
Contains 4,200 black-and-white photos along with complete cultural tips and requirements for both indoor and outdoor plants.

Grounds, Roger. *Ornamental Grasses.* London: Pelham Books, 1979.
A detailed account of ornamental grasses in the garden but unfortunately from the English viewpoint.

Grout, A. J. *Mosses with Hand-Lens and Microscope.* Ashton, Maryland, 1965.
> A reprint of a classic book on mosses written in a non-technical manner and full of wonderful lore.

Hale, Mason E. *How to Know the Lichens,* 2d ed. Dubuque, Iowa: Wm. C. Brown, 1979.
> An especially good field guide to identifying lichens with many clear illustrations.

Harkness, Bernard E. *The Seedlist Handbook,* 2d ed. Bellona, New York: Kashong, 1976.
> A listing of all the plants usually found in seed exchanges of the American Rock Garden Society.

Harper, Pamela and Frederick McGourty. Perennials, *How to Select, Grow & Enjoy.* Tucson, Arizona: HP Books, 1985.
> The best in pictures by an accomplished garden photographer and the finest instructions by a master American gardener.

Hay, Roy, and Patrick M. Synge. *Color Dictionary of Flowers and Plants.* New York: Crown, 1975.
> A very valuable addition to any plant library, with hundreds of small but clear photos of perennial and annual plants and flowers.

Hortus Third. New York: Macmillan, 1976.
> This is the monumental revision of L. H. Bailey and Ethel Zoe Bailey's original work of nomenclature for the American gardener and horticulturist, overseen by the staff of the L. H. Bailey Hortorium at Cornell University. Very expensive but worth talking your local library into acquiring it, if they haven't already.

Jekyll, Gertrude. *Annuals and Biennials.* London: Country Life, n.d.
> The classic English gardener talks about the classic English garden approach to annual flowers. Since climate vary rarely enters into the life of an annual, this is a valuable book to have.
> *Colour Schemes for the Flower Garden.* London: Country Life, 1936.
> Another gem of a book with good photos and good advice about principles that apply in any climate. Many of Miss Jekyll's books have been reissued by the Ayer Company in Salem, New Hampshire.

Johnson, Hugh. *The Principles of Gardening.* New York: Simon & Schuster, 1979.
> A fine guide to gardening, covering art, history, and science with fine illustrations, good advice, and readable text.

Koch-Isenburg, Ludwig. *Garden Guide.* New York: The Viking Press, 1964.
> A German garden book that is more of a diary of one gardener's experiences, translated for England, then brought to America. If you ever find one in a used book store, pick it up for it's full of wonderful stuff.

Lacy, Allen. *Home Ground, A Gardener's Miscellany.* New York: Farrar Straus Giroux, 1984.
A fine garden writer's stories about plants and people in the garden.

Longwood Gardens Plant and Seed Sources. Kennett Square, Pennsylvania: Longwood Gardens, 1983.
Longwood Gardens have one of the finest garden displays in America. This booklet tells where they buy their plants and seeds.

Lloyd, Christopher. *Foliage Plants.* London: Collins, 1973.
A very literate discussion of plants to grow for leaves instead of flowers. English, but the philosophy works anywhere.
The Well-Tempered Garden. New York: Dutton, 1970.
A wonderful book to read. Should be consulted every year before picking up a shovel.

Meyer, E. T. *Rock & Water Gardens.* New York: Charles Scribner's Sons, n.d.
How to build rock gardens and ponds the old way with rocks and very hard work.

Miles, Bebe. *Wildflower Perennials for Your Garden.* New York: Hawthorne, 1976.
A classic book on wildflowers for the garden, written by a fine American gardener.

Parsons, Frances Theodora. *How to Know the Ferns.* New York: Charles Scribner's Sons, 1899.
Rambling through the woods when they were clean, with notes by a fern lover and quotes from great American poets.

Perry, Frances. *The Water Garden.* New York: Van Nostrand Reinhold Company, 1981.
A complete discussion of plants, fish, and construction of a water garden.

Pizzetti, Ippolito, and Henry Cocker. *Flowers: A Guide for Your Garden.* 2 vols. New York: Harry N. Abrams, 1975.
Using the fine color plates from the great eighteenth- and nineteenth-century botanical periodicals for a starting-off point, these books cover both history and culture of a host of garden annuals and perennials. Books for consultation when winter winds blow.

Robinson, W. *The English Flower Garden and Home Grounds.* London: John Murray, 1901.
The flyleaf says "from Rosemary," the pictures are wood engravings from photographs, many of the names are out of date, many of the plants either unavailable or unable to live through a winter in the Northeast, but this book would never leave my library. A reprint is available from Kraus Reprint & Periodicals, Rte. 100, Millwood, New York 10546.

Sabuco, John J. *The Best of the Hardiest.* Flossmoor, Illinois: Good Earth Publishing, Ltd., 1985.
A new climate zone map for America that is far closer to reality than the U.S.D.A. map. The book describes 917 plants for hardiness. It's a tremendous value to the northern gardener.

Schacht, Wilhelm. *Rock Gardens.* New York: Universe, 1981.
An updated classic book on rock gardens that's full of fine information.

Schenk, George. *The Complete Shade Gardener.* Boston: Houghton Mifflin Company, 1984.
The owner of the fabled Wild Garden, one of the more unusual nurseries to be found in the United States (now unfortunately out of business), writes a complete book on growing plants in the shade.

Sources of Native Seeds and Plants. Ankeny, Iowa: Soil Conservation Society of America, 1982.
A booklet that lists all the nurseries that carry native wildflowers and grasses.

Taylor, Norman, ed. *The Practical Encyclopedia of Gardening.* New York: Garden City Publishing Company, Inc., 1936.
This is the book to look for, not the fourth edition which does not contain the marvelous asides that the older editions did. A book for dipping into when you cannot go out to garden but the muse is sitting on your shoulder.

Tools & Techniques for Easier Gardening. Burlington, Vermont: The National Association for Gardening, 1984.
A book that covers all the products available in the United States to help the handicapped gardener.

Verey, Rosemary. *The Scented Garden.* New York: Van Nostrand Reinhold Company, 1981.
A beautifully packaged book about plants with fragrance, and where to grow them.

Wilder, Louise Beebe. *Hardy Bulbs.* New York: Dover Publications, Inc., 1974.
One of those books that are fun to read even if you will never grow a bulb or watch a crocus push up through the snow.

Wolgensinger, Bernard, and Jose Daidone. *The Personal Garden: Its Architecture and Design.* New York: Van Nostrand Reinhold, 1975.
A picture book that suffers with translation but is still full of wonderful gardens.

INDEX

Bold type denotes illustrations